Korean Confucianism

CEACOP East Asian Comparative Ethics, Politics, and Philosophy of Law

Series editors: Philip J. Ivanhoe, Chair Professor of East Asia Comparative Philosophy and Religion and Director of the Center for East Asian and Comparative Philosophy (CEACOP) at City University of Hong Kong; Sungmoon Kim, Associate Professor of Political Theory at City University of Hong Kong; Eirik Lang Harris, Assistant Professor of Philosophy at City University of Hong Kong

This is a series of path-breaking and field-defining works in East Asian comparative philosophy with a special interest in works of normative and applied ethics, political theory, and philosophy of law. This series is published in partnership with the Center for East Asian and Comparative Philosophy (CEACOP) at City University of Hong Kong.

Titles in the Series

Korean Confucianism

The Philosophy and Politics of Toegye and Yulgok

Hyoungchan Kim

Translated by
Shon Yoo-taek, Yoon Heeki, and
Dara Seamus Fox

ROWMAN &
LITTLEFIELD
——— INTERNATIONAL

London • New York

This work was supported by a grant from The Academy of Korean Studies funded by the Korean Government (MEST) (AKS-2011-AAA-2102).

Published by Rowman & Littlefield International Ltd
Unit A, Whitacre Mews, 26-34 Stannary Street, London SE11 4AB
www.rowmaninternational.com

Rowman & Littlefield International Ltd.is an affiliate of Rowman & Littlefield
4501 Forbes Boulevard, Suite 200, Lanham, Maryland 20706, USA
With additional offices in Boulder, New York, Toronto (Canada), and Plymouth (UK)
www.rowman.com

British Library Cataloguing in Publication Data
A catalogue record for this book is available from the British Library

ISBN: HB 978-1-7866-0860-4
      PB 978-1-7866-0861-1

Library of Congress Cataloging-in-Publication Data Is Available

ISBN 978-1-78660-860-4 (cloth)
ISBN 978-1-78660-861-1 (pbk)
ISBN 978-1-78660-862-8 (electronic)

Contents

Preface

In the history of every country, there is a period when its people are faced
with a critical task, on the fulfillment of which the future may depend. Such
challenges unexpectedly surface in the turmoil of history, and they must be
surmounted to ensure the survival of the people concerned. If there appear
some iconic figures who are capable of coping with such grave undertak-
ings in the midst of the raging storms of history, Koreans usually say that
the country is indebted to the Providence of Heaven. From this perspective,
it was due to the Providence of Heaven that there emerged the figures of
Yi Hwang (李滉, 1501–1570), who is referred to by his pen name Toegye
(退溪), and Yi I (李珥, 1536–1584), whose pen name was Yulgok (栗谷),
in the mid-sixteenth century during the Joseon (朝鮮) Dynasty (1392–1910).
At that time (five generations after the foundation of Joseon), the revolutionary ideals of the dynasty had faded away and those with vested interests
monopolized political power and accrued the lion's share of the economic
benefits of the era. Moreover, the situation worsened when the Japanese
invaded the country in 1592.

Toegye reflected on the problems Joseon was faced with and tried to fundamentally solve them by rejuvenating the philosophy and ideology of the
nation. In this context he proposed his theory on the achievement of a morally perfect society based on the advanced learning of Neo-Confucianism.
According to his theory, self-reflection on the status and workings of the mind
should be conducted in such a way as to lead to voluntary action or practice
in accordance with universal principles, which would ultimately bring about
the morally ideal society. In addition, he established Confucian academies to
educate students and enshrine sages and worthies, which he believed would

help to curb the immoral actions of the elite. He was the epitome of the sober-minded scholar pursuing the way of the sage, who was aloof from the compromises and temptations of secular power. Toegye's reflections on the contemporary tasks the country was faced with and his thinking on real-world practice had decisive influence on the formation of a national philosophy and ideology and on the development of new modes of governance.

According to Toegye, ideal governance, based on the wholeheartedness and sincerity of the king, propagates the king's virtue throughout the nation. In other words, his form of ideal governance, focusing on man's innate and spontaneous moral impulses, is constituted of just rule, which originates from the disciplined mind of the king, who consistently cultivates good morality.

Yulgok was similar to Toegye in that he tried to realize the ideal society on the basis of the moral mind cultivated through engagement with the Confucian system of value. However, he focused on the role of scholar-officials who were imbued with Confucian knowledge rather than that of the king exclusively, and he argued for the cooperative governance of the king and his retainers. He was interested in the human capacity to rectify the perverse impulses of the mind rather than in spontaneous moral drives. Therefore, in accordance with his political philosophy, Yulgok emphasized the role of retainers who could propose to the king policies befitting the times and promote necessary reform measures. In the monarchy of Joseon, the role of the king was very important, but Yulgok assigned more significance to the need for royal succession based on adherence to Confucian scholars' philosophies and ideals rather than to the succession of kings according to consanguinity. As a result, on the basis of Toegye's establishment of Korean Confucianism, Yulgok attempted to achieve governance by scholar-officials, in pursuit of which he took the initiative in urging the reinstatement in their positions at court of those who had been expelled during the period of Toegye.

This difference in emphasis between Toegye and Yulgok was mirrored by the divergence in thinking between the Toegye School and the Yulgok School, and subsequently between the two political factions, the Southerners and the Westerners. Toegye and Yulgok took the lead in overcoming the crisis of Joseon in the mid-sixteenth century, which was caused by the monopolization of power on the part of the maternal relatives of the king. Both of them contributed to the development of Korean Confucianism, but politically their varying views resulted in the formation of factional parties that played a leading role in the politics of the Joseon Dynasty. The duty of the king to pursue profound self-cultivation, the dignity and sense of responsibility of scholar-officials as exponents of Confucian ethics, and the political system of Joseon based on checks and balances between the king and his retainers were systemic elements of good governance that were advanced by Toegye and Yulgok. As a result, the two political factions established by the two scholars led Joseon for three hundred years, even while criticizing and competing with each other.

In this book I will review the lives and thought of Toegye and Yulgok from their first meeting as master and disciple until their relationship appeared to become antagonistic in terms of both their scholarly and political views. I will examine, primarily from the philosophical point of view, why they took different pathways though they had the same ideals and how they tried to deal with contemporary tasks in their respective ways. Through the academic correspondence and the theoretical debates between the two, I will examine in detail the philosophical and critical thinking and the theoretical achievements of both. This will be the basis of the various discussions in this book. I will also analyze their views on the morally right way for both a human being and a nation to conduct itself through an examination of their philosophies and the relationship between their views and their real-world practices. Although, fundamentally, this study will be based on their philosophies, I will also consider not only contemporary realities and the political situation but also the two scholars' individual circumstances and dispositions, as well as their essential spirit and mission and those of other scholars who made contributions during the Joseon Dynasty.

Although for a long period I have studied Korean Confucianism, including the philosophies of Toegye and Yulgok, I believe this focus on the reality of their lives and the systematic exposition of my thesis has clarified my understanding of Korean Confucianism even further. Thus, I hope that this work on Toegye and Yulgok, who grasped the tasks of the period in spite of the immensity of the challenge, will be meaningful to many.

II.

Korean Confucianism was the governing philosophy and ideology of the Joseon Dynasty for five hundred years. I began this book on the basis of my interest in the ways in which Korean Confucianism reflected the political and social realities of the Joseon Dynasty and in the reciprocal influence philosophy and practical reality had on each other during that period. Such concerns, which had been gradually forming since my initiation into the study of Korean Confucianism, became more defined while I was engaged in joint studies with scholars from various fields. A philosophical discussion may sometimes appear to be a solely metaphysical exercise disconnected from reality. However, if a philosophy is not understood as a part of our lives, its formative process and context cannot fully be grasped. The scholars of Joseon, including Toegye and Yulgok, discussed philosophical topics such as "the four beginnings (四端) and the seven feelings (七情)" and "the human mind (人心) and the moral mind (道心)," but they, as scholar-officials, devoted themselves to the foundation and governance of Joseon, achieved through the adoption of Confucianism as a national ideology. As they attempted to study, practice, and realize Neo-Confucian ideals during the stages of their own lives, if we do not comprehend their scholarly debate as a part of their thought and lives, our understanding will be fragmentary.

In this context, it may be said that Korean Confucianism is a rare example that enables us to investigate the formative process of philosophy in its immersion in the real world, the influence of philosophy on reality, and the consequences of philosophical debates. As Joseon was founded and governed on the basis of Neo-Confucian philosophy and ideology, scholar-officials engaged in both academic debates and the governance of the nation for five hundred years. As a result, we can trace the thought and achievements of these scholar-officials in their connection to practical affairs through multiple extant records.

III.

This book is based on my work on a joint project ("Korean Philosophy from Comparative Perspectives") with Professor Philip J. Ivanhoe (City University of Hong Kong), Kim Youngmin (Seoul National University), Kim Sung-moon (City University of Hong Kong), and Richard Kim (Loyola University Chicago). Professor Ivanhoe, who took the lead in the joint team, is a committed and enthusiastic scholar, and the debates I engaged in with him and with many other scholars at academic conferences were an added impetus in the writing of this book. Because I had studied mainly in Korea, the joint work with these respected scholars offered a fruitful opportunity to widen my perspective.

While studying Korean Confucianism with these scholars, I felt the keen need to connect relatively disparate themes in a single volume, and this book was written to satisfy this imperative. I am hopeful that my efforts at elucidation may make a real contribution to the study of Korean Confucianism.

Hyoungchan Kim
March 2018

The History of Korean Confucianism and the Status of Toegye and Yulgok as Confucian Scholars

THE HISTORY OF KOREAN PHILOSOPHY AND THE RISE OF NEO-CONFUCIANISM

During the era of Toegye and Yulgok, Neo-Confucianism was the predominant governing ideology or philosophy of Joseon (1392–1910). Before the foundation of Joseon, the Korean Peninsula had been occupied for about a thousand years by Buddhist countries such as the Three Kingdoms of Goguryeo, Baekje and Silla (first century BC~seventh century AD), the North-South States (Balhae and the Unified Silla: 698–926), and Goryeo (918~1392).

Korean philosophy, whose genesis has been traced to the foundation of Gojoseon (in around 2000 BC), is composed of Korea's indigenous shamanism as well as foreign religions and philosophies such as Taoism, Buddhism, Confucianism, and Catholicism. These religions and philosophical strands of thought, while competing or becoming amalgamated with one another, helped in the maintenance of social order and the governance of the state.

Confucianism, which had been introduced to the Korean Peninsula even before the fourth century AD, had some considerable effect on the formation of political institutions and social morality, even during the period when Buddhism exercised overwhelming influence as the national religion. Buddhism was fundamentally a religion that stood aloof from the quotidian world. On the other hand, the practical tendencies of Confucianism were thought to be appropriate to the governance of secular society because they were oriented toward the realization of a moral and ideal nation in the actual world.

It was during the Goryeo Dynasty that Confucian intellectuals began to present themselves as the main force underpinning social progress. Although Goryeo had been a Buddhist country since its foundation and had been governed by the aristocracy, from the year 958 forward government officials were selected through the state examination, and Confucian intellectuals began to take on the mantle of the main driving force of society. These intellectuals began to accept and observe the Neo-Confucianism formulated in China in the eleventh and twelfth centuries and adopted its tenets as the philosophical and ideological basis for the reform of their society. Furthermore, they criticized corrupt aristocrats and Buddhist monks and dreamed of constructing a new ethical state based on Neo-Confucianism.

As a country, Joseon was established by Confucian intellectuals. They crowned the war hero Yi Seong-gye (1335~1408) as their king and in fact founded Joseon through a bloodless revolution. In order to realize their ideals systematically, they codified laws that stipulated the national ideology, the administrative structure of the state, and the responsibilities of the king and government officials. In accordance with these laws they established new institutions. Jeong Do-jeon (鄭道傳, 1342~1398, pen name: Sambong 三峯), who took the lead in the foundation of Joseon as an intellectual and public official, was killed by Yi Bang-won (李芳遠), who later became King Taejong, the king himself, in the last analysis, could not but adhere to the vision promulgated by Jeong Do-jeon and other scholars for the consolidation of a Neo-Confucian ideal state.

Neo-Confucianism is a corpus of learning that, on the basis of Confucius's and Mencius's Confucianism, systematically theorizes the mechanisms of nature and society that comprise the origin of the universe and of all things, the ethics and forms of discipline necessary for human society to sustain itself, and the optimal forms of organization and governance of a nation. On the basis of their understanding of the principles of the universe and nature, Neo-Confucian scholars in the past aimed at discerning and establishing the most fruitful principles underpinning human society and strove to cultivate intellectuals and officials who could promote and apply these principles and govern society and the nation in accordance with these principles. They believed they could thereby ultimately realize an ideal state in this world. Joseon was a country founded by Confucian and Neo-Confucian scholars, who became the main group responsible for the governance of the nation and who were imbued with the clear aims of enhancing the level and quality of education, learning, and self-cultivation. The aim of education in their view was to foster talented people who would administer society in accordance with Neo-Confucian ideals, and the aim of learning and self-cultivation was for individual members of the elite to prepare themselves to govern society and the nation on the basis of the Neo-Confucian value system.

Philosophical currents in the Joseon Dynasty were deepened and developed through large and small controversies among scholars. Their learning was fundamentally and broadly based on that of Cheng Yi (程頤) and

Zhu Xi (朱熹), which originated in China. But some scholars accepted or crit-icized the teaching of Lu Jiu-yuan (陸九淵) and Wang Shou-ren (王守仁), which was popular in the contemporary Chinese Ming (明) era. There were also scholars who recognized the limit of Cheng-Zhu's learning and studied new branches of philosophy or ideology. However, all these scholars con-tributed to the development of the unique Confucianism and philosophy of Joseon. As a consequence of their studies, learning, and debates, scholars could participate in state affairs as officials or take the lead in disseminating culture and approved customs to rural districts. Moreover, their experiences in practical matters were reflected in their theoretical discussions.

The intellectual ferment that arose in the Joseon Dynasty can be seen as the motor of the academic achievements that resulted in the greater pro-fundity and development of Korean Confucianism. However, it should not be overlooked that the scholars who took the initiative in the controversies of the period were also the main figures in the foundation and governance of Joseon, the promotion of culture and politics, and the evolution of state administration. If we regard their philosophical positions and controversies as purely academic or theoretical preoccupations or merely as methods of self-cultivation, we might not gain a full appreciation of the essential meaning and role of the Confucianism of Joseon.

The history of philosophy in the Joseon Dynasty was composed of con-troversies that revolved around Neo-Confucian tenets.[1] Through this intense process, scholars established universal moral and practical values and the desirable course for the nation and society to take, and in this context the main strands of Korean Confucianism came to be formulated. The represen-tative controversies included the debate on "Confucianism and Buddhism" that arose soon after the foundation of Joseon and the debates on "*Taegeuk / Tai-ji* (太極, the Supreme Polarity)" in the early sixteenth century, on "the four beginnings and seven feelings (四端七情)" from the mid- to the late sixteenth century, on "mourning rites (喪禮)" in the mid-seventeenth century, on "human nature and the thing's nature" in the first half of the eighteenth century, on "Catholicism (西學)" from the eighteenth to the nineteenth cen-turies, on "the doctrine of mind (心說)" in the nineteenth century, and on the tension between "the open-door policy and anti-Western ideology" in the nineteenth century.

THE CONTROVERSY ON CONFUCIANISM
AND BUDDHISM

The details of this controversy could be ascertained in "Bulssi jabyeon (佛氏雜辨, Various Arguments against the Buddhists)," which was written by Sambong in 1398, immediately after the foundation of the Joseon Dynasty. Although there were only a few counterarguments against the contents of "Various Arguments against the Buddhists" from some Buddhist monks such as Gihwa (己和, 1376~1433), the text was a polemic rather than a fully considered argument against Buddhism. Sambong, as a successful revolutionary leader, denounced in theoretical terms the dominant ideology of Buddhism. Before he wrote it, in his essay titled "Simmun cheondap (心問天答, The Mind Asks for and Heaven Responds to It)," he had emphasized the active role of human beings in history and had compared Confucianism (Neo-Confucianism) with Buddhism and Taoism and maintained the supremacy of Neo-Confucianism in another essay, "Simgiri pyeon (心氣理篇, On the Mind, Matter, and Principle)." He believed that Neo-Confucian scholars should take the initiative in the governance of society and the nation and that full-fledged criticism of Buddhism, which had a thousand-year tradition as the national ideology, should precede this changing of the intellectual guard.

His "Bulssi jabbyeon" was accepted in Joseon as a major component of the critique of Buddhism. In this essay, composed of nineteen chapters, Sambong pointed out in concrete terms the absurdity of the Buddhist theory of reincarnation, the immorality of the theory of the hellish inferno that was used to coerce believers into making donations, the evil of practices such as mendicancy that allowed those who engaged in it to live a parasitic life without labor, and the injustice of the proscription against Buddhist priests maintaining any ties to their families.

Needless to say, as "Bulssi jabbyeon" denounced Buddhism from a biased Confucian or Neo-Confucian point of view, it cannot safely be said that the arguments of the essay together constituted a fair criticism of Buddhism. However, the text was highly regarded as a typical example of the critique of heretical Buddhism from a Neo-Confucian perspective in that it systematically criticized the core principles and social abuses of Buddhism. As Sambong was killed soon after he finished the essay, "Bulssi jabbyeon" posthumously played a role in vitiating the influence of Buddhism in Joseon and in lending greater legitimacy to Confucianism, ultimately enabling the foundation of a state based on Neo-Confucian ideology.

THE CONTROVERSY ON THE SUPREME POLARITY

While Sambong's criticism was intended to deprive Buddhism of its influence by denouncing its main doctrines, the controversy on *Taegeuk* (太極, the Supreme Polarity) was focused on guiding contemporary intellectuals in their understanding of Neo-Confucianism as the philosophy or ideology of the new dynasty. The controversy was motivated by the debate between

Zhu Xi (朱熹) and Lu Jiu-yuan (陸九淵) in 1188 in Chinese Southern Song (南宋). This debate revolved around the proposition "The Ultimate Non-Being Is the Supreme Polarity (無極而太極)," which had been set forth in Zhou Dun-yi (周敦頤)'s "The Explanation of the Diagram of the Supreme Polarity (太極圖說)."

Yi Eon-jeok (李彥迪, 1491–1553, pen name: Hoejae 晦齋) heard about a dispute between his maternal uncle, Son Suk-don (孫叔暾, pen name: Mang-jae 忘齋) and a friend of his uncle's named Jo Han-bo (曹漢輔, pen name: Manggidang 忘機堂) concerning Zhu Xi's and Lu Jiu-yuan's interpretations of the proposition "The Ultimate Non-Being Is the Supreme Polarity." Hoejae wrote an essay on this dispute. The controversy on the Supreme Polarity began when Manggidang read Hoejae's essay and sent a letter to Hoejae. The latter, reasoning that Mangjae's and Manggidang's interpretations were based on Taoism, Buddhism, and Lu Jiu-yuan's thinking, criticized them from the viewpoint of the Cheng-Zhu School (程朱學).

While the core subject of the dispute between Zhu Xi and Lu Jiu-yuan was the ontological meaning of the Ultimate Non-Being (無極) and the Supreme Polarity (太極), Hoejae and Manggidang transfigured these onto-logical concepts into the subjects of cultivation and practice in the course of their controversy. In other words, they debated not only understanding and mastering the original and absolute principle "The Ultimate Non-Being Is the Supreme Polarity" but also the relationship between the mastery and the practice of the principle. Through this controversy, Hoejae could refute the attitude of understanding Neo-Confucianism on the basis of Buddhism and the philosophy of Lao-Zhuang (老莊) and consolidate the philosophical position of Cheng-Zhu in Joseon. Later, Toegye, in his posthumous biography of Hoejae, appraised him highly, writing: "[Through this controversy] Hoejae illuminated the origin of Confucianism and refuted a heretical fallacy."[2]

Hoejae held successive high-ranking government posts such as Minister of Personnel, Minister of Justice, and Gyeongsang Provincial Governor. When some officials and scholars were in danger of being killed in 1545 owing to severe party strife, he, as the Head of Special Justice, attempted to save the lives of Sarimpa (士林派) scholars who had already been sentenced to death. However, he failed in his efforts and he himself was sent into exile. Until he died in exile he devoted himself to his studies. Later, his tablets were enshrined in both the Confucian Shrine and the Royal Shrine, together with Yi Hwang (李滉), Yi I (李珥), Kim Jip (金集), Song Si-yeol (宋時烈), and Park Se-chae (朴世采). Throughout the entire history of the Joseon Dynasty, only these six retainers were enshrined in both shrines, which was considered to be the greatest honor that could be bestowed on scholar-officials. These scholar-officials are generally called "the six sages."

THE CONTROVERSY ON THE FOUR
BEGINNINGS AND SEVEN FEELINGS

The controversies on "the four beginnings and seven feelings (四端七情)" between Yi Hwang (李滉, 1501–1570, pen name: Toegye 退溪) and Gi Dae-seung (奇大升, 1527–1572, pen name: Gobong 高峯), and then between Yi I (李珥, 1536–1584, pen name: Yulgok 栗谷) and Seong Hon (成渾, 1535–1598, pen name: Ugye 牛溪), showed that Korean Confucianism had already passed through the stage of the adoption of Chinese Neo-Confucianism and had entered the stage of its own unique and profound development.

These controversies were concerned with explicating the emergence of moral feeling from moral nature, and with the constitution and function of mind, original nature, and feeling, and the relations between them in order to effectively oversee the manifestation of moral feeling. While the controversy between Toegye and Gobong was mainly focused on the constitution and function of moral feeling or "the four beginnings and seven feelings," the controversy between Yulgok and Ugye developed into a debate on the human mind and the moral mind, which was concerned with the control of moral feelings through the mind. With these controversies as a form of momentum, theories on mind and nature became the main themes of the Confucianism of Joseon. Furthermore, it might be said that the controversies facilitated the cultivation of ethical men of talent who would contribute to the constitution of the Neo-Confucian ideal state.

The eight-year controversy between Toegye and Gobong started when Toegye as a representative senior scholar retired from his official post to live in his hometown and when Gobong had just passed the state examination as a young scholar-official. Their heated controversy, which transcended age and social position, is still considered to be the apotheosis of scholarly discussion in Korea. The philosophical viewpoints of Toegye and Yulgok formulated through these controversies became institutionalized in the form of the Toegye School and the Yulgok School, and politically they gave rise to the Southern Faction (*Namin*) and Western Faction (*Seo-in*), respectively. In this way the controversies had great influence on the intellectual milieu and on the political domain in Joseon. These controversies will be dealt with in detail in the course of this book.

THE CONTROVERSIES ON MOURNING RITES

The controversies on mourning rites, which erupted twice in the Court of Joseon in the late seventeenth century, reflected the influence of Confucianism on contemporary political affairs. The controversies, centering around the funeral rite of Queen Dowager Ja-ui, who was the second wife of King Injo, arose when King Hyojong, the second son of King Injo, died in 1659 and when Queen Inseon, the wife of King Hyojng, died in 1674. Heo Mok (許穆) and Yun Hyu (尹鑴), who belonged to the Southern Faction, argued that the funeral rite of the royal family should be different from that of an ordinary official's family. On the other hand, Song Si-yeol (宋時烈) and Song Jun-gil (宋浚吉), who belonged to the Western Faction, argued that the funeral rite of the royal family should not differ. This vehement controversy about Confucian propriety, which arose from one of the practical implications of Confucianism, reflected the accumulated studies conducted on propriety in Joseon. The retainers belonging to the Southern Faction embraced the position of Toegye, who supported king-centered rule and argued that all political measures should be initiated on the basis of the mind of the king. On the other hand, the retainers belonging to the Western Faction supported Yulgok's position in that he emphasized the importance of scholar-officials who were well-versed in ethics and of the political cooperation of the king and retainers rather than the authority of royal blood. In the first controversy, the Western Faction was victorious and the Southern Faction was ousted from the court, but in the second controversy, the result was reversed.

In Confucianism, the exercise of propriety was a form of embodying heavenly principles in the actual world through appropriate actions and institutions. Therefore, a man who properly understood and practiced propriety was one who recognized the principle of Heaven. Such a man was accepted as a virtuous person who was qualified to lead the state and society in accordance with the Neo-Confucian value system. On the other hand, a man who did not understand propriety was considered to be a narrow-minded person who did not have any such qualifications. In the first controversy, the opinion of those belonging to the Western Faction was acknowledged to be right, and as a result this group came to power. However, in the wake of the second controversy, the Southern Faction succeeded in transferring power to itself.

The theoretical controversies on the interpretation of propriety became associated with the alternating wielding of power because of the direct or indirect relationship of the king with the two political factions. However, the fact that the interpretation of propriety was accepted as a legitimate cause that ultimately determined the location of power in the court demonstrated that Confucianism was deeply rooted in the administration of the state. On the other hand, from this period on, Confucian discussions in Joseon, which should have been occasions of free intellectual inquiry, came to be restricted because of the excessive intervention of political players in scholarly discussions.

THE CONTROVERSY ON HUMAN NATURE
AND THE THING'S NATURE

In the early eighteenth century, the controversy on human nature and the thing's nature was composed of vehement theoretical arguments regarding some aspects of the original human nature between Yi gan (李柬, 1677~1727, pen name: Oe-am 巍巖) and Han Won-jin (韓元震, 1682~1751, pen name: Namdang 南塘), who were the disciples of Kwon Sang-ha (權尙夏, 1641~1721, pen name: Su-am遂菴). Oe-am argued that the original natures of the human being and the animal are identical because they originate from the same *li / li* (理, principle), while Namdang maintained that the original natures of the two are different because the original nature of each entity signifies that *li* as the universal principle is inside *gi / qi* (氣, material force) as physical matter (質料). The two scholars justified their own standpoints through their respective interpretations of Zhu Xi's and Yulgok's writings and theories, which were favorable to their own positions. Their controversy eventually encompassed issues such as the constitution of ethical "original nature (本然之性)," "physical nature (氣質之性)," "the five constants (五常: benevolence, righteousness, propriety, wisdom, and sincerity)," and "the substance of mind not yet manifested (未發心體)."

Originally, the various philosophical strands pursued by Cheng Yi and Zhu Xi implied ambiguous conceptualizations of original nature, and so many scholars including Toegye and Yulgok raised questions about Cheng-Zhu's ideas in this regard. After the series of controversies between Oe-am and Namdang, which spanned ten years, their debates on human nature and the thing's nature became full-scaled and spread to other scholars. Scholars around Kim Chang-hyeop (金昌協, 1651~1708, pen name: Nongam 農巖) in the capital area aligned themselves with Oe-am's perspective, while scholars around Su-am in the Chungcheong area mainly supported Namdang. As the Chungcheong area was called Hoseo (湖西) and the capital area was Rakha (洛下), this debate was also called "the Ho-Rak controversy."

Both Nongam and Namdang regarded themselves as the disciples of Song Si-yeol, who claimed that he was the orthodox successor of Yulgok and who became the central political figure in the Western Faction. Namdang, who advocated the difference between human nature and the thing's nature, argued that Yulgok was in the orthodox ethical lineage that originated with Zhu Xi, and he became the central figure of the hardliners who denounced the other factions as heretics. On the other hand, Nongam and other scholars in the capital area who maintained the identity of human nature and the thing's nature had an open-minded attitude and admitted not only the reasonableness of Toegye's theory but also of Zhu Xi's, and they introduced new Chinese learning and culture. Later, the central political power of the state was transferred to the Kim clan from Andong, who belonged to the lineage of Nongam. From the ranks of this clan emerged Bukhakpa (北學派) scholars, who advocated the assimilation of cultural developments abroad and constituted a pivotal axis of the trend toward the Practical Learning (實學) in the late period of Joseon.

THE CONTROVERSY ON SEOHAK (CATHOLICISM)

The controversy on Seohak (西學, Catholicism)[3] arose in the eighteenth century when the intellectuals of Joseon displayed interest in Western civilization, which had established a foothold in China. A group of intellectuals together studied books on Catholicism that had been translated into Chinese, and among them the first Catholics in Korea were produced. Given that this occurred without the intervention of any missionaries, this was an exceptional development in the history of Catholicism. These first Catholics belonged to the school of Yi Ik (李瀷, 1681~1763, pen name: Seongho 星湖), which was centered on the capital area. Although Seongho was born to a family that had produced high civil officials or vassals for many generations, as his elder brother was killed on account of party strife, he devoted his life to learning and declined to take up any official post. Professing that he was the successor of Toegye's learning, Seongho publicly criticized Yulgok and opened the door to new learning. As a result, many brilliant young adherents gathered around him, becoming his disciples. Some of them studied Catholicism. Jeong Yak-yong (丁若鏞, 1762~1836, pen name: Dasan 茶山), who compiled the corpus of practical learning in the late period of Joseon, was among them, as were his brothers. According to Toegye, moral nature might spontaneously be manifested by the mind through its understanding of the principles of the universe and nature and by its retaining a reverent attitude toward the Lord on High. Perhaps as a result of this teaching, it seems that quite a few scholars from the Seongho School could accept, without any particular reticence, a Catholicism that entailed the worship of the one and only God thanks to their acceptance of Toegye's viewpoint.

However, some scholars of the Southern Faction thought that it might be dangerous for young intellectuals of their faction to embrace Catholicism in the face of political struggle with the majority party or the Western Faction. Therefore the controversy between those who warned against Catholicism and those who eagerly accepted it started within the Seongho School. As Catholicism was a religion and strand of thought formed in a cultural milieu that was quite different from that of Joseon, it entailed many practices that conflicted with Confucianism. Could the Heavenly Father of Catholicism be understood as the Lord on High of Confucianism? If Catholicism regarded the Heavenly

God as a higher authority than the king, could it be permitted in a Confucian country? If Catholicism did not admit the core Confucian ethical injunctions of "benevolence, righteousness, propriety, and wisdom (仁義禮智)," didn't it radically deny the order of Confucian society? These questions conveyed the risk that the introduction of Catholicism might bring about conflict with the core Confucian tenets of Joseon. And in fact, this latent possibility offered the Western Faction an opportunity to oppress the Southern Faction on the pretext of extirpating heresy.

After the death of King Jeongjo, who favored the Southern Faction, the Western Faction came to power, while the Southern Faction was ousted from the court and the academic arguments regarding Catholicism came to an end. However, in exile Dasan, on the basis of his experience of Catholicism, reviewed voluminous Confucian classics one after another, and his work constituted a core element of the new Practical Learning of the late period of Joseon. His writings also subsequently influenced the formation of the "School of Enlightenment (開化派)."

Throughout the nineteenth century, when Joseon found itself in a critical situation, constantly at the risk of being plundered by foreign invaders, there were philosophical controversies on issues such as the doctrine of mind and on the tension between the open-door policy and anti-Western ideology. However, such controversies were little influenced by the thought of Toegye and Yulgok because the age of Confucianism was coming to its end.

NOTES

1. It is very useful for the understanding of Korean philosophy to survey representative theoretical controversies among scholars in the Joseon Dynasty. It is in this context that I contributed to devising and writing *Nonjaeng-euro boneun han-guk cheorak* (Korean Strands of Philosophy in View of Salient Debates, 1995). In the present text, I draw on this book for the selection of the main controversies that arose in the period of development of Korean Confucianism and for the presentation of the ideas at the core of these debates.

2. "Haeng-jang (Posthumous Biography)," *Hoejae jip* (The Collected Works of Hoejae) in *Han-guk munjip chonggan* (The Comprehensive Collection of Korean Literature), 24:503b.

3. Seohak (西學) refers to the body of learning introduced to Korea from the West. In its broad sense, Seohak is composed of natural and medical science, as well as Catholic teachings, while in its narrow sense it designates only Catholicism. As most contemporary intellectuals did not oppose the introduction of science and technology, the status, legitimacy, and implications of Catholicism were the crux of the argument centered on Western learning. Therefore, hereinafter Seohak refers only to Catholicism.

Notes on Dates and Quoted Texts

- The dates referred to in this book are based on the lunar calendar because this is the dating system used in most records relevant to Toegye and Yulgok and the collections of their works.
- The three-volume *Toegye jip* 退溪集 (*The Collected Works of Toegye*) and the two-volume *Yulgok jeonseo* 栗谷全書 (*The Complete Works of Yulgok*) contained in *Han-guk munjip chonggan* 韓國文集叢刊 (*The Comprehensive Collection of Korean Literature*) (Seoul: Minjok munhwa chujinhoe, 1988) were used.
- For the translations of sections of *Toegye jip*, I referred to the sixteen-volume *Gugyeok Toegye jeonseo* (The Complete Works of Toegye in Korean), edited by Toegyehak chongseo pyeon-gan wiwonhoe (Seoul: Toegyehak yeon-guwon, 2003).
- For the translations of sections of *Yulgok jeonseo*, I referred to the seven-volume *Gugyeok Yulgok jeonseo* (The Complete Works of Yulgok in Korean), edited by The Reference Office at Han-guk jeongsin munhwa yeon-guwon (Seongnam, Gyeonggi: Han-guk jeongsin munhwa yeon-guwon, 1996).
- The Romanization of Chinese terms follows Korean pronunciation. In the case of terms used in both Korea and China, "Korean Romanization/Chinese Romanization" is indicated when they appear for the first time.
- For the titles of books or articles written in Chinese, Korean Romanization is used if the author is Korean, while Chinese Romanization is used if the author is Chinese.

- When transcribing Korean text in the Roman alphabet, the Romanization of Korean, revised in 2000, is adhered to, while Chinese text is rendered in the Roman alphabet through Hanyu Pinyin Romanization.
- All photos of diagrams were taken from rare books at the Korea University Library in Seoul, Korea.

Chapter 1

The First Encounter

Twenty-three-year-old Yulgok called on fifty-eight-year-old Toegye in the early spring of 1558. At that time Toegye was one of the most eminent scholars in the Joseon Dynasty. Yulgok, having visited his father-in-law in Seongsan (星山, present-day Seongju in Gyeongbuk Province), and while on his way to his mother's hometown in Gangneung in Gangwon Province, visited Toegye's house in Ye-an (禮安, present-day Andong in Gyeongbuk Province). Yulgok stayed at the house for three days, a longer sojourn than had been planned owing to the unexpected early spring rain. When the rain turned to snow, Yulgok said goodbye to the old scholar and went on his way.

After Yulgok left his house, Toegye wrote a letter to one of his disciples named Jo Mok (趙穆, 1524–1606), whose pen name was Wolcheon (月川):

A few days ago Yulgok, who lives in Hanseong (漢城: present-day Seoul), called on me after his visit to Seongsan. He stayed at my house for three days owing to rain. He was cheerful, intelligent, and seemed to have read and remembered much, and to have devoted himself to learning. Indeed, he reminded me of the saying, "Youth is to be regarded with respect (*husaeng ga-oe* / *hou-sheng-ke-wei* 後生可畏)."[1]

From that time on, Toegye and Yulgok exchanged letters and discussed learning, the moral life, and the righteous path of the scholar. Yulgok sincerely respected Toegye and periodically asked advice of him. In addition, after he entered government service, Yulgok earnestly asked Toegye to participate in government administration. And after Toegye died, Yulgok attempted to enshrine his tablet in Confucian academies and in the National Shrine of Confucius.

Toegye reciprocated in his respect for Yulgok and wished that his intellectual talents might not be wasted on trifling secular affairs. Hoping that he would grow to be a great scholar, Toegye attempted to persuade Yulgok, whose personality he felt was too scrupulous and rigid, to devote himself to his studies and scolded him for not doing so sufficiently.

After Toegye passed away, Yulgok consolidated his position as a statesman while deepening his learning through scholarly debates. He tried in vain to prevent the division of political factions into Easterners and Westerners but was obliged to become the leader of the Western Faction. By contrast, Toegye was posthumously nominated as the leader of the Eastern Faction. After Toegye's passing, Yulgok criticized only a few of his theories. However, in the context of the political divisions of the time, Toegye's learning was regarded as the philosophical underpinning of the Eastern Faction, while Yulgok's was seen as that of the Western Faction.[2] Eventually, the intelligentsia and political elite of Joseon came to be divided into the two camps of Toegye's and Yulgok's schools of learning, and they led Joseon society through alternating periods of mutual conflict and accommodation.

The two scholars devoted their entire lives to the embodiment of the Confucian ideal of "sage on the inside, virtuous king on the outside (*naeseong oewang / nei-sheng-wai-wang* 內聖外王)." However, they pursued their own paths in accordance with the different social circumstances of the times in which they were immersed. Though Toegye had once been in government service, he looked on helplessly at the purge of scholars and the arbitrary actions of the king's maternal relatives of that period. Like Confucius (孔子) and Mencius (孟子), in his later years Toegye returned to his native town, pursued his studies, mentored his disciples, and suggested the righteous direction for the country to take regardless of the characteristics of those who came to power. On the other hand, Yulgok entered government service when the overweening influence of the king's maternal relatives had been supplanted and the purged scholars had been rehabilitated. During his lifetime of forty-eight years, he paved the way for the embodiment of Confucian ideals in Joseon society, achieved mainly in the persons of erudite scholars who had a sense of duty in terms of the pursuit of truth.

The exchange of ideas between Toegye and Yulgok through letters continued for thirteen years, from 1558 when Yulgok called on Toegye in early spring until the winter of 1570 when Toegye died. However, it may be said that their relationship persisted when Yulgok wrote a funeral oration for Toegye and presented a memorial to the king in order to persuade him to enshrine Toegye's tablet in the National Shrine of Confucius. Their relationship may be said to have continued by proxy even after Yulgok died, when the Easterners entered a confrontation with the Westerners, and further, when the political factions divided into the Southern Faction and the Western Faction and confronted each other.

I will now carefully examine the main strands of the two scholars' thinking through their most important writings and the letters they exchanged for thirteen years. Radically misreading their intentions, later scholars believed that they were exclusively opposed to and critical of each other, and recently such a perspective has become more prevalent. However, careful reading of their writings enables us to understand that their relationship was that of a master and disciple who earnestly exchanged views on the moral life and the path of learning. They were also comrades who took pains to transform the Joseon into an ideal nation based on the values of Confucianism and Neo-Confucianism. At first the young Yulgok asked for guidance and the more elderly Toegye responded, but later Yulgok answered Toegye's questions about the contemporary social situation.

A DIFFICULT DECISION: TO ADVANCE INTO THE WORLD OR RETREAT FROM IT

Yulgok introduced his first encounter with Toegye in an essay entitled "Swae-eon (瑣言)," which means "miscellaneous stories." It seems that Yulgok wanted to record the first meeting with Toegye in the form of an apparently anecdotal text that did not involve profound learning or engage in systematic commentary on the contemporary situation.

Miscellaneous Stories (I)[3]

When I read the history of the Han (漢) Dynasty, I suspected that strangely enough, the advance into and retreat from the world of "the four hoary old men" were unjustifiable, but I dared not reveal my view to anyone. However, I expressed my opinion without reserve to Master Toegye and he agreed with me. I did not know that ancient sages had commented on this matter until I read Zhu Xi's thoughts in *Xing-li da-quan* (性理大全). Zhu Xi said, "The four hoary old men might not be Confucian scholars but merely quick-witted intellectuals."[4] Only then could I feel sure that I was right.

Some people maintained that "the four hoary old men" disguised themselves as sages only to help the prince in accordance with the tactics of Zhang Liang (張良),[5] of which almost all the retainers of the Imperial Court of the Han Dynasty were ignorant. I could not agree with them because their view presupposed that Zhang Liang, who had been loyal to the king, betrayed him impetuously. In general, at the end of "the Warring States period (戰國時代)," scholars were not well versed in moral principles but extolled those who displayed fortitude. The four old scholars disappeared solely to avoid being insulted by Emperor Gaozu (高祖). How could their retreat from the world be considered equal to that of Yi Yin (伊尹)[6] or of Tai-gong (太公)?[7] If they could be highly esteemed merely by rejecting the meeting with Emperor Gaozu, can it also be said that tacticians such as An Qi-sheng (安期生)[8] and Kuai Che (蒯徹)[9] were lofty and solemn scholars? Once, I wrote the following poems about the four old men:

Oh, gone are the age-old paragons Yao and Shun,
As futilely, the four hoary old men left Mt. Shang behind.
For, alas, having lost his once generous nature,
The king consigned them into the hands of Duke Jian-cheng.[10]
唐虞世遠更何求 一出商顏亦浪游
可惜龍顏空大度 得賢終讓建成侯

Like Qin Shi Huang, the king pissed into scholars' hats.[11]
So why did they feign to become vassals of the Han Dynasty?
No one knew, however, the hoary men's real intention.
Willingly, they wanted to serve the cause of the prince.
溲溺儒冠亦一秦 如何更作漢家臣
那知四皓商山老 盡是東宮願死人

The four old men who were inducted in the Court of Han
Should feel ashamed, recalling the verdancy of Mt. Shou-yang.[12]
Alas, hoary old men from Mt. Shang, what did you earn thus?
Was it only your lifelong disgrace, as "the attendants of the prince"?
聘幣慇懃出漢廷 商山應愧首陽青
可憐四皓成何事 贏得生平羽翼名

In his first encounter with Toegye, Yulgok commenced by asking him about the hoary old men's steps into and retreat from the world because understanding the circumstances surrounding their advance or withdrawal could be helpful to his decision about the wisdom of entering government service.

It was quite natural for a Confucian scholar who had cultivated his philosophical capacities through learning to be concerned with public affairs and to enter government service because one of the purposes of Confucian learning was to become "a sage on the inside and a virtuous king on the outside." So for a Confucian scholar to step into the world of practical affairs was to embody the ideals and values he had pursued through learning and self-cultivation. If a Confucian scholar was confident that he was well versed in learning and had cultivated virtue, he would naturally attempt to advance into the world. However, if he was surrounded by unfavorable social circumstances in which he could only with great difficulty embody his ideal, it would be ill-advised for him to engage in practical affairs, and he would be better advised to continue his studies and to teach his disciples, in this way deferring his entry into the world of realpolitik until some future date. This was a Confucian tradition from the times of Confucius and Mencius, so for a Confucian scholar to enter government service even in times of confusion seemed solely designed to satisfy his personal ambition. Nevertheless, it might also have incurred censure if a scholar lived in solitude, aloof from the confusion of the world. Therefore it was acknowledged that sometimes a scholar should engage practically and strive to propose the right path for the nation, though his attempt might end in failure. Regardless of the times, it was a very difficult balance for scholars to strike in deciding on their level of engagement or withdrawal in consideration of their capabilities and social circumstances.

Yulgok, who had been preparing for the state examination as a young scholar, recalled first of all this matter of practical engagement during his first encounter with Toegye. At that time Toegye, as a highly respected scholar, had been pursuing his studies and mentoring his disciples for ten years, since his retirement to his hometown at the age of forty-nine. Sometimes, owing to the earnest requests of the king, Toegye resumed his government service, but only for short periods. Yulgok questioned Toegye about the advance into and retreat from the world of the "four hoary old men." As Yulgok was preparing for the state examination, he may have wanted to meet Toegye to ask for guidance on whether and to what extent he should engage with the practical affairs of the world.

The "four hoary old men" refers to Dong-yuan-gong (東園公), Lu-li (甪里), Qi-li-ji (綺里季), and Xia-huang-gong (夏黃公). All of them were more than eighty years old and they were called Si-hao (四皓: four hoary old men) because their hair, beards, and eyebrows were all gray. Emperor Gaozu of Han wanted to have them near, but they did not enter the court because the emperor regarded courageous men more highly than learned men. Emperor Gaozu wanted to depose Prince Liu Ying (劉盈), the son of Queen Lu (呂后), and instead install Liu Ru-yi (劉如意), the son of Royal Concubine Qi (戚), as the new prince. Queen Lu's elder brother, Duke Jian-cheng (建成侯), in accordance with the advice of Zhang Liang (張良), cordially invited the four hoary old men to become retainers at the court in the expectation that they would be of some help to his nephew. As the duke hoped, the old men supported Prince Liu-Ying and channeled Emperor Gaozu into revoking his plan to replace the prince.[13]

Yulgok doubted whether the four old men's acceptance of positions at the court was appropriate behavior. At that time the Qin (秦) Dynasty had disintegrated and Emperor Gaozu had founded the Han Dynasty. Therefore, in view of the contemporary situation, it can hardly be said that it was a period when moral justice could not be attained. Rather, it was an era when talented persons felt an onus on them to enter government service in order to consolidate the foundations of the new dynasty. However, Emperor Gaozu, who had conquered the central districts of China, favored men of action and was indifferent toward those who pursued learning. Moreover, the emperor is said to have insulted scholars by "pissing into their hats."[14]

Yulgok thought that the four old men entered the Court of Emperor Gaozu not to embody moral principles but only to support the prince. He was convinced of the justice of his thinking, as Toegye agreed with him on this matter.[15] Furthermore, by quoting Zhu Xi's remark that the four were merely quick-witted and calculating old men, he maintained that they were mere tacticians and not authentic Confucian scholars pursuing moral principles.

The dilemma of whether to engage in worldly affairs or to withdraw from them was the subject of discussion between Toegye and Yulgok until the later years of the former's life, perhaps because it was the starting point of the process of deciding how to embody the lessons of their lifelong learning in the social circumstances with which they were faced. While Yulgok attempted to enter government service as a scholar-official, Toegye retired to his hometown, disappointed with the contemporary political situation. Yulgok told Toegye that people eagerly wanted him to help administer state affairs and entreated him to participate in the Royal Court. However, Toegye declined most of Yulgok's requests.[16] This might have been due to the difference in their judgments on the contemporary state of affairs and in their own capabilities and personal situations.

The prime of Toegye's life coincided with the mid-sixteenth century, about 150 years (five generations) after the foundation of Joseon in 1392. The first generation of Joseon, who criticized the ills and abuses of Buddhism and the aristocracy and professed a desire to construct a Neo-Confucian[17] ideal state, had already died. During the lifetime of Toegye, after several coups that were caused by conflicts centering on the accession to the throne, severe factional struggles continued between vassals who attempted to preserve their vested interests and those in favor of reform who argued for the realization of Neo-Confucian ideals. During Muo sahwa (the literati purge in the fourth year of King Yeonsan's reign in 1498), Gapja sahwa (the literati purge in the tenth year of King Yeonsan's reign in 1504), and Gimyo sahwa (the literati purge in the fourteenth year of King Jeongjong's reign in 1519), many scholar-officials including Kim Jong-jik, Kim Goeng-pil, Jo Gwang-jo, and Yi Eon-jeok were killed. In addition, King Myeongjong's maternal relatives, who had come to the fore as a strong political faction, brought about Eulsa sahwa (the literati purge in the year of King Myeongjong's accession to the throne in 1545) and Jeongmi sahwa (the literati purge in the second year of King Myeongjong's reign in 1547).

As mentioned earlier, during the period from 1534 to 1549 when Toegye took up various government posts, the Neo-Confucian political ideal of governance by sage-kings and scholar-officials was frustrated. Toegye's elder brother Yi Hae (李瀣, 1496–1550, pen name: Ongye 溫溪) was flogged for having criticized the despotism of the king's maternal relatives and died on his way into exile.[18] It seems that Toegye decided to resign from his government post because he witnessed the intellectual class growing helpless owing to the increasing political dominance of the king's maternal relatives since Eulsa sahwa.[19]

The year 1549, when Toegye resigned from his post and went to his hometown, corresponds to the initial period when scholar-officials were excluded from major government posts, that is, the period from 1545, when Eulsa sahwa was carried out, to 1565, when Queen Munjeong died and her relatives were expelled.[20] During this period, Yulgok called on Toegye in 1558. Yulgok, who wanted to enter government service by taking the state examination, had to mull over whether he should take a government post or not, and he might have wanted to ask the advice of Toegye on this matter.

However, political conditions began to change in 1564, soon after Yulgok entered government service at the age of twenty-nine. As Queen Dowager Munjeong, who had provided patronage to her relatives, died in 1564, King Myeongjong attempted to expel the relatives and reinstate the scholar-officials. Though Myeongjong passed away without fulfilling his goals, King Seonjo, who came to the throne in 1567 at the young age of sixteen, sincerely tried to assimilate the expertise of scholar-officials and achieve political reform. At this time, Toegye was already in his late sixties. As King Seonjo had repeatedly invited him to join the Royal Court, he went to the capital city of Hanyang in 1568. However, after he had an audience with the king, he seems to have been somewhat disappointed with the monarch. He presented a memorial to the king titled "Mujin yukjo so (戊辰六條疏, Memorandum on Six Points in 1568)" in which he suggested six thoughts that might help the king to rule wisely, and he participated in *gyeong-yeon / jing-yan* (經筵, a lecture for the king) nine times. However, after he dedicated *Seonghak sipdo* (聖學十圖, *Ten Diagrams on Sage Learning*) to the king, which he composed in the hope that the monarch would become a sage king, he returned to his hometown.

Dedicating *Seonghak sipdo* to the king, Toegye wrote as follows:

> As your Majesty's servant, I feel sorry that my memorial about learning could not move your Majesty and that my humble advice was of little help to your Majesty's sagacious judgment. This petty servant is so embarrassed that I cannot make any excuse.[21]

Though Toegye had presented "Mujin yukjo so" to the king and had directly expressed himself to him, he became aware that the king would not listen to what he suggested. So as his final service to the king, he dedicated *Seonghak sipdo* to him in the hope that it would be of some help to the young monarch in growing to be a sage-king.

Toegye's decision to retire from the world mirrored the dilemma that had faced many, with varying results. Yi Yin and Tai-gong, who Yulgok mentioned in his story concerning the poem about the four old men as the paragons of "advance into and retreat from the world," had retired from practical affairs but ultimately had achieved their aspirations in the world. Yi Yin, while engaged in farming, received invitations three times from King Tang (湯) and helped the king to found the Yin (殷) Dynasty. He said, "Isn't it the case that any king who I serve is my king and any people who I administer are my people?"[22] And he took it on himself to strive to manage the state well. Mencius esteemed him as a sage.[23] Jiang Tai-gong (姜太公) was a sage who was biding his time fishing at the Wei-shui River (渭水) when the Yin Dynasty went into decline owing to King Zhou's (紂王) tyranny. He helped King Wu (武) to subdue the Yin Dynasty and to found the Zhou (周) Dynasty. Subsequently, Tai-gong was invested with the title of Duke of Qi (齊). On the contrary, An Qi-sheng and Kuai Che from the Qin (秦) Dynasty were known as excellent tacticians.

Yulgok regarded the four old men not as statesmen like Yi Yin and Jiang Tai-gong, who helped end tyranny and embodied just rule, but merely as tacticians like An Qi-sheng and Kuai Che. Furthermore, he maintained that they should be ashamed of themselves, bearing in mind the examples of Bo-yi (伯夷) and Shu-qi (叔齊), who retired on Mt. Shou-yang (首陽) and starved to death in order not to live under a tyrant. Yulgok thought that the four old men entered the Court of Emperor Gaozu only to form a faction that would curry favor with the prince. He excoriated them based on his belief that if one could not embody the right path to pursue in the world, one should starve to death rather than step into the practical world and attempt to rise to power armed only with one's petty talents.

Yulgok, who seriously considered entering government service, and Toegye, who had already withdrawn from official posts and retired to his hometown, found themselves in different situations. However, Yulgok believed that Toegye was not fundamentally opposed to entering government service. Toegye's critical judgment on the four old men implied that if a lord was unwilling to pursue the embodiment of the righteous way with the assistance of his retainers, it was not right to enter the court. He implied that one should advance into the world and attempt to achieve one's worldly aspiration only in an age when one can pursue the embodiment of the righteous way. However, although Toegye warned that one should not study for the purpose of rising in the world, he said that one should willingly accept the opportunity to take up a government post in which one's learning and self-cultivation could be put to use.[24] In the winter of 1558, when Yulgok first met Toegye, the former gained first place in the Special State Examination. The officials administering the examination read his answer titled "Cheondo chaek (天道策, A Proposal on the Way of Heaven)" and are said to have praised Yulgok as a genius.[25] However, he took up a government post in 1564, six years after the Special State Examination, because he had to observe the three-year filial mourning period for his deceased father and overcome one more hurdle, the civil service examination.

"EXCESSIVE PRAISE"

Yulgok believed that Toegye, on the pretext of having contracted a disease, wanted to retire to his hometown until he died. Yulgok, who had been preparing for the Special State Examination that was the prerequisite for entering government service, called on Toegye in his hometown and dedicated a poem to him. The poem is replete with somewhat excessive praise of Toegye, which reflected the young student's respect for the elderly scholar.

Miscellaneous Stories (II)[26]

Master Toegye, being sick, returned to his hometown in Ye-an and built a house in a valley, in which he would live for the rest of his days. In the spring of 1558 (the thirteenth year of King Myeongjong's reign), on my way from Seongsan to Imyeong (臨瀛, present-day Gangneung in Gangwon Province), I visited Ye-an to meet the master. While staying in his house I wrote a poem for him.

The water flowing in the dale may originate in Zhu-shui and Si-shui,[27]
The eminent peak may well be compared to Mt. Wu-yi.[28]
Though his learning is gleaned from one thousand classics,
He desires no more than life in a shabby, small house.
He cherishes the lucid moon shining in the sky after rain,
His cheerful talk pacifies the rough waves of the world.
This paltry mind wishes only to hear words on the Way,
Not to steal a few idle hours from the master.

溪分洙泗派 峯秀武夷山
活計經千卷 行藏屋數閒
襟懷開霽月 談笑止狂瀾
小子求聞道 非偸半日閒

Master Toegye responded to my poem as follows:

Ill in bed, the admiration of spring scenes was beyond my means,
You came to me, however, to refresh my spirit.
And now I know a renowned scholar who is worthy of the name.
What a shame I was lacking in my study of *gyeong* /
    jing (敬, reverent mindfulness).
A good harvest can't be expected in the midst of thickly grown weeds,
A mirror can't be polished well in a miasma of rising dust.
Shall we halt our exchange of excessive praise,
And instead study diligently morning and night, day after day?

病我牢關不見春 公來披豁醒心神
始知名下無虛士 堪愧年前闕敬身
嘉穀莫容稊熟美 游塵不許鏡磨新
過情詩語須刪去 努力功夫各日親[29]

In his poem Yulgok says that Toegye's learning succeeded to that of Confucius, and he praises the characteristics and profundity of his learning by
comparing him with Zhu Xi on Mt. Wu-yi. He also admires Toegye's devotion to his studies by contrasting the voluminous classics he had read with
his simple life. He continues by suggesting that Toegye's cultivated mind
and cordial words might pacify the disorderly world full of sound and fury
and earnestly asks for his advice. Yulgok's somewhat florid diction reflects
his admiration for Toegye. He concludes that he visited Toegye as a young
student in pursuit of the righteous way.

Toegye could not but feel burdened by Yulgok's laudatory poem. He might
have been prepared to accept that he had inherited the scholastic mantle of
Confucius but may have thought that it was excessive to be compared with
Zhu Xi. In his poem Toegye welcomes the bright young man who visited
his humble house and says that Yulgok has stimulated him intellectually.
He also encourages Yulgok by saying that he is worthy of the reputation of
a respected scholar. And his self-deprecatory remark "I was lacking in my
study of *gyeong* (敬: 敬身 in the original Chinese poem)" reflected Toegye's
modest attitude even toward a young man or a man of lower status. After
alluding to the magniloquence of Yulgok's poem, Toegye ends his poem by
concluding that they should try to diligently pursue learning.

In his poem Toegye says that he should have tried harder in his studies of
gyeong (reverent mindfulness). *Gyeongsin / jing-shen* (敬身) in the original
Chinese poem may be translated as "reverent behavior" or "polite greeting."
In the context of the poem, it seems to be more accurate to interpret it as "per-
sonally learning and practicing the attitude of *gyeong*." Toegye always emphasized *gyeong* as the fundamental attitude or means of study and self-cultivation.
It was also in this context that whenever he met Yulgok, he used to encourage
the younger man by saying that Yulgok roused him to study.[30] So in his poem
Toegye seems to regard the study of *gyeong* as the subject of his further study.

Gyeong was so important in Toegye's studies that some scholars defined
his teachings as the philosophy of *gyeong*.[31] The concept refers not only to
the fundamental attitude toward the primacy of learning but also to the ideal
method of study that can be applied to the whole gamut of Neo-Confucian
learning and self-cultivation. Therefore *gyeong* has a profound meaning that
cannot be translated into mere respect or reverence.

It originally referred to the stance of welcoming a god with reverence
and solemnity.[32] In Neo-Confucianism it was reinterpreted as "the reverent

attitude of being mindful of the impending subject or situation, as in the case of welcoming a god."[33] Toegye repeatedly emphasized to his disciples that *gyeong* was a stance applicable to both theoretical study and practical cultivation.

In his first encounter with the young and high-spirited Yulgok, Toegye humbly confesses that he regrets neglecting the study of *gyeong*. And after the two lines, "A good harvest can't be expected in the midst of thickly grown weeds, / A mirror can't be polished in a miasma of rising dust," Toegye advises Yulgok not to neglect his studies.

EXPECTATION AND RESOLUTION

Toegye seems to have been deeply impressed by the young Yulgok, who stayed at his house in a valley in Ye-an for three days. After Yulgok went to Gangneung, the two scholars exchanged letters and poems. In his letters Yulgok posed some questions to Master Toegye. The master answered them in his letters and also wrote poems for Yulgok. In the poems the master alluded to his worries about the damaging trends of contemporary learning, together with his expectations for Yulgok. For his part, Yulgok recorded the letters and poems exchanged with Master Toegye in his "Miscellaneous Stories."

Miscellaneous Stories (III)[34]

I stayed at Master Toegye's house for two nights and then left for Gangneung. When I arrived there, I received the following letter and poems from the Master.

Aren't there numerous talented persons in the world? However, the prevalent trend of contemporary society is that they are reluctant to pursue learning. Of those rare people who have not adapted themselves to this trend, some lack in talent and some are too old. If young men as brilliant as you begin to follow the righteous way, how great the resultant achievements will be. I sincerely hope that you will not be satisfied with slight accomplishments but devote yourself to the fulfillment of your lofty aims.

Master Toegye's poem is as follows:

Old people wondered and doubted about learning of the Way,
And now the Way fades away for study is only for profit.
Fortunately, however, you can discern a clue to reviving the Way,
I wish they would follow you and acquire new knowledge.[35]
從來此學世驚疑 射利窮經道益離
感子獨能尋墜緒 令人聞語發新知

Another poem from the master:

Returning home, I deplore my long wandering.
Staying in a quiet nook, I barely peep at a ray through a crack.
I pray you will pursue the righteous Way before it is too late.
Never regret setting foot in a secluded place.[36]
歸來自歎久迷方 靜處才窺隙裏光
勸子及時追正軌 莫嗟行脚入窮鄉[37]

I wrote a poem in reply to the master.

Who may ever reach the supreme stage in the study of *gyeong*?
Alas, I can't dispel all the causes of my disease.
In retrospect, only after drinking cold water in a stream
Could I feel refreshed, as it washed away the dregs in my heart and belly.
When young, I wandered through every quarter and corner,
And only after man and horse became gaunt could I look back on myself.
As the setting sun naturally hangs over the western hill,
How can a wayfarer worry when his home is still a long way off?
學道何人到不疑 病根嗟我未全離
想應捧飲寒溪水 冷澈心肝只自知
早歲春糧走四方 馬飢人瘦始回光
斜陽本在西山上 旅客何愁遠故鄉

In the first poem Toegye criticizes the corrupted contemporary trend of learning and hopes that Yulgok, young and talented, will pursue the righteous way of learning in order to enlighten the world. Toegye sent the second poem to Yulgok together with a letter[38] in which he encourages Yulgok by confessing that he also wandered in his youth. On the other hand, Yulgok, in his first encounter with Toegye and in his letter, claims that he repented of his fascination with Buddhism. So Toegye modestly says in his poem that he could glimpse the true way of learning only after a long period of wandering and advises Yulgok not to blame himself too much for his immersion in Buddhism but to try to pursue righteous learning.

In his poem written in response to Toegye's advice, Yulgok says that previously he could not have confidence in his study of the Way but that his doubt was washed away after meeting with Toegye. In addition, Yulgok says that he has ceased his wandering and that he is no longer interested in miscellaneous fields of study. Finally, he shows his resolution not to be frustrated in his pursuit of the Way, though it is a long journey.

When Yulgok was sixteen years old, his mother Sin Saimdang (申師任堂) died and he observed the three-year filial mourning period for her. Subsequently, he withdrew to Mt. Geumgang and became immersed in Buddhism.[39] He seems to have been shocked at the death of Sin Saimdang, who had great influence on him as a mother and mentor. Although the founding and governing ideology of the Joseon Dynasty was Confucianism, Buddhism, introduced a thousand years before, was deeply rooted in people's lives. Though the dynasty officially rejected Buddhism, many people still put great store in its teachings, as the young Yulgok did.

Nevertheless, it was not a trifling matter that a scholar who desired to enter government service evidently had a passionate affinity for Buddhism. About one year after he went to Mt. Geumgang, Yulgok realized the limits of Buddhism and took up the study of Confucianism once again. However, his immersion in Buddhism, more than any wandering in his youth, seems to have left the deepest impression on him. In his poem to Toegye Yulgok confesses that he repented of his wandering and expresses his resolution not to be frustrated in the long pilgrimage toward truth.

The two lines of this poem, "In retrospect, only after drinking cold water in a stream, / Could I feel refreshed, as it washed away the dregs in my heart and belly," have been variously interpreted. Some scholars have considered the lines to mean that "Toegye drank cold water and refreshed his heart" or "Toegye repented of the wandering of his youth and recovered his spiritual core."[40] If twenty-three-year-old Yulgok intended to convey this implication in these lines, he may well be criticized as impudent.

Professor Yi Gwang-ho argues that "these lines might have been inserted by someone in a later era."[41] However, this possibility is not supported by any evidence. Therefore it is reasonable to interpret the lines in the context of the situation in which Yulgok met Toegye. In that case, a plausible assessment is that it is not Toegye but Yulgok who reflects on his wandering in his youth, drinks cold water, and refreshes his heart.

The argument about the interpretation of these lines may have arisen owing to their ambiguity on one hand and the differing views on the relationship between Toegye and Yulgok on the other. While those who have evaluated Yulgok tried to interpret his posture toward Toegye as not excessively con-descending, those who believe that Yulgok frequently disparaged Toegye in *Yulgok jeonseo* (栗谷全書, *The Complete Works of Yulgok*) have seen Yulgok's writings in a skeptical light.

However, Yulgok advocated his theories while criticizing Toegye's ideas only after the latter had died. The notion of an intense rivalry between them was established by later scholars, after Yulgok had died. During their lifetime when they exchanged ideas, their relationship was that of master and disciple who respected and encouraged each other rather than harboring any sense of rivalry and competition.

The following poems are vivid descriptions of their relationship. These poems, written when Toegye first met Yulgok, are contained in *Toegye jip* (退溪集, *The Collected Works of Toegye*).

Mr. Yi, a Young Genius, Visited My House at Gyesang and
  Stayed Here for Three Days Owing to Rain[42]

You, renowned as a young genius, live in Seoul
While I, a sick old man, live in a remote village.
How could I anticipate that you would call on me today
To intimately exchange profound thoughts with me?
早歲盛名君上國 暮年多病我荒村
那知此日來相訪 宿昔幽懷可款言

I was pleased to meet you on a spring day in February,
Heavenly grace and mutual trust caused your delay for three days.
Streaks of rain like silvery bamboo struck the bank of a stream,
Flakes of snow like floral beads whirled around the trunks of trees.
The muddy lanes into which horse hoofs sank are too trying to allow a journey,
As the scenery seems refreshed by a bird's call for a bright day.
Again I offer you a cup, filling it to the brim,
Forgetting our ages, let's be more intimate with each other
     through our righteous pursuits.
才子欣逢二月春 挽留三日若通神
雨垂銀竹捎溪足 雪作瓊花裹樹身
沒馬泥融行尚阻 喚晴禽語景纔新
一杯再屬吾何淺 從此忘年義更親

These two poems seem to have been written before Yulgok left Toegye's
house after his three days' stay. In the first poem Toegye expresses his happiness at unexpectedly meeting and talking with Yulgok, who was renowned
as a young prodigy, in his humble house in a remote village. In the second
poem Toegye, after stating his impressions of the three rainy days spent with
Yulgok, displays his affection for Yulgok by saying, "Now, forgetting our
ages, let's be more intimate with each other through our righteous pursuits."
    While the two poems depict the atmosphere of the day before Yulgok left,
the following three poems depict Toegye's feelings immediately after Yulgok
left.[43]

Three days after his visit, raindrops turned into crystal-clear jade stones,
Plants pushed out new shoots amid snowflakes drifting in the air.
The spring god, ashamed that he had little to show to the poet,
Decorated hills and groves with a variety of flowery snowflakes.
三日霪霖變玉華 滿空飄絮地滋芽
東君愧乏詩人賞 粧點園林替萬花

Drifting snowflakes hid the contours of distant mountains,
A hungry magpie crowed and flapped toward its nest.

Blue water and fecund fields could have washed your eyes,
But, alas, I couldn't enjoy fair and luminous weather with you.
靄靄斯須失遠山 噪飢鳥鵲自飛還
飜嫌不共晴妍日 綠水芳郊洗眼看

Leaving my hut surrounded by clouds,
You may trudge along a mountain path.
Overcoming hardships with perseverance,
You may learn also local customs during your journey.
A deep root promises full blossoms,
A deep fountain ruffles the water spontaneously.
Please don't forget to write to me betimes,
And console this laggard a thousand leagues away.
別我雲中屋 行穿海上山
忍心艱險際 諳俗旅遊間
本厚華應曄 源深水自瀾
煩君時寄札 千里慰憛閒

In the first poem Toegye writes that Yulgok could go on his journey because spring rains have turned into snow. Toegye describes the landscape covered with snow as a gift from the god of spring. In the second poem he expresses his sorrow that he cannot enjoy with Yulgok the splendid scenes smothered in white. In the third poem he hopes that Yulgok will learn more about the troubled world and that their relationship will last indefinitely.

Though Toegye was well known as a scholar-official who greatly contributed to the establishment and development of the Neo-Confucianism of the Joseon Dynasty, he was also a writer who composed poems throughout his life. His poems, recorded in works such as *Naejip* (內集), *Byeoljip* (別集), *Oejip* (外集), and *Sokjip* (續集), amount to about two thousand pieces.[44] His poems may be the source that can best enable us to grasp the truest impulses of his heart and intellect.

NOTES

1. Yi Hwang (李滉), "Dap Jo Sa-gyeong" 答趙士敬 (Response to Jo Sa-gyeong), in *Toegye jip* 退溪集 (The Collected Works of Toegye) of *Han-guk munjip chonggan* 韓國文集叢刊 (The Comprehensive Collection of Korean Literature), 30:46c. (Volume 30 of *Han-guk munjip chonggan*, the right side of the lower column on page 46. Subsequent citations from *Han-guk munjip chonggan* will follow this format.)

2. Compared to the members of the Southern Faction (the former Eastern Faction) who lived in the Yeongnam region and subscribed to the teachings of the Toegye School, the members of the Western Faction had a weak academic identity. In the late seventeenth century, they divorced the Yulgok School from the teachings

of Jo Gwang-jo (趙光祖, pen name: Jeongam 靜菴) and of Toegye and adapted themselves to the thinking of Zhu Xi in order to secure their identity as an academic and political force and to establish an independent school. For details refer to Yu Sae-rom, "17-segi seo-in-ui haktong uisikgwa Yulgok yeonbo-ui pyeonchan" (The Seo-in Members' Consciousness of Their Scholastic Mantle and the Publication of the Chronology of Yulgok), *Han-guksaron* 52 (Seoul: Department of Korean History at Seoul National University, 2006).

3. Yi I, "Swae-eon" 瑣言 (Miscellaneous Stories), in *Yulgok jeonseo* 栗谷全書 of *Han-guk munjip chonggan*, 44:301d–302a. Though "Miscellaneous Stories" is a single work of interconnected texts, I divide it into three sections, I, II, and III, in accordance with its varied contents.

4. "Li-dai san—Xi-han" 歷代三—西漢, in *Xing-li da-quan* 性理大全, Vol. 61.

5. Zhang Liang (張良, courtesy name Zi-fang 子房: ?–189 BC) assisted Emperor Gaozu of the Han Dynasty (漢高祖) to defeat Xiang-yu (項羽). Zhang Liang together with Xiao-he (蕭何) and Han-xin (韓信) were known as the three meritorious retainers present at the foundation of the Han Dynasty. Later, Zhang Liang was appointed premier.

6. Yi Yin (伊尹), who had retired to the country, after the third invitation from King Tang (湯王) to join the Royal Court, helped the king to found the Shang (商) Dynasty.

7. Tai-gong (太公) had been waiting for an opportunity to enter government service, whiling away his time by fishing. When he had the opportunity, he helped King Wen (文王) and King Wu (武王) to defeat the Shang Dynasty, which was governed by a tyrant named King Zhou (紂王). As his family name was Jiang (姜), he is usually called Jiang Tai-gong (姜太公). Later, he was made a duke.

8. An Qi-sheng (安期生) lived during the period of the Qin (秦) and Han (漢) Dynasties. He is said to have followed the tenets of Taoism and to have sold medicine for his livelihood. Some said that he later became a Taoist hermit. Kuai Che (蒯徹) was one of his friends.

9. Kuai Che (蒯徹) was a tactician who had helped Han-xin (韓信) in the early period of the Han Dynasty. Later, in order to avoid the use of the letter designating "che (徹)" in his name, which was the same as the "che" in the autonym of Emperor Wu of Han (漢武帝), Liu "Che" (劉徹), people called him Kuai Tong (蒯通).

10. Duke Jian-cheng (建成侯) was the elder brother of Queen Lu (呂后), who was the wife of Gaozu of the Han Dynasty.

11. It is said that Emperor Gaozu hated Confucian scholars so much that when he saw one wearing a Confucian hat, he had the scholar take it off and he urinated into it. In the poem that describes this action, Gaozu's misconduct is compared to the attempt of Qin Shi Huang (秦始皇) to banish Confucian scholars and to censor Confucian books.

12. This phrase suggests the integrity of Bo-yi (伯夷) and Shu-qi (叔齊), both of whom retired to Mt. Shou-yang (首陽) and died there when the Yin (殷) Dynasty was vanquished by the Zhou (周) Dynasty.

13. Sima Qian 司馬遷, "Liu-hou-shi-jia" 留侯世家, in *Shi Ji* 史記, Vol. 55.

14. Sima Qian, "Li-sheng-lu-jia-lie-zhuan" 酈生陸賈列傳, in *Shi Ji*, Vol. 97.

15. It seems that Yulgok, after he had met Toegye, sent him a story about the four old men and three poems, all of which were included in "Miscellaneous Stories."

In *Toegye jip*, Toegye's brief answer to Yulgok is recorded and is quoted here. "The matter of the advance into and the retreat from the world of practical affairs of the four old men, and the three poems which you sent to me, precisely reflect the opinion I held at the time when we talked face to face. How could you write like so if you did not focus carefully on my words? You compel me to exert myself to study more diligently. I am much obliged to you for your poems, though I feel sorry that I cannot reply to each of them" (Yi Hwang, "The Appended Response to Yi Sukheon (Yulgok)," in *Toegye jip*, 31:130c).

16. Even after the age of forty-nine, Toegye was offered and accepted various government posts and was obliged to stay in the capital city. However, he used to entreat the king to allow him to retire and returned to his hometown. From the age of forty-nine, when he was the magistrate of Pung-gi until the age of seventy, he presented petitions seeking permission to resign to the king a total of fifty-three times. For information on the offices and the periods during which he held each of them, refer to Yi Sang-eun, *Toegye-ui saeng-aewa hangmun* (Toegye's Life and Learning) (Seoul: Yemun seowon, 1999), 29–34.

17. Korean Confucianism is based on Neo-Confucianism, especially the Zhu Xi (朱熹) School of Neo-Confucianism. However, it was not a simple reproduction of Zhu Xi's learning, as it accepted a critique of this school of thought based on Wang Yangming's philosophy, and its unique philosophical system was developed on the basis of the theories of *li-gi / li-qi* (理氣), mind-nature (心性), and the study of propriety. Therefore it is unreasonable to characterize Korean Confucianism as simply adhering to Zhu Xi's philosophy. As a result, this book argues that Neo-Confucianism is composed of both Zhu Xi's and Wang Yangming's thought. However, the term "Zhu Xi's learning" is used when it is necessary to distinguish it from Wang Yangming's thought. In addition, in this text the term "Korean Confucianism" refers to Korean Neo-Confucianism throughout.

18. "Yeonbo" 年譜 (Chronology), in *Toegye jip*, 31:224d.

19. Jo Mok (趙穆), a disciple of Toegye's, delivered his master's remark on the contemporary circumstances of scholars, as follows: "In my twenties when I was a Jinsa (進士, a low-level official) at Seong-gyun-gwan (成均館, the highest-status educational institute in the Joseon Dynasty), scholars indulged themselves to the point of dissipation after the purge of the Confucian scholars in 1545." "Toegye seonsaeng eonhaengnok" 退溪先生言行錄 (Memoirs of Master Toegye's Words and Deeds), trans. Jeong Sun-mok, in *Toegyehak yeon-gu nonchong* 退溪學 研究論叢 (Collected Studies on Toegye's Learning) 10 (Daegu: Toegye yeon-guso of Kyungpook National University, 1997), 162–63.

20. For the contemporary situation of Joseon and Toegye's attitude to it, refer to Kim Hyoungchan, "Han-guk cheorak-eseo-ui segyehwa galdeung" (The Conflicts within Korean Philosophy Ensuing from Globalization), in *Cha-i-wa galdeung-e daehan cheorakjeok seongchal* (A Philosophical Reflection on Differences and Conflicts), ed. Han-guk cheorakhoe (Seoul: Cheorakgwa hyeonsil sa, 2007).

21. Yi Hwang, "Jin Seonghak sipdo cha" 進聖學十圖箚 (On the Dedication of *Seonghak sipdo*), in *Toegye jip*, 29:198c–d. For the translation of quotations from *Seonghak sipdo*, I referred to *Yeokjuwa haeseol Seonghak sipdo* (Ten Diagrams on

Sage Learning: Translation Notes and Interpretations), ed. Han-guk sasang yeon-guso at Korea University (Seoul: Yemun seowon, 2009). I altered some of the quotations in light of their specific contexts.

22. Mencius, "Gong-sun-chou I" 公孫丑 上, *Mencius.*

23. Ibid.

24. For the relationship between a scholar's learning and his assumption of official positions, refer to Kim Hyoungchan, "Toegye-ui seowon-gwan-e daehan cheorakjeok haemyeong" (A Philosophical Elucidation on Toegye's View on the Confucian Academies), *Toegye hakbo* 136 (2014): 110–14.

25. "Chronology I," in *Yulgok jeonseo* 栗谷全書, 45:284b.

26. Yi I, "The Miscellaneous Story," in *Yulgok jeonseo,* 44:302a–b.

27. Si-shui (泗水) and its tributary Zhu-shui (洙水), where Confucius used to teach his disciples.

28. The mountain on which Zhu Xi built Wu-yi jing-she (武夷精舍). Here he taught his disciples and composed a poem titled "Wu-yi jiu-qu-ge (武夷九曲歌)."

29. This poem is one of those contained in "Four Poems Dedicated to Yi Sukheon," in *Toegye jip.* A few Chinese characters in this poem are different from those in the dedicated poem but the contents are very similar. *Toegye jip,* 031:058b. For the translation of this poem I relied on "Toegye si yeokae (74)" (An Interpretation of Toegye's Poetry [74]), trans. Yi Jang-wu and Jang Se-hu, *Toegye hakbo* 130 (2011).

病我牢關不見春 公來披豁醒心神
已知名下無虛士 堪愧年前關敬身
嘉穀莫容濟熟美 纖塵猶害鏡磨新
過情詩語須刪去 努力工夫各日親

30. Yi Hwang, "The Appended Response to Yi Sukheon," in *Toegye jip,* 31:130c.

31. Refer to Takahashi Susumu (高橋進), "Dong-asia-e isseo-seo 'gyeong' cheorak-ui seongnipgwa jeon-gae" (The Formation and Development of the Philosophy of *Gyeong* [敬] in East Asia), *Toegye hakbo* 44 (1984); *Toegye gyeong cheorak* (Toegye's Philosophy of *Gyeong*), trans. Choe Bak-gwang (Seoul: Dongseo munhwasa, 1993).

32. Zhen De-xiu (眞德秀) and Cheng Min-zheng (程敏政), "Shi lu-song" 詩魯頌 (Praise Odes of Lu in the *Book of Odes*), in *Xin Jing fu-zhu* 心經附註 (Daejeon: Hangmin munwhasa, 2005). "詩曰 上帝臨女, 無貳爾心. 又曰 無貳無虞, 上帝臨女.... 【附註】程子曰 毋不敬, 可以對越上帝."

33. Zhen De-xiu and Cheng Min-zheng, "Yi Kun-liu-er" 易坤六二 (The Second Sign of Kun [坤] in the *Book of Changes*), in *Xin Jing fu-zhu.* "伊川先生曰… 主一之謂敬, 直內, 乃是主一之義, 至於不敢欺不敢慢, 尙不愧又屋漏, 皆是敬之事也."

34. Yi I, "Swae-eon," in *Yulgok jeonseo,* 44:302b–c.

35. This poem is also recorded in Toegye's Collection. Though three characters in line three of the poem in the collection are different from those in the version of the poem in Yulgok's "Miscellaneous Stories," the contents of the two poems are very similar. Yi Hwang, "Yi Sujae Sukheon gyeonbang gyesang" 李秀才 叔獻 見訪溪上 (On the Young Genius Yi Sukheon's Visit to Gyesang), in *Toegye jip,* 29:96d.

36. The phrase "setting foot in a secluded place" refers to Yulgok's withdrawal to Mt. Geumgang at the age of nineteen, during which period he was fascinated with Buddhism.

37. This poem is also introduced in Toegye's Collection ("Jeung Yi Sujae Sukheon" 贈李秀才叔獻 (Dedicated to the Young Genius, Yi Sukheon), in *Toegye jip*, 31:11ld. In May, about three months after he met Toegye, Yulgok sent his first list of questions in relation to some issues in Confucian learning, and Toegye sent his reply with these poems. Refer to Jeong Seok-tae, *Toegye seonsaeng yeonpyo irwol jorok* 退溪先生年表日月條錄 (The Chronology of Toegye's Daily Records) (Seoul: Toegyehak yeon-guwon, 2006), 2:485.

38. Yi Hwang, "Response to Yi Sukheon," in *Toegye jip*, 29: 37la–372c.

39. "Chronology I," in *Yulgok jeonseo*, 45:282d–283b.

40. The Reference Office at Han-guk jeongsin munhwa yeon-guwon, ed., *Gugyeok Yulgok Jeonseo* (The Complete Works of Yulgok in Korean), Vol. 4 (Seongnam: Han-guk jeongsin munhwa yeon-guwon, 1996), 39.

41. Yi Gwang-ho, trans. and ed., *Toegye-wa Yulgok, saeng-gageul datuda* (The Exchange of Opinions between Toegye and Yulgok) (Seoul: Hong-ik Publishing Company, 2013), 35.

42. Yi Hwang, "Yi Sujae Sukheon gyeonbang gyesang uryu samil" 李秀才 叔獻 見訪溪上 雨留三日 (The Young Genius, Yi Sukheon Visited My House at Gyesang and Stayed Here for Three Days Owing to Rain), in *Toegye jip*, 31:048a–b. For the translation of these poems I referred to *Toegye si puri* (The Interpretations of Toegye's Poetry), Vol. 6, trans. Yi Jang-wu and Jang Se-hu (Gyeongsan: Yeungnam University Press, 2011), 581–82.

43. Yi Hwang, "Four Poems Dedicated to Yi Sukheon," in *Toegye jip*, 31:045b–c. As the first of the four poems is introduced in Yulgok's "Miscellaneous Stories," I present here the other three poems.

44. Since 1986, Professors Yi Jang-wu and Jang Se-hu have translated all of Toegye's poetry over the course of thirty years. Some of the translations were published in separate volumes of *Toegye hakbo*. According to these scholars, the total number of Toegye's poems amounts to 1,987. *Toegye si puri* (The Interpretations of Toegye's Poetry), 6 Vols. (Gyeongsan: Youngnam University Press, 2007–2011).

Chapter 2

Yulgok Asks and Toegye Answers 1 (May 1558)

At the end of their first encounter, Yulgok left for his mother's home and Toegye remained in his hometown, both perhaps realizing that it was the beginning of a lasting relationship through which fundamental philosophical questions were teased out, primarily the goal of learning and the method of achieving it, and its role in the practical world. They exchanged letters regardless of where Yulgok was staying, whether it be in the house of his mother's relative in Gangneung, in the area where his father's office was located, or in Hanyang where he took up a government post and served in the Royal Court.

Yulgok persistently asked Toegye questions about Confucian classics and the latter replied via letters. Yulgok, through the guidance Toegye provided, evolved in his philosophical understanding over time. Toegye's answers to Yulgok's shrewd questions not only helped Yulgok open for himself a new horizon of understanding but also sharpened his own philosophical insight. Though typically Yulgok posed questions and Toegye responded, Yulgok's questions sometimes also stimulated Toegye's thinking.

In May 1558, Toegye completed his *Jaseongnok* (自省錄, The Record of Self-Reflection). In November of the same year Gi Dae-seung (奇大升, pen name: Gobong 高峯, 1527–1572) called on Toegye. In January of the following year, when Toegye wrote a letter to Gobong, "the debate on the four beginnings and the seven feelings (四端七情論爭)" commenced between Toegye and Gobong.[1] At this time Toegye had been devoting himself to his studies for ten years since he had resigned from his official post. On the strength of his accumulated learning, he established his own philosophical position and unfolded his philosophy through the exchange of learned ideas with other scholars. In 1568, when Toegye compiled the *Ten Diagrams of Sage Learning* (*Seonghak sipdo*), Yulgok asked him questions about it and commented on its diagrams. In light of Yulgok's comments, Toegye corrected and supplemented the diagrams several times. In this way Toegye pursued the path of learning until the end of his life. And throughout this period, his intellectual apprentice Yulgok insistently inquired about and commented on Toegye's theories.

The philosophical questions Yulgok posed were collated in his *munmok / wen-mu* (問目, a list of questions), along with Toegye's responses. A *munmok* was usually a list of questions that a disciple sent to his master, but there were some exceptions to this model. For instance, Toegye sent one to Gobong who was twenty-six years younger than he and reexamined his own views after receiving Gobong's responses.[2]

According to an extant record, Yulgok sent a single *munmok* sheet in May 1558 and two sheets of *munmok* in 1570. May 1558 was about three months after his first encounter with Toegye. At this time Yulgok was diligently studying the classics in order to prepare for the Special State Examination, while Toegye was in the process of announcing his mature philosophical positions to the world. Toegye died on December 8, 1570, twelve years after he received the first sheet of *munmok* from Yulgok. It is presumed that Toegye received two sheets of *munmok* from Yulgok and answered him in the period from May to November 1570.[3] During this period Yulgok, having entered government service, was immersed in assisting King Seonjo, who had acceded to the throne at the age of sixteen in 1567 and had thrown the court open to the return of scholar-officials, while Toegye was seeing out his last years, after he had dedicated to the king the *Ten Diagrams on Sage Learning* that he had compiled. Through the sheets of *munmok* and the answers exchanged between them over the course of twelve years, we may gain a glimpse of their relationship and the changes in their thinking. First, let's review Yulgok's *munmok* written in 1558 and Toegye's responses to it.

THE GOAL OF LEARNING

About three months after his first encounter with Toegye, Yulgok drew up a sheet of *munmok* with four categories of questions. In this first *munmok* sent to Toegye, we may gain insight into the critical mind and studious attitude of twenty-three-year-old Yulgok, and in his responses to Yulgok we can confirm Toegye's philosophical point of view, elaborated over the course of the ten years since he had returned to his hometown.

In "The Appended Notes Presented to Master Toegye in 1558" in *Yulgok jeonseo* (栗谷全書, *The Complete Works of Yulgok*),[4] which contains Yulgok's questions and Toegye's answers, not a few sections of the questions and answers exchanged between them are omitted. If we compare "The Appended Notes" with Toegye's answers recorded in *Toegye jip*

(退溪集, *The Collected Works of Toegye*),[5] we discover that only central questions and answers are presented in "The Appended Notes." Therefore it is necessary to review "The Appended Notes" in *Yulgok jeonseo* with reference to *Toegye jip* in order to discover the elements that were omitted.

Yulgok's first question was about the first chapter of *The Great Learning* and was formulated as follows:

【Question】 Zhu Xi said, "Though the practices of 'the determination (定) of the object of pursuit,' 'the attainment of calmness (靜),' and 'attainment of tranquil repose (安)' are independent of each other, it is not difficult to engage in all of them. However, 'careful deliberation (慮) after tranquil repose' and 'the attainment (得) of the highest good after careful deliberation' are the most difficult qualities to master. 'Careful deliberation after tranquil repose' could be mastered by no one but Yan Zi (顔子)." (The succeeding part of the question was omitted in Yulgok's *munmok*.)

【Answer】 You seem to have doubted Zhu Xi's remark "'Careful deliberation after tranquil repose' could be mastered by no one but Yan Zi." However, as the remark of the sage makes sense from start to finish and implies both specificity and generality, those with superficial knowledge as well as those with profound knowledge can grasp it in accordance with their own levels of knowledge. Generally speaking, even those with only very moderate knowledge may endeavor to put into practice the sage's remark "Careful deliberation after tranquil repose can be mastered." However, strictly speaking, no one except a great sage can indeed put this counsel into practice. Zhu Xi's remark about Yan Zi held good only in connection with his strict division of the stages of knowledge. If someone, on the pretext of recognizing the import of Zhu Xi's remark, abandons his studies, his views and disposition are not adequate to the task of expounding on the Way. Why on Earth should we listen to his excuses and adjust our viewpoints to his? (I say "on the pretext of" in the sense that those who show the slightest indication of abandoning their studies are not qualified to pursue the Way of Yao and Shun).[6]

The first part of *The Great Learning*, with which Yulgok's question is concerned, is as follows:

The Way (Dao) of great learning consists in illustrating illustrious virtue; renovating the people; and abiding in the state of highest good. The point where to abide being known, the object of pursuit is then determined; and, that being the case, an unperturbed calmness may be attained. To that calmness there will succeed a tranquil repose. After that repose, there may be careful deliberation, and that deliberation will be followed by the attainment of the highest good.[7]

This suggests very concisely and systematically the aim of studying Confucianism and the method of its study. There are a variety of interpretations of this quotation. However, as both Toegye and Yulgok were influenced by Zhu Xi in this respect, our interpretation also follows Zhu Xi's.

The great learning of Confucianism pursues the rehabilitation of the illustrious and pure mind endowed by Heaven, the enlightenment of the people in accordance with Confucian teachings, and ultimately the embodiment of a life that fulfills the highest good. In order to attain such a state, first of all, the point to abide or the highest good must be known. Then the object of the pursuit is determined. The object being determined, an unperturbed calmness may be attained. To that calmness there will succeed a tranquil repose. After that repose, there may be careful deliberation, and that deliberation will be followed by the attainment of the highest good or the ultimate aim of living.

Yulgok seems to have doubted Zhu Xi's remark "'Careful deliberation after tranquil repose' could be mastered by no one but Yan Zi." Yan Zi is the pseudonym of Yan Yuan (顏淵), the disciple who was most highly regarded by Confucius. So Zhu Xi's remark may be recalibrated in the form of the phrase "Careful deliberation after tranquil repose could be mastered only by highly cultivated men." However, one of the fundamental premises of the Neo-Confucianism of Cheng Yi and Zhu Xi is that the innate nature of all human beings is endowed with the universal principle of nature and of the universe. It may even be said that "Seongnihak (性理學, The Study of Human Nature and Neo-Confucian Principles)" originated from the premise that "human nature is endowed with the principle of the universe and of nature (性卽理)." In this respect, Confucianism, since Confucius himself and Mencius, has taught that every human being can become a sage through study and self-cultivation.

However, Zhu Xi distinguished the stage of attaining calmness and repose after determining the object of pursuit from that of attaining the highest good after careful deliberation and said that the latter stage could be fulfilled by no one but Yan-zi. The former stage, according to Zhu Xi, is a process that functions in the mind while the latter stage is a process whose purpose is to cope with external circumstances. So it may be said that Zhu Xi's intention here was to emphasize that the spiritual dimensions of the latter stage are different from those of the former.

Perhaps an ordinary man who regarded the sustaining of a humble attitude toward the ancient sages as a great virtue would have accepted Zhu Xi's remark without any objection. However, Yulgok seems to have been not a little displeased with this stance, and so his first question in the *munmok* was about Zhu Xi's dictum.

The young Yulgok was a startlingly talented boy who wrote, at the age of eight, a poem titled "Hwaseokjeong (花石亭),"[8] the mood of which was a startling accomplishment on the part of an eight-year-old boy. He was renowned as a child prodigy and later repeatedly attained first place in the state examinations.[9] From his first encounter with Toegye, Yulgok seems to have displayed his talent. However, he did not dare to say that he was as talented as Yan Zi. Nevertheless, it might have been difficult for him to accept Zhu Xi's remark that ordinary men, including himself, could not fulfill the Way of *The Great Learning* however assiduously they might strive to do so.

Considering that nobody had been called a sage since Confucius died, it may be said that the Way of Confucianism or the highest good discussed in *The Great Learning* was not an object to be attained but only a lofty ideal to be pursued. According to Confucian principles, every human being is born with the attributes to become a sage and can achieve this through his or her best endeavors. However, throughout the entire history of Confucianism, there were only a few sages, including the last one, Confucius. Historically, as Confucianism began to take the ideological role of checking the absolute power of the king, it was almost impossible for a Confucian scholar to attain the status of a sage. Confucian scholars were mainly concerned with limiting the power of rulers by insistently demanding that they should cultivate virtue, as had Confucius, who became venerated as the paragon that rulers should emulate. So Confucius's status of sage was consolidated as the historical ideal to be perennially pursued,[10] and even Mencius and Zhu Xi were regarded as figures who failed to attain the status of sage. It was argued that Yan Zi, if he had not died prematurely, would have exceeded the achievements of Confucius. So Zhu Xi's remark "Careful deliberation after tranquil repose could be mastered by no one but Yan Zi" implied that it was fundamentally impossible for ordinary human beings to attain Yan Zi's status.

But Yulgok seems to have been unwilling to accept the implication of Zhu Xi's remark. Seen in the light of Confucian and Neo-Confucian theories, Yulgok's attitude on this matter was quite correct. However, the Confucian circle regarded such an attitude as presumptuous because it could be seen as a challenge to the prestige of Zhu Xi and Yan Zi.

Therefore Toegye, in warning Yulgok not to interpret Zhu Xi's remark in a narrow way, encouraged him in his studies and tried to broaden his horizon of understanding. Toegye's answer, "as the remark of the sage makes sense from start to finish and implies both specificity and generality, those with superficial knowledge as well as those with profound knowledge can apply the statement in accordance with their own levels of knowledge," was a quintessentially Confucian statement. Truth, as seen through the prism of Confucianism, is not defined by the binary formula "If 'A' is correct, 'Not A' is incorrect." Confucianism teaches that one should pursue truth in accordance with the parameters of one's own capacities and circumstances. Therefore in this light truth in Confucianism is viewed in various ways.

As mentioned earlier, Yulgok's question about Zhu Xi's remark was in a sense reasonable. According to the principles of Neo-Confucianism, anyone who is endowed with "the original moral nature (道德的 本性)" derived from nature can practice and follow the stages of study suggested in *The Great Learning*. In this respect Yulgok was right that the path to the Way was open to him. Strictly speaking, however, we should understand Zhu Xi's remark in view of the distinct stages of study. Even an ordinary man, through his endeavors, can understand the ultimate aim of "the highest good," determine his direction in life, and attain the calmness of mind and repose. However, deliberating on matters at hand in a calm state of mind and embodying the highest good are far more difficult tasks than the earlier-mentioned ordinary man's potential attainments. In this respect, Toegye explained that Zhu Xi's remark about Yan Zi held good only in connection with his strict division of the stages of study.

In addition, Toegye warned contemporary scholars, including Yulgok, "If someone, on the pretext of recognizing the import of his [Zhu Xi's] remark, shows the slightest indication of abandoning his studies, he is not qualified to pursue the way of Yao and Shun."

Toegye's point was clearly that the establishment of a productive aim of study is very important. By conceiving of a desirable aim, one can have confidence in one's capabilities regardless of adverse circumstances, direct one's attention to the aim, and overcome difficulties in the process of fulfilling it. When one establishes a positive goal, the power of one's self-control and diligence becomes stronger than any external coercive power.

Yulgok might have felt that Toegye's answer was satisfactory. In fact, it wasn't because of youthful precocity that he asked about Zhu Xi's dictum. Not only in his *Seonghak jibyo* (聖學輯要, *The Essentials of Sage Learning*), which he dedicated to King Seonjo, but also in his *Gyeongmong yogyeol* (擊蒙要訣, *The Secret to Dispelling Ignorance*), in which he devised the optimal method of study for the beginner, Yulgok emphasized that the beginner, first of all, should commit to the lofty aim of becoming a sage with the firm resolution that he would not abandon his studies on some pretext or other.

The first chapter of *Gyeongmong yogyeol* titled "Establishing the Aim of Study" begins as follows:

> A man who begins his studies should, first of all, commit to his aim of becoming a sage without underestimating himself and procrastinating over some pretext. In general an ordinary man and a sage have the identical original nature. Though the physical matter or material disposition (*gijil / qi-zhi* 氣質) of everyone is different in its clarity or purity, if a man puts into practice what he truly knows and abandons old habits and recovers his original nature, he can spontaneously complete with all kinds of goodness. So even an ordinary man should conceive of the aim of becoming a sage.[11]

GYEONG: REVERENT MINDFULNESS

Yulgok's second question to Toegye was about *gyeong / jing* (敬, reverent mindfulness). Toegye alluded to *gyeong* in a poem when Yulgok called on him for the first time. The fundamental attitude underlying Toegye's learning was *gyeong*, and he emphasized it above all else to his disciples as a method of study. According to Yulgok's *munmok*, before Yulgok mentioned *gyeong*, Toegye asked him a question about it with the intention of guiding him toward the right path of study, as if Yulgok were his own disciple.

【Question】Master, you said, "*Gyeong* (敬) is *ju-il mujeok / zhu-yi wu-shi* (主一無適, focusing the mind and not allowing it to wander)," and you asked, "If things or events converge in your mind at a single point in time, what should you do?" I pondered on your question and came to understand your intention.

Ju-il mujeok is the cardinal method of *gyeong*, and the response to various changes that it enables is the way *gyeong* is put into practice. If a man has pondered beforehand on things or events that converge on him, he can respond to each of them like a mirror that reflects things with great fixity. While he is responding to the concatenation of things or circumstances, if his mind itself remains undisturbed, it proves that he has already grasped clearly the principles of various phenomena and events. On the other hand, if he has not deliberated on these principles, the moment he ponders a state of affairs, other phenomena will pass without notice. So how can he respond to all of the surrounding phenomena? Figuratively speaking, when the five colors in the spectrum of a ray of light appear at the same time in the center of a mirror, it reflects all of them simultaneously, though the brightness of the mirror does not change owing to these colors. The method of putting *gyeong* into practice is like the placid action of a mirror. This method underpins the necessary method of study when things congregate.

While studying amid a stable state of affairs, a man should devote himself to one thing. However, if he thinks of shooting an arrow at a flying goose or swan while reading a book, he no longer displays the attitude of *gyeong*. "Focusing the mind and not letting it wander (*ju-il mujeok / zhu-yi-wu-shi* 主一無適)" when things stand still is the essence of *gyeong*. On the other hand, responding to various changes without losing control when phenomena accumulate is the application of *gyeong*. Without *gyeong* the highest good cannot be attained, while through the maintenance of *gyeong* the highest good exists. Standing still here does not mean acting like dry wood or wood burned to ashes; moving here does not mean acting in confusion or in the midst of commotion. Therefore maintaining a consistent attitude when things or events accumulate or are at a standstill, and maintaining an inseparable relationship between *che / ti* (體, essence) and *yong / yong* (用, function), is the highest good of *gyeong*.

The eyes and ears of King Shun (舜) were utterly attuned to all directions and he observed "the seven heavenly bodies (*chiljeong / qi-zheng* 七政),"[12]

rearranged "the five ceremonies (*orye / wu-li* 五禮)," and standardized "the five tools (*ogi / wu-qi* 五器)."[13] The king achieved many things because he maintained the attitude of *gyeong* at every moment and concentrated on only one thing at any given time. What do you think about his achievement, sir? Fang shi (方氏)[14] said, "Though his mind might be empty, the king's duty of supervision remained sure in his mind." And Zhu Xi said, "The sage-king's mind was empty but lucid; and when confronted with significant or minor things or events, he responded to each of them as they approached from all directions, though not one of them had been kept foremost in his mind."[15]

Toegye's question to Yulgok was very puzzling. In Neo-Confucianism *gyeong* is interpreted as *ju-il mujeok*, that is, the focusing of the mind on one thing and not allowing it to wander. *Gyeong* originally meant the attitude of "reverent mindfulness" necessary for the worship of a god.[16] One should worship a god sincerely and wholeheartedly in a disciplined mood, without permitting idle thoughts for even a moment. But "if other things or events enter one's mind at a single point in time, what should one do?" It is a very puzzling question.

Toegye mentioned the significance of studying with the attitude of *gyeong* in "The Diagram of The Great Learning (大學圖)," which is chapter 4 of *Ten Diagrams on Sage Learning*, one of the representative works of his later years. *Gyeong* was not especially emphasized in *The Great Learning*, but Toegye underscored it as a method of study and self-cultivation in order to ameliorate the effects of contemporary scholarship, which he felt was too biased toward theoretical studies.

In "The Diagram of The Great Learning" Toegye focused on *gyeong* instead of the method of *The Great Learning* as a whole. Here, in addition to *ju-il mujeok* suggested by Cheng Yi (程頤),[17] he introduced the following three interpretations of *gyeong*.

To maintain an orderly and focused body and mind (*jeongje eomsuk / zheng-qi yan-su* 整齊嚴肅).

— Cheng Yi[18]

To engage in a method of self-cultivation aimed at always maintaining a clear-minded and alert state (*sangseongseong beop / chang-xing-xing-fa* 常惺惺法).

—Xie Liang-zuo (謝良佐)[19]

To concentrate the mind, never permitting an idle thought (*gisim suryeom buryong ilmul / qi-xin shou-lian bu-rong yi-wu* 其心收斂, 不容一物).

—Yin Tun (尹焞)[20]

These three quotations, together with *ju-il mujeok*, had been the accepted Neo-Confucian interpretations of *gyeong* since Zhu Xi's theorization of it. *Xin Jing fu-zhu* (心經附註, *The Supplementary Annotation to the Classic of the Heart-Mind*), which attracted Toegye's attention, also interpreted *gyeong* in detail while citing these quotations.[21] They may be summarized and synthesized as follows: *Gyeong* is "a method of concentrating on study while always maintaining a focused body and mind through a reverent attitude." Zhu Xi explained *gyeong* as follows:

> *Gyeong* (reverent mindfulness) is one's mastery over one's mind and is the foundation of all one's undertakings. If one masters the method of study incorporating the attitude of *gyeong*, one will understand that *The Elementary Learning* (*Xiao-xue* 小學) relies on *gyeong* to make a beginning; if one understands this, one will also know that *The Great Learning* necessarily relies on *gyeong* in order to achieve completion. One will be able to see it as the one thread running through all, and one will have no doubts. Once one's mind is secure in this state, one may proceed with *gyeongmul / ge-wu* (格物, the investigation of things) and *chiji / zhi-zhi* (致知, the extension of knowledge), and thereby exhaustively comprehend the principle (*li* 理) as it is present in things and states of affairs: this is what is meant by "cultivating virtuous nature and theoretical studies (尊德性而道問學)." Then one may proceed to make one's intentions sincere and perfect one's mind, and thereby cultivate one's morality: this is what is meant by "First establish what is greater, and lesser things will not be able to detract from it." One may further proceed to regulate the family and properly govern the state, and thereby even attain the tranquility of the world: this is what is meant by "Cultivate morals and then give ease to the people; make yourself reverent and faithful and thereby the world will enjoy tranquility." All of these dimensions show that one should not absent oneself from the practice of *gyeong* for even a single day. This being the case, *gyeong* cannot but be the essence of penetrating the beginning and the sum of sage learning.[22]

In this light, *gyeong* can be seen as a method of study that can be applied to *The Elementary Learning, The Great Learning*, "the investigation of things and the extension of knowledge," "the cultivation of virtuous nature," "theoretical studies," "the cultivation of sincerity," "the perfection of the mind," "the cultivation of morals," "the regulation of the family," "the proper governance of the state," and "the attainment of the tranquility of the whole world." That is, *gyeong* is a method of study intrinsic to the cultivation of virtue, theoretical studies, and the governance of the state and the world. Toegye, after quoting Zhu Xi's statement, summarized the meaning of *gyeong* in "The Diagram of The Great Learning" as follows:

> *Gyeong* penetrates both elementary and advanced learning. So from the start of one's studies to the reaping of their fruits, one must devote oneself to the study of *gyeong* and not be remiss in this endeavor.[23]

According to this summary, we may say that from the daily work of cleaning the house inside and out or entertaining a guest to the metaphysical study of the moral heart-mind or the structure and principle of the universe, and further to the administration of the state and the world, that is, from the beginning to the end of one's studies one should consistently maintain the attitude of *gyeong*. Toegye emphasized that *gyeong* is the pivot of or the key to all methods of study in several chapters of *Ten Diagrams on Sage Learning* such as "Chapter Eight: The Diagram of the Study of the Heart-Mind (心學圖)," "Chapter Nine: The Diagram of the Admonition for Mindfulness Studio (敬齋箴圖)," and "Chapter Ten: The Diagram of the Admonition on Rising Early and Retiring Late (夙興夜寐箴圖)," in addition to "Chapter Four: The Diagram of The Great Learning (大學圖)." So it may not be implausible to say that Toegye's learning is in a word "the study of reverent mindfulness (敬學)."[24]

If *gyeong* entails concentrating on a phenomenon or a state of affairs while maintaining the alertness of one's consciousness, what should one do when various circumstances surround one simultaneously? To this question Yulgok differentiated between the form of *gyeong* in times when the mind is active and in times when it is tranquil and explained their relationship. The study of *gyeong* in times of mental tranquility, according to him, entails the investigation of the principle of each thing and the recognition of "the inevitable law of morality (當然之則)." In view of the Confucian sense of value, this law refers to the most ideal standard of moral value. If one has already studied the standard, one can comply with the inevitable law of morality without being confused when various circumstances arise at once. In this case one's mind seems to be empty because one does not focus on the knowledge of concrete things but recognizes their ineluctable principles. As a result, as one apperceives these principles, one can respond to any situation without agitation.

In the following answer Toegye seems to agree with Yulgok's view. However, if we carefully look into his response, we can see that he prioritizes a somewhat different method of study from that of Yulgok.

【Answer】 When one has no work to do, one should "sustain one's mind and cultivate one's nature (存心養性)" and maintain an alert consciousness. Only when one studies a classical book or is faced with a set of circumstances does one deliberate on *uiri / yi-li* (義理, righteous principle) because it is only right to do so in that context. In general, as soon as one thinks about *uiri*, one's mind becomes active and does not display the state of tranquility. Though such a change in one's state of mind is evident and not difficult to understand, few, if any, comprehend it. The majority of people believe that the disposition not to think in times of tranquility is coterminous with the state of absentmindedness or stupefaction, and that to think and deliberate in times of activity involves an engagement with superficial or transient things and a lack of focus on *uiri*. If this is the case, many self-professed scholars cannot reap the fruits of their studies. Only when *gyeong* penetrates one's studies both in times of mental tranquility and mental activity may one's method of study be said to be true.[25]

While Yulgok explained *gyeong* by dividing it into the activities of "focusing the mind and not allowing it to wander (主一無適)" and "responding to various changes (酬酢萬變)," Toegye conceptualized it by dividing it into the activities of "sustaining and cultivating one's mind and nature (存心養性) while maintaining the alertness of one's consciousness" and "deliberating on righteous principle."

Toegye emphasized that one should always maintain the alertness of mind even in times of tranquility. In other words, one's mind, even when there is no onus to respond to events or circumstances, should not remain in an absentminded or stupefied state. As Yulgok understood the undertaking of study in the state of tranquility as *gyeongmul gungni / ge-wu qiong-li* (格物窮理, the investigation of things and principles), his view of the undertaking of study in times of tranquility was a little different from that of Toegye. *Gyeongmul gungni* is a method of studying the universal principle through one's confrontation with each thing outside one's mind and through one's pursuit of the principle or essence of each thing. Such a determined focus on grasping the principle of each thing is different from Toegye's view of the ideal mode of study in times of tranquility. As evidenced in his remark quoted earlier, Zhu Xi also thought that one should first establish an ideal attitude of mind through *gyeong* and then "investigate things and extend knowledge."

Toegye thought that one should cultivate one's original nature, which is immanent in the mind, before one responds to the stimuli of phenomenal things because the highest good is manifested in one's original nature. In Toegye's terms, this is the form of study carried out "before the issuance of mind (*mibal / wei-fa* 未發)," that is, the form of study before the response of one's original nature immanent in the mind to the outer world. Toegye emphasized this form of study, which he believed would ensure that one's moral disposition may be spontaneously manifested under the stimuli of phenomenal things. In order to explain the process of the manifestation of a moral disposition, in later years Toegye proposed concepts such as "the manifestation of *li / li* (*libal / li-fa* 理發)" and "the spontaneous advent of *li* (*lijado / li-zi-dao* 理自到)." In contrast to Toegye's view, Yulgok's "investigation of things and principles (格物窮理)" is a form of study that accompanies conscious effort in order to investigate the principle of things. In other words, Yulgok's recommended form of study is carried out "after the issuance of mind (*yibal / yi-fa* 已發)" or after the response of one's original nature to external phenomena.

At the time when they began to exchange letters Toegye, should have clearly explained that Yulgok's method of the study of *gyeong* was different from his. If he had done so, they could have continued to discuss this matter and might have arrived at a more productive conclusion. However, at that time they could not discuss this matter on equal terms because of their great difference in age and the brevity of their friendship. As a result, their debate was nonreciprocal, with Yulgok asking questions and Toegye responding.

The difference in their views on the study of *gyeong* could not be overcome because Toegye laid emphasis on the form of study before issuance, while Yulgok prioritized the form of study after issuance of mind. Toegye's position was that one should study the mind and one's original nature sufficiently before offering a response to the phenomenal world, while Yulgok's stance was that the study of *gyeong* begins from one's response to the external world and from one's conscious attempt to recognize the principles of phenomena. Yulgok's attitude toward Toegye's response is not known, but from that time forward Yulgok pursued his own method, which was informed by views that were different from Toegye's in terms of the optimal methods of study and self-cultivation. The difference in their views also caused subsequent disputes between Toegye and Gobong (高峯), Yulgok and Ugye (牛溪). Moreover, the disputes between the Toegye and Yulgok Schools, which persisted for hundreds of years, on the interpretations of *ligi / li-qi* (理氣, principle and matter), "the four beginnings and the seven feelings (四端七情)," and "the human mind and the moral mind (人心道心)" fundamentally originated from the distinctive views of Toegye and Yulgok.

THEORY INTO PRACTICE

Toegye sent an additional response to Yulgok, as follows:

> 【Additional Answer】 You talked about "focusing the mind and not allowing it to wander (主一無適)" and then about "responding to various changes (酬酌萬變)." It was a meaningful statement. Your citing of Zhu Xi's statement, ". . . he responded to each of them [things] . . . though not one of them had been kept in his mind," and the statement of Mr. Fang (Fang-shi 方氏), "Though his mind might be empty, the . . . supervision remained . . . in his mind," was also reasonable. However, I think that while the principles implied in such statements are not difficult to understand, they are onerous to practice, and more difficult still to practice persistently with a sincere mind.[26]

Toegye praised Yulgok's answer concerning the interpretation of *gyeong*. In view of Yulgok's view that one should respond to various changes without being reactive and without being obsessed by them, Toegye admitted that

Yulgok understood *gyeong* correctly. However, it may be that Toegye felt that Yulgok should not be too proud of his understanding. In this context Toegye said that while the comprehension of principles is not difficult, putting them into practice and doing so consistently with a sincere mind is. Here Toegye understood the root of most of the ethical problems that arise in a society, which are caused by people choosing the wrong path, being blinded by selfish interests, and not by their being incapable of exercising moral judgment. It seems likely that Toegye would agree that, furthermore, one is prone to rationalize one's misdeeds through one's accumulated knowledge and logic. In this way the ethical weakness in a society is propagated and reproduced. It is common to see people who hold forth about fairness and justice but who, when the time comes to rectify wrongs, decline to seek justice and instead choose to pursue their own interests. The aim of Neo-Confucianism is to educate people in such a way as to ensure they can unswervingly make fair and just judgments and choices while restraining their greed.

Neo-Confucianism, based on Confucianism, is a body of learning that systematizes the viewpoint that human beings can and must live in a harmonious society in accordance with the natural endowment of their original ethical nature. If we accept some of its premises, it may prove to be a very persuasive theoretical system capable of explaining why we should lead our lives in a society oriented toward a strong sense of morality. Some of the major premises of Neo-Confucianism are as follows:[27]

1. All entities and functions are formed by the combination of *li / li* (理: principle, law, or norm) and *gi / qi* (氣: matter or energy).
2. Both physical and ethical principles exist in nature and are represented by the "four virtues (*sadeok / si-de* 四德—*wonhyeongyijeong / yuan-heng-li-zhen* 元亨利貞: origination, flourishing, advantage, and firmness)."
3. Each entity, or product of nature, comes into being by adopting a certain principle of nature as its original nature, which is composed of "the five constants (*osang / wu-chang* 五常—*yinuiyejisin / ren-yi-li-zhi-xin* 仁義禮智信: benevolence, righteousness, propriety, wisdom, and fidelity)."
4. The more pure and authentic is the *gi* that combines with *li* (or the original nature), the more perfect *li* becomes in the phenomenal world.
5. The *gi* of a human being is clearer and purer than that of any other entity. Of all the forms of *gi* that compose the human body, the *gi* that composes the heart-mind is the most clear and genuine.

One facet we should bear in mind is that the ultimate aim of Neo-Confucianism is not to establish a logically perfect theoretical system on the basis of these premises but to put Neo-Confucian ideals into practice in the real world through self-cultivation on the basis of philosophical study and concrete experiences. In other words, to establish a logically consistent theoretical system is one type of pursuit, but to lead a life based on such a theoretical system is quite another. This is because our lives are too complicated to be comprehensively explained by abstract theories. Moreover, even those who are well versed in theoretical discourse frequently judge and behave in ways that are incompatible with the logic of their theoretical system.

In Toegye's era, the Joseon Dynasty had suffered from several purges of the intelligentsia, extending over 150 years since its foundation in 1392, and the Neo-Confucian founding ideology of the dynasty was declining in influence. As the king's maternal relatives monopolized national power, Toegye resigned from the magistracy of Pung-gi and retired to his hometown of Andong. He still regarded Zhu Xi's philosophy, which had been adopted as the founding ideology of Joseon, as the basis of real learning and education. At that time in China, criticism of Zhu Xi's learning was mounting while the philosophy of Wang Yang-ming (王陽明) began to attract the attention of scholars. Nevertheless, Zhu Xi's learning was still regarded as the most influential philosophy in Northeast Asia. Toegye edited Zhu Xi's major work in his *Juja seo jeoryo* (朱子書節要, *The Essential Elements of Zhu Xi's Writings*) and set forth the lineage of Zhu Xi's learning in *Songgye won myeong ihak tongnok* (宋季元明理學通錄, *A History of Neo-Confucianism in the Song, Yuan, and Ming Dynasties*).[28] These works demonstrated that Toegye was evidently a faithful scholar of Zhu Xi's philosophy. In his study of Zhu Xi's works, what is noticeable is that he attached more importance to *Xin Jing fu-zhu* (心經附註, *Supplementary Annotations to the Classic of the Heart-Mind*) than to *Xing-li da-quan* (性理大全, *The Complete Collection of the Doctrines on Human Nature and Principle*) and *Zhu Zi chuan-shu* (朱子全書, *The Complete Works of Master Zhu*). While these two books were generally evaluated as the seminal texts of Zhu Xi's philosophy, *Xin Jing fu-zhu* was not highly regarded by scholars of Zhu Xi and was even criticized for its similarity to Wang Yang-ming's writing. However, Toegye rejected such criticism, maintaining that the book was as essential as the Four Books (Si-shu 四書) and *Jin-si lu* (近思錄, *Reflections on Things at Hand*). So he encouraged young scholars to read this text.[29]

Toegye highly regarded *Xin Jing fu-zhu* because he thought that it was a necessary handbook for both theoretical study and for the cultivation of virtue. Toegye believed that Confucianism and Neo-Confucianism originally pursued the paths of study and self-cultivation simultaneously but that most scholars had become biased toward theoretical study.[30] Such a bias, according to Toegye, had propagated widely since Zhu Xi's era, and *Xin Jing* (心經, *The Classic of the Heart-Mind*) and *Xin Jing fu-zhu* were compiled to correct it.[31] Zhen De-xiu (眞德秀, 1178–1235), Zhu Xi's second-generation disciple, collected writings on the cultivation of mind culled from various classical texts and edited *Xin Jing*, and during the Ming Dynasty Cheng Min-zheng (程敏政, 1445–1499) annotated *Xin Jing* and compiled *Xin Jing fu-zhu*. These books, in contrast to Zhu Xi's emphasis on the strict analysis and reinterpretation of the classics on the basis of a specific theoretical system, were focused on the cultivation of personality.

The cultivation of mind is a matter to which a conceptual and theoretical methodology cannot rigorously be applied. The theoretical study of Confucian classics is one kind of pursuit while the cultivation and practice that has been learned on the basis of theoretical discourse is another. The cultivation of *gyeong*, which occupies a cardinal position in Toegye's system of learning, corresponded to the cultivation of virtue emphasized in *Xin Jing fu-zhu*. The method of cultivating *gyeong*, in which one maintains an alert consciousness and concentrates intently on things at hand, was focused on forms of training and practice that connect Neo-Confucian theoretical study with daily life. Toegye emphasized the study of *gyeong* in order to complement Zhu Xi's learning, which was biased toward theoretical study, and to intensify the cultivation of virtue.

Although Toegye consolidated his system of learning theoretically, he emphasized concrete practice more than any other Neo-Confucian scholar. He criticized Wang Yang-ming's philosophy because, although it seemingly emphasized moral practice, it neglected to suggest concrete methods of carrying this out. However, he agreed with Wang's criticism that "these days people insist that they should put their principles into practice only after gaining accurate knowledge, but in fact they neither achieve knowledge nor engage in moral practices until the end of their lives."[32] Both Toegye and Wang believed that knowledge that was not accompanied by practice was meaningless and could not in fact be true knowledge. In this context, Toegye thought that while Wang's learning attached importance to the cultivation of mind, it did not consider the method of engaging in moral practices in daily life. He said, "Yang-ming was only concerned about the way the phenomenal world could trouble the mind," and that he "talked ambiguously by coalescing all things into the realm of the mind," and he added that Wang's learning was essentially Buddhist.[33]

Although Toegye agreed with Wang's criticism that Zhu Xi's learning was biased toward theoretical study, instead of adhering to the tenets of Wang's learning, he endeavored to build, on the basis of Zhu Xi's philosophy, an elaborate theoretical system that he believed enabled people to actively practice moral virtue in their daily lives. While Toegye's view on "the cultivation of virtue" was consolidated through the concept of *gyeong*, his "theoretical study" was elaborated through his controversy with Gobong on "the four beginnings and the seven feelings." In November of the year when Yulgok sent his first *munmok* to Toegye, Gobong visited Toegye and asked a question, and in January of the following year Toegye answered. This was the beginning of "the controversy on the four-seven" between them.

In accordance with Toegye's teaching, Yulgok repeatedly emphasized that what was important in Neo-Confucianism was practice as well as theoretical study. It would not be accurate to say that Yulgok's advocacy of "practical endeavor, performed with sincerity (*musil yeokhaeng / wu-shi-li-xing* 務實力行)" was influenced solely by Toegye's teaching. However, it may be said that Yulgok inherited and developed Toegye's attempt to recuperate the practicability of Confucianism by sublating the tendency of Zhu Xi's learning, which was biased toward theoretical study, and by reinforcing the cultivation of virtue. Yulgok's concern for practice may have partly been due to his personal disposition, which was more positive than Toegye's, but above all else it resulted from the changing situation of the times. That is, the circumstances of Yulgok's lifetime required more engagement in concrete practice on the part of intellectuals and made it easier to put philosophical knowledge into practice than was the case during Toegye's lifetime. It may also be said that scholar-officials in Yulgok's lifetime could attempt to establish the ideal Neo-Confucian state through partisan politics (*bungdang jeongchi / peng-dang zheng-zhi* 朋黨政治) on the basis of Toegye's scholarly achievements and his views on contemporary circumstances.

UNDERSTANDING AND MASTERY

Yulgok's third question was about the recognition of truth. As we have seen in discussing the first chapter of *The Great Learning*, in Confucianism "the highest good" is regarded as the ultimate aim of life that human beings should pursue. Zhu Xi said that one should pursue and recognize what "the highest good" is before one can embody it. It is quite natural that one must correctly understand one's necessary direction before one embarks on a journey. So Zhu Xi thought that in *The Great Learning* an explanation of *gyeongmul chiji / ge-wu zhi-zhi* (格物致知, the investigation of things and the extension of knowledge) that corresponds to the methodology involved in recognizing "the highest good" was missing. So he wrote his own explanation of *gyeongmul chiji*, which was contained in "Bu-wang zhang (補亡章, A Supplementary Chapter)."

The Great Learning was originally a part of *Li Ji* (禮記, *The Book of Rites*), and is considered to have been written by a sage. Because Confucius said, "I do not try to create, but simply refer to the sages' works (述而不作),"[34] Confucian circles have thought it very impolite to change or supplement the sages' writings. However, anticipating reproaches that would be directed against him, Zhu Xi supplemented his explanation of *gyeongmul chiji*, which was so important in his theoretical system.

In Neo-Confucianism, "the highest good" or the ultimate aim of human beings can be embodied by first recognizing *li* or the universal truth and then by living in accordance with the standard *li* establishes. According to Zhu Xi, the pursuit of *li* is called *gungni / qiong-li* (窮理) and the method of engaging in *gung-li* is called *gyeongmul chiji*. Therefore *gyeongmul gungni* (格物窮理) was the pivotal process in the practice of Neo-Confucianism, especially for elementary learners. However, as it entailed the recognition of the ultimate truth, it was seen as perhaps too difficult a process for elementary learners to assimilate. In fact, later scholars like Bak Se-dang (朴世堂, 1629–1723) criticized the emphasis on *gyeongmul chiji*, suggesting that its promotion as the starting point of study placed an excessive demand on elementary learners.[35]

Yulgok asked Toegye about *gyeongmul* (格物):

【Question】 Cheng Yi said, "While reading a book, one pursues and learns morals and righteousness, evaluates the attitudes of historical figures, and responds to phenomena and events in order to determine their rectitude or evil. If one has difficulty in the investigation of a state of affairs, one turns one's attention to another." And Si-ma Wen-gong (司馬溫公)[36] said, "The principles of forms still in the process of shaping themselves, as well as the principles of things and events emanating from all directions and from immeasurable distances have appeared before my eyes. In this way I learn what is right." Wen-gong seems to be talking about a process akin to *gyeongmul* (格物), but his statement that "I learn what is right" is quite different from Cheng Yi's or Zhu Xi's remarks. I believe a more productive avenue would have been for him to study the subtle difference between "natural principle (*soyiyeon / suo-yi-ran* 所以然)" and "normative principle (*sodang-yeon / suo-dang-ran* 所當然)" than to focus on what is right. *Li* (principle) originally refers to "the highest good." So how can there be any *li* that is not "right"? Doesn't "learning what is right" really mean that one should exert oneself ceaselessly by observing the regular movements of celestial bodies and cultivate virtue by following the example of the fertile Earth that benevolently embraces and nurtures all things? Wen-gong seems to have understood the *gyeok / ge* (格) of *gyeongmul* (格物) as "protection (*haneo / han-yu* 扞禦)," and he could not grasp the essential idea of *gyeongmul* that Cheng Yi discussed. Master, I dare to write to you as I remember you once talked about this matter. I humbly ask for your response to my view.[37]

In Neo-Confucianism, *li* refers to universal truth. It means the ontological and operative principle and the fundamental norm of all things. All phenomena in the universe inevitably come into being, subsist, function, change, and cease to exist in accordance with *li*. The *li* that exists at any time and in any place cannot but be right for it is the universal and normative principle of the universe and of nature. According to the modern Western view of nature, physical laws govern the existence of all things in nature and their movements or functions, while moral norms or imperatives that are created by human beings regulate human affairs. However, in Neo-Confucianism all the entities in nature, including human beings, are subject to *li*, which comprises both physical laws and moral imperatives. In other words, in Neo-Confucianism all entities that follow the physical laws of nature must also observe the moral norms of nature as constituents of the universe. In reality, we cannot but follow natural physical laws, but many of us act against the universal moral norms. Neo-Confucianism, however, considers that moral norms fundamentally comply with physical laws, so we are therefore required to observe both moral norms and the physical laws of nature to the same degree.[38] The physical laws of nature are called *soyiyeon* (所以然, the reason for the form of the existent = the ineluctable logic) and the universal moral norms *sodang-yeon* (所當然, the ethical corollary = the preordained consequence).

Yulgok, thinking that *li* cannot but be the highest good, asked whether Wen-gong's focus on selecting and learning what is right among various principles was mistaken. He also believed that Wen-gong's statement was not compatible with Cheng Yi's or Zhu Xi's view that while one reads a book, evaluates the attitudes of historical figures, and responds to things and events, one should also seek after abstruse and omnipresent *li*, which is the universal principle through which physical laws and moral norms reach agreement with each other.

Yulgok's criticism of Wen-gong's statement seems reasonable at first glance. However, it was actually a criticism of the attitude that elementary learners of Neo-Confucianism were liable to adopt. When elementary learners heard about the sages' teachings on the omnipresence of the highest principle, many were satisfied with their knowledge of the abstract principle itself. They subsequently studied theories on "benevolence, righteousness, propriety, and wisdom (仁義禮智)," "the five moral disciplines in human relations (五倫)," and so on, and they assimilated theories of *li* and thought that they had understood and mastered the subject. However, in Neo-Confucianism recognizing and learning truth does not simply mean its conceptual or theoretical understanding but instead the achievement of mastery over it through practical efforts and experience. To have an intellectual grasp of truth is quite different from practically recognizing and experiencing it.

In fact, most people, by accepting a system of thought such as a philosophy or religion, believe that they understand or recognize the truth the system pursues. However, most of them regard only the plausible or internally consistent explication of the system as truth; they do not actually recognize or experience truth itself. Their false belief that they recognize profound truth may lead to arrogance, prejudice, and dogmatism. Though it is very dangerous for a scholar to maintain a dogmatic attitude, most scholars cling to such a stance. Neo-Confucianism suggests various methods of learning such as reading, introspection, observation, experience, and practice so that scholars may overcome slavish adherence to theory and attain real recognition and mastery of truth.

Toegye resolved to write a long answer to Yulgok, and I will first examine the initial part of his response.

【Answer】 As there are many methods of pursuing principle, you should not restrict yourself to only one. When a person neglects his studies, he loses interest in his pursuits when he cannot understand a situation in spite of his efforts. He will likewise lose interest in his studies, and in the end will abandon his study of fundamental principles. On the other hand, when a person finds his subject of study too difficult to understand or uncongenial, he should set this subject aside and take up a new one. If he continues to study in this way, his learning will accumulate and deepen, and he will consequently attain maturity. Thus, he will naturally gain insight and gradually see the real aspect of righteous principles. Then he will again take up the subject he had set aside and minutely examine clues for the understanding of the subject, while referring to the learning he has already delved into, and he will unconsciously be more attuned to the subject he had set aside. This is the precise method of pursuing fundamental principles. So don't ever abandon what seems to be too great a challenge. The suggestion of Yan-ping (延平)[39] that "after achieving the complete understanding of one thing, advance little by little in sequence" is a fundamental rule worth observing in the pursuit of principle. As the profound meaning of this remark is not contrary to Cheng Yi's statement, there is no need to doubt Ge-an's (格菴)[40] opinion.[41]

Toegye began his explanation of *gyeongmul gungni* (格物窮理) with Cheng Yi's statement, which Yulgok had quoted. According to his explanation, the sequential study of the principles (*li*) of subjects (circumstances and things) is the most fundamental method of learning. If one is brought to a standstill in one's study of a subject, one should set it aside for a later date and instead commence one's study of another subject.

This explanation seems to be contrary to Yan-ping's suggestion, "After achieving the complete understanding of one thing, advance little by little in sequence." However, Toegye explained that the two statements were not contrary to each other because Yan-ping's statement referred to the fundamental rule of study while Cheng Yi's statement referred to the concrete method of study.

We can plausibly infer from Toegye's answer that Yulgok raised a question about the differing statements of Cheng Yi and Yan-ping. However, Yulgok's question cannot be found in his extant letters. And presumably, Toegye's remark at the end of his response, "There is no need to doubt

Ge-an's opinion," might have been his answer to Yulgok's missing question. The following is a note in *Da Xue huo-wen* (大學或問, *Questions and Answers on The Great Learning*) for scholars like Yulgok, who Toegye felt may have misunderstood the statements of Cheng Yi and Yan-ping:

> Zhao Ge-an (趙格菴) said the following: "Cheng Yi advised that if one is brought to a standstill in one's study of a subject, one should commence one's study of another subject. Yan-ping said that after achieving the complete understanding of a subject, one should attempt to study another subject. Their statements are different from each other. On the whole, Cheng Yi's statement implies that each person has his own favored and unfavored fields, so if he studies his favored field, he can easily progress. This does not mean that one can divide one's mind into two in studying two different subjects and into three with three different subjects, even if one has not yet understood the first subject of one's study. Yan-ping's statement may be a piece of advice for those who cannot concentrate on one subject. We should not misunderstand his intention."[42]

THE TRANSMUTATION OF KNOWLEDGE INTO PRAXIS

Toegye responded to Yulgok's criticism of Si-ma Wen-gong as follows:

> 【Additional Answer】 You said in your letter that the statement of Wen-gong, ". . . the principles of things and events have appeared before my eyes. . . . In this way I learn what is right," implies a sentiment akin to *gyeongmul* (格物). But you firmly rejected the remark "I learn what is right." I don't recall precisely what I said about Wen-gong's statement when I met you. Now, however, I find that I don't agree with you.
>
> Basically, all the principles of things and events together constitute the highest good. However, good and evil and right and wrong inevitably coexist. Therefore, generally speaking, *gyeongmul* and *gungni* (窮理) refer to the illumination of or discrimination between good and evil and right and wrong. In this context Shang-cai (上蔡)[43] described *gyeongmul* as "the pursuit of what is right." So to say that "all the principles of things and events together constitute the highest good" and to denounce the remark of Wen-gong, "Learn what is right," reveal a biased attitude resulting in unbalanced learning.[44]

Toegye explained that all the principles of things and events together constitute the highest good and that the illumination of or discrimination between good and evil and right and wrong, which coexist, constitute the study of *gyeongmul* and *gungni*. In this context, he also interpreted Shang-cai's remark about *gyeongmul* as the pursuit of what is right. So Toegye scolded Yulgok for his denunciation of Wen-gong's remark. This response of Toegye is set forth in the *munmok* of *Yulgok jeonseo*. Although Toegye's answer seems plain, it may be regarded as a stock explanation to some readers.

However, in *Toegye jip* there is a lengthy interpretation that is omitted in this "Additional Answer." In that interpretation, Toegye advised Yulgok to scrupulously examine the stages of the journey from the recognition of the highest good to its practice. Toegye reviewed Wen-gong's "Du-le-yuan-ji (獨樂園記, A Record of the Solitary Enjoyment of Pastoral Life)," about which Yulgok had raised a question, and explained the writer's intention in the chronicle. Toegye's considered explanation was in contrast with young Yulgok's casual question because he acutely pointed out and criticized the latter's logical inconsistency. The following is part of Toegye's answer that is omitted in the *munmok* of *Yulgok jeonseo*:

Si-ma Wen-gong misinterpreted the *gyeok* (格) of *gyeongmul* (格物) as "protection." So his theory couldn't but be different from Cheng Yi's or Zhu Xi's. However, his general comment on learning was based on an ethical principle. His innate character was so pure and humane that he could attain the abstruse Way by himself.

I reviewed and pondered on "Du-le-yuan-ji" on the basis of the theory of knowledge and practice and interpret its contents as follows: "Looking into the origin of benevolence and righteousness and tracing the clue to propriety and music" is a process of *gyeongmul*; "the principles of things and events gathering before my eyes" refers to the effect of *chiji* (致知); "to learn what is right" is to practice diligently; "still being incapable of attaining what is right" implies that one is yet unable to put the principles one has recognized into practice and so one should continue to make strenuous efforts in this regard. "The principles of things and events gathering before my eyes" are impossible to discern without the profound study of these principles. If this study is performed, the principles of Heaven and Earth can be grasped at a glance and right or wrong can be differentiated. "To learn what is right" is to act in accordance with knowledge. Here, "what is right" is equal to "goodness" and "to learn" is equivalent to "to practice." "Still being incapable of attaining what is right" refers to the state of being incapable of attaining the highest good, even if some kinds of goodness have already been realized in the heart-mind. If "to learn what is right" is also concerned with *gyeongmul chiji* (格物致知), this phrase together with the preceding two phrases ["looking into the origin of benevolence and righteousness and tracing the clue to propriety and music" and "the principles of things and events gathering before my eyes"] would unnecessarily overlap in their implication of "knowledge (知)." On the other hand, if the phrase "to learn what is right" is concerned with *gyeongmul chiji*, the adjacent phrase ["still being incapable of attaining what is right"], which is interpreted as a dearth of the practice of goodness and so the necessity of making strenuous efforts in this regard, may look abrupt and senseless. So it is only logical not to interpret the phrase "to learn what is right" and the adjacent phrase with respect to practice (行), in the context of *gyeongmul* or knowledge (知). Si-ma Wen-gong might not have attained spiritual enlightenment, but he would never have made the mistake of interpreting "to learn what is right" in terms of knowledge, not practice.

I infer from these two phrases that Wen-gong seems to have studied diligently because he was conscious of his lack of learning. He felt joy only in studying himself, so he said, "How can I expect to learn from others or from the outside world?" And he enjoyed studying alone. In the passage beginning with "With my weakened will . . . ," he wrote about miscellaneous events that accompanied his enjoyment. Seen in this respect, the phrases I have interpreted above are not mistaken but very reasonable.[45]

The passage about which Yulgok raised a question appears in Si-ma Guang's (Wen-gong's) "Du-le-yuan-ji (獨樂園記)." Si-ma Guang was the leader of the faction advocating "Conservative Policies," which was opposed to the faction promoting "New Policies" in the Northern Song Dynasty. He was famous as the compiler of *Zi-zhi tong-jian* (資治通鑑, *Comprehensive Mirror in Aid of Governance*). He wrote "Du-le-yuan-ji" when he retired from the central government and took a post dealing with trifling tasks in Luo-yang (洛陽). He called a hill on which he used to stroll after work "Du-le-yuan (獨樂園)" and wrote "Du-le-yuan-ji," which relates the origin of the hill's name and his state of mind at that time. The essay is well known for the elegant and refined taste it displays.

The section Yulgok was concerned with is as follows:

I, Yu-sou (迂叟, 司馬光), usually read books, look to sages as my masters and generous men as my friends. I have looked into the origin of benevolence and righteousness and traced the clues to the realization of propriety and music. The principles of forms still in the process of shaping themselves, as well as the principles of things and events emanating from all directions and from immeasurable distances have appeared before my eyes. Although I learn what is right, I am still incapable of attaining what is right. Nevertheless, how can I expect to learn from others or the outside world?[46]

Toegye answered Yulgok's question as follows: "Looking into the origin of benevolence and righteousness and tracing the clues to the realization of propriety and music" is the process of *gyeongmul*; "the principles of things and events gathering before my eyes" refers to the effect of *chiji*; "to learn what is right" requires diligent practice; "still being incapable of attaining what is right" implies being yet unable to put recognized principles into practice and the consequent necessity of making strenuous efforts to do so. According to Toegye, "To learn what is right," the phrase about which

Yulgok inquired, should be understood apart from *gyeongmul chiji*, which is a stage of recognition, because it is a stage of putting the principles that have been grasped through *gyeongmul chiji* into practice.

Yulgok thought that one has only to recognize a principle that is fundamentally right. Such a view is not itself mistaken. However, faced with the problem of how to perceive or experience omnipresent principles, his view proved to be untenable. For this reason, Zhu Xi's *gyeongmul* (格物, the investigation of things), suggested as a method of *gungni* (窮理, the investigation of principles), was severely criticized by Wang Yang-ming in later years. When one is confronted by a thing, if one only concentrates on understanding the universal principle inherent in it, there is no way of verifying whether or not one has properly understood the universal truth. Ultimately, one's understanding can only be verified through one's practice in daily life. If one has recognized principles in the world through *gyeongmul* and *gungni* but cannot put these principles into practice in daily life, one's recognition of truth may be said to be incomplete or mistaken. In that case, one's *gyeongmul* and *gungni* should be subject to revision.

As Yulgok, focusing on the issue of the recognition of truth, criticized Si-ma Guang's view, Toegye explained that this recognition cannot be separated from its practice and interpreted Si-ma Guang's view in accordance with the relationship between the stage of recognition and that of practice. Toegye's explanation that truth is not an abstract idea but the highest good that one should pursue and that the recognition of the highest good should be accompanied by practice is based on his view that theoretical studies and the cultivation of virtue must be carried out simultaneously. In later years Yulgok developed Toeye's view and suggested three stages of study, namely *geogyeong / ju-jing* (居敬, the maintenance of reverent mindfulness), *gungni* (窮理, the investigation of principle), and *yeokhaeng / li-xing* (力行, the undertaking of strenuous endeavor).[47]

THE SAGES' AUTHORITY

Yulgok's fourth question was whether sages like Confucius and Mencius sometimes assumed an arrogant attitude toward others. His question was concerned with Zhu Xi's statement in "Chapter 8 of Chuan (傳)," *Da Xue zhang-ju* (大學章句, *The Great Learning in Chapters and Verses*). It was one of the questions Yulgok formed while he was studying the classics.

Ostensibly, it was a question about the perception and display of arrogance and indolence, but substantially it was a question of whether even sages like Confucius, Mencius, and Zhu Xi could be in error. If Confucius and Mencius were not arrogant, it was wrong for Zhu Xi to have taken them as examples of overbearing sages; if Zhu Xi did not make a single mistake, it might be true that Confucius and Mencius were arrogant. Yulgok posed his question as follows:

> 【Question】 In the passage in Chapter 8 of *The Great Learning* that deals with arrogance and indolence, Zhu Xi said, "It is an ordinary feeling and the natural course of events that one who deserves to be treated arrogantly should be treated arrogantly." He supported his position by using as illustrations the episodes in which Confucius played the *seul / se* (瑟, a kind of stringed instrument) while singing and in which Mencius reclined on his cushion when a guest visited him. And Hu-shi (胡氏)[48] said, "The traits of arrogance and indolence are not attributable to sages but to ordinary persons. Among ordinary persons there are those who are excessively arrogant and indolent." What can I conclude from these instances? Won't it be problematic if a person who deserves to be treated arrogantly is actually treated arrogantly? Through their actions, don't Confucius and Mencius only intend to teach the person concerned, not to treat him arrogantly? I do not doubt their intention. In addition, Zhen shi (陣氏)[49] said, "Arrogance refers only to the simplicity displayed in the observance of a ceremony and indolence only to the delay in the observance of a ceremony." So is the meaning of arrogance in this chapter different from the perspective of Han Zi (韓子)[50] when he said, "Though arrogance is vice"?[51]

It is quite natural to treat a person arrogantly who deserves to be dealt with in such a manner. One may believe that even sages like Confucius and Mencius might have done so. However, as they are deified sages in Confucianism, it is unthinkable that they arrogantly behaved contrary to the dictates of propriety. Nevertheless, if one says that Zhu Xi's descriptions of their behavior were mistaken, one is implying that Zhu Xi's explanation was wrong. This is also unthinkable. The original text of *The Great Learning* and Hu Bingwen's (胡炳文) and Zhen Chun's (陳淳) perspectives imply that arrogance and indolence are characteristics that are far removed from the behavior of sages. Yulgok might have intended to embarrass Toegye with his question. However, it is a question that is often raised in Confucianism.

Confucian scholars usually portray sage-kings such as Yao, Shun, Yu, Tang, and Wen, as well as Regent Chou-kung and sages such as Confucius and Mencius, as paragons who recognized and practiced truth, and that the attempt to adhere to their words and deeds is the most important focus of study. The fact that the sages, who understood, elucidated and practiced truth, existed historically contributes to the authenticity and concreteness of the truth they preached. However, the assumption of the infallibility of these sages because they are believed to have attained truth without displaying any faults sometimes paradoxically functions as an obstacle to the recognition and interpretation of truth.

Zhu Xi said, "It is an ordinary feeling and the natural course of events that one who deserves to be treated arrogantly should be treated arrogantly." He supported his position with his description of the episodes involving Confucius and Mencius ostensibly behaving arrogantly. Seen in this context, Zhu Xi seems to have thought that arrogance is a feeling every human being is capable of and not a breach of propriety. However, is it possible for sages to treat arrogantly those who treat others likewise?

Chapter 8 of *The Great Learning* denounces arrogance and indolence, explains the relationship between "self-cultivation (修身)" and "the management of a family (齊家)," and offers the reason why self-cultivation is the key to the governance of the latter, the smallest unit of society.

"The governance of a family depends on self-cultivation" because most people adhere to their judgment of what is intimate and valuable, what is vulgar and detestable, what they should be afraid of, what is respectable, what is lamentable, what should arouse pity and what is arrogant and indolent. Therefore people who can see the evil aspects of those they like or who can see the good aspects of those they hate are seldom found.[52]

According to this, the unity of a family depends on self-cultivation and the cast of mind of family members toward each other. When a member of a family recognizes the merits of other members and treats them with courtesy, it is necessary for that family member to also see their defects. Conversely, when a family member is aware of the defects of other members and treats them with disdain, that person should also perceive their merits. Generally speaking, avoiding the adoption of a fixed conception about others and treating them impartially is the key to self-cultivation. Only when all members of a family endeavor to practice such self-cultivation can they become a harmonious unit.

This quotation from *The Great Learning* teaches that a harmonious family is achieved through self-cultivation and by the jettisoning of animosity and arrogance toward others. However, Zhu Xi seems to have seen Confucius's and Mencius's responses to their guests as instances of an arrogant attitude. So Yulgok might well have doubted whether or not Confucius and Mencius displayed an arrogant and discourteous attitude toward their guests.

The original versions of Zhu Xi's accounts of the behavior of Confucius and Mencius are as follows:

Ru-bei (孺悲) wanted to talk with Confucius. But Confucius refused on the pretext of illness. However, as the page who was to deliver Confucius's message went out, Confucius played the se (瑟) and sang to Ru-bei.

—"Book 18 (微子)," *The Analects*

> A man called on Mencius and tried to obstruct him from leaving the
> king. But Mencius did not reply to him and reclined upon his cushion.

—"Gong-sun-chou (公孫丑) II," *Mencius*

In the first episode Confucius refused to meet a guest and let him know
that he intentionally did so because Confucius wanted the guest to reflect on
himself. In the second episode Mencius also pretended that he was arrogant
so that his guest might grasp his intention and engage in introspection.

According to Zhen Chun's interpretation, *o / ao* (敖, arrogance) refers only
to simplicity in the observance of a ceremony and *ta / duo* (惰, indolence) to
delay in the observance. Even if one knows how to observe a ceremony in
accordance with proprieties, one may simplify the procedures intentionally or
omit some recklessly. *O* corresponds to the former and *ta* to the latter. Both *o*
and *ta* connote discourtesy but *o* in particular refers to "intentional arrogance"
and *ta* to "lack of sincerity" in the practice of propriety.

Ultimately, Yulgok's question was whether sages like Confucius and
Mencius could adopt the negatively connoted attitude of *o*. In addition,
the intention of Zhu Xi, who related these episodes, should be clarified.
Of course, Zhu Xi does not seem to have recounted these episodes in order to
denounce Confucius's and Mencius's unethical deeds. Then is it the case that
Zhu Xi had another meaning of the word *o* in mind? This does not seem to
be the case because Zhu Xi explained in his annotation to *The Great Learning* that arrogance and indolence refer to the traits of ordinary men. So why
did Zhu Xi recount episodes in which not ordinary men but Confucius and
Mencius looked arrogant and indolent? In order to answer Yulgok's question,
Toegye had to explain and defend Zhu Xi's position.

【Answer】 The remark of Hu shi (胡氏) that arrogance and indolence are
displayed by ordinary men is true. Zhu Xi interpreted the word "men," which
was employed in the first part of *The Great Learning*, as "ordinary men." He
also said, "Ordinary men do not deliberate on what they intend to do." So Zhu
Xi did not have in mind the arrogance and indolence of superior men or sages.
However, he thought that sages may assume an arrogant and indolent attitude
in order to correct ordinary men's biased inclinations and to guide them to the
pursuit of the "unprejudiced Way (中道)." Therefore what should be addressed
from the standpoint of superior men is the way to respond to ordinary men's
arrogance and indolence. Ordinary men usually say, "I treat a person arrogantly when he deserves to be treated so" or "Arrogance is a natural feeling of
humans," though they continue to engage in evil conduct because of their preju-
diced disposition. In the case of superior men, their possible lack of courtesy
toward ordinary men is a quite natural response, which is based on their just and
genuine intentions. Their seemingly discourteous responses in fact reveal their

gentle, sincere, righteous, and amicable temperaments. Zhu Xi's relation of the behavior of Confucius, who sang and played the *seul / se* (瑟), and of Mencius, who reclined on his cushion, do not imply Confucius's and Mencius's arrogance and indolence but their intention of guiding ordinary men to the pursuit of the righteous way. So [in light of Zhu Xi's accounts] why should we worry that superior men's arrogance and indolence are like those of ordinary men or that scholars may be arrogant and engage in rash and thoughtless acts? (Toegye's additional note: *O* means ill conduct but it came to have a slightly different meaning when it was applied to superior men.)[53]

The phrase in chapter 8 of *The Great Learning*, "men inclined toward arrogance and indolence," refers to "ordinary men," as Hu Bing-wen explained. Though Zhu Xi agreed with Hu, Yulgok raised a question about Zhu Xi's intention because of his accounts of the behavior of Confucius and Mencius. In response to Yulgok's question, Toegye explained the arrogant attitude of ordinary men and that of superior men.

According to Toegye, chapter 8 of *The Great Learning* warns ordinary men of the pitfalls of their chronic prejudice on the one hand and on the other enjoins superior men to correct ordinary men's biased inclinations. Therefore Toegye assessed that Zhu Xi's accounts implied that Confucius's and Mencius's intention was to correct the inclinations of ordinary men. Ultimately, Toegye answered insightfully while advocating the infallibility of Zhu Xi as well as of Confucius and Mencius. The sages' apparent arrogance and indolence, according to Toegye, though it seems wrong and biased, are in fact unbiased responses to ordinary men, given in order to guide them.

Acute and logical criticism of even the sages' statements with the ambition of superseding them may be a productive method of study, while acknowledgment of the authority of sages, which was strengthened over the course of generations, and self-reflection guided by this authority, may be another beneficial method of study. Yulgok's method seems to correspond to the former and Toegye's to the latter. Such a difference may typically be seen in the differing views on established authority of the young and the old generation.

The specific reason for highlighting the authority of the sages in Confucianism was that as a philosophy it aimed at the construction of an ideal society in the real world without relying on transcendental gods and the rendering of judgment after death. The authority of the sages may have been exaggerated to some degree, but it helped people to aspire to higher ideals and to restrain the excesses of despotism. Until the governing system of the state was fundamentally reformed, the authority of the sages operated as an imperceptible defense against social depravities, enabling society to move incrementally toward the ideal. The destruction of established authority was justified only when the chronic ills of a society could not be rectified or when there was no hope of progressing toward a better society. However, there was a case to be made that the acceptance or consolidation of the sages' authority was necessary in order to criticize and provide a counterweight to those in power. Though the sages as mortal human beings could not achieve perfection, they greatly contributed to the societal well-being when ordinary people focused on their great virtues rather than their slight defects.

NOTES

1. After he had passed the civil service examination in 1558, Gobong visited Toegye. Toegye sent Gobong a letter in January of the following year, and the controversy between them on the four-seven commenced. According to "Gobong seonsaeng yeonpyo" 高峯先生年表 (The Chronological Records of Master Gobong), in *Gobong jip* 高峯集 (The Collected Works of Gobong), Gobong visited Toegye in October. But this is inaccurate, as Gobong's visit was made in November, as is stated in *Toegye seonsaeng yeonpyo irwol jomok* 退溪先生年表日月條錄 (The Chronology of Toegye's Daily Records). And in any case, as the civil service examination was held on either October 28 or 29 every year, it is reasonable to assume that Gobong visited Toegye in November after he passed the examination. For more on this, refer to Jeong Seok-tae, *The Chronology of Toegye's Daily Records 2*, 516–17.

2. In *Gobong jip*, Gobong's response to Toegye's list of questions is recorded. Gi Dae-seung, "Response to Master Toegye's List of Questions," in *Gobong jip*, 40:130a–d.

3. Jeong Seok-tae, *The Chronology of Toegye's Daily Records 4*, 674.

4. Yi I, "The Appended Notes Presented to Master Toegye," in *Yulgok jeonseo*, 44:178a–180d.

5. Yi Hwang, "The Appended Response to Yi Sukheon," in *Toegye jip*, 29:372c–374d.

6. Yi I, "The Appended Notes Presented to Master Toegye," in *Yulgok jeonseo*, 44:178a–b.

7. "Shou zhang" 首章 (the first chapter), in *Da Xue zhang-ju* 大學章句 (*The Great Learning in Chapters and Verses*).

8. "Chronology I," in *Yulgok jeonseo*, 45:282a.

9. Yulgok was a brilliant scholar who gained first place in more than seven civil service examinations. Geum Jang-tae, *Yulgok pyeongjeon* (The Critical Biography of Yulgok) (Seoul: Jisik-gwa gyoyang, 2011), 84; Han Yeong-wu, *Yulgok Yi I pyeongjeon* (A Critical Biography of Yulgok Yi I) (Seoul: Minum sa, 2013), 79.

10. Concerning the formative process of the mythology surrounding Confucius, refer to Mark Edward Lewis, *Writing and Authority in Early China* (Albany, NY: State University of New York Press, 1999), 218–20.

11. Yi I, "Ipji jang" 立志章 (The First Chapter titled "Resolution") in *Gyeongmong yogyeol* 擊蒙要訣 (The Secret to Dispelling Ignorance) of *Yulgok jeonseo*, 45:83a–b.

12. Quoted from "Shun-zhan" (舜典, A Story of King Shun), in *Shu Jing* (書經, *The Book of Documents*). "The seven methods of governance (七政)" here refer to the sun, the moon, and the five stars. The king is said to have observed astrological phenomena in order to govern people in accordance with the providence of Heaven.

13. The five ceremonies and the five tools are introduced in "Shun-zhan (舜典)," in *Shu Jing* (書經). The five ceremonies refer to the ceremony of worship, the ceremony appropriate to calamity and mourning, the ceremony appropriate to hosting guests of the state, the ceremony appropriate to war, and the festive ceremony. The five tools refer to the implements used in the five ceremonies. Simply put, King Shun observed the five ceremonies and used suitable tools for each ceremony.

14. Mr. Fang (方氏) refers to Fang Feng-chen (方逢辰, 1221–1291), who was a scholar of the classics in the late period of the Song Dynasty and the early period of the Yuan Dynasty. His original name was Meng-kui (夢魁) and his pseudonym was Jiao-feng (蛟峰). He primarily studied Zhu Xi's thought.

15. Yi I, "The Appended Notes Presented to Master Toegye in 1558," in *Yulgok jeonseo*, 44:178b–c.

16. Refer to notes 30 and 31 of chapter 2.

17. Cheng Yi (程頤, pseudonym: 伊川 Yi-chuan, 1033–1107) was one of the representative scholars of Neo-Confucianism in the Northern Song Dynasty. He had great influence on Zhu Xi.

18. Michael C. Kalton translated this phrase in his *To Become a Sage* (New York: Columbia University Press, 1988) as follows: "well-ordered and even-minded, grave and quiet."

19. Xie Liang-zuo (謝良佐, 1050–1103) was a disciple of the brothers Cheng Hao (程顥) and Cheng Yi. Michael C. Kalton translated this phrase in his *To Become a Sage* as follows: "the method of always being clear-minded and alert."

20. Yin Tun (尹焞, 1071–1142) was a disciple of Cheng Yi. His pseudonym was Hua-jing (和靖). Michael C. Kalton translated this phrase in his *To Become a Sage* as follows: "possessing one's mind in a condition of recollection and not permitting anything [to have hold on it]."

21. Zhen De-xiu (眞德秀) and Cheng Min-zheng (程敏政), "Yi Kun-liu-er Jing-er-zhi-nei-zhang" 易 坤六二 敬而直內章 (A Chapter Concerning the Axiom, "Leading to an Honest Mind with Reverent Mindfulness" Implied in the Second Sign of Kun [坤]), *Xin Jing fu-zhu* 心經附註.

22. Toegye quoted Zhu Xi's dictum in *Da Xue huo-wen* (大學或問, *Questions and Answers on The Great Learning*) in his "Daehakdo" (大學圖, Diagram of the Great Learning), in *Seonghak sipdo* (聖學十圖, Ten Diagrams of Sage Learning), in *Toegye jip*, 29:205a–b.

23. Yi Hwang, "Ten Diagrams of Sage Learning: Chapter 4. The Diagram of The Great Learning," in *Toegye jip*, 29:205c.

24. However, *lihak / li-xue* (理學, the study of *li*), *simhak / xin-xue* (心學, the study of the heart-mind), and *dohak / dao-xue* (道學, the study of the Way) are more frequently employed than *gyeonghak / jing-xue* (敬學, the study of reverent mindfulness) as definitional characteristics of Toegye's learning. In particular, *lihak*, which means the study of *li* as the core concept of Neo-Confucianism, is the most

representative term that most fully displays the characteristics of Toegye's learning. *Dohak* is mainly focused on by scholars who emphasize Toegye's consistent pursuit of the conduct of moral practices in real life, and *simhak* is emphasized by scholars who maintain that the aim of Toegye's positive interpretations of *li* was ultimately to stress the importance of the cultivation of the mind. Refer to Kim Hyoungchan, "Toegye's Philosophy as Practical Ethics: A System of the Learning, Cultivation, and Practice of Being Human," *Korea Journal* 47, no. 3 (2007).

25. Yi I, "The Appended Notes Presented to Master Toegye in 1558," in *Yulgok jeonseo*, 44:178d.

26. Ibid., 44:178d–179a.

27. Kim, "Toegye's Philosophy as Practical Ethics," 167–71.

28. Concerning the influence of books about Zhu Xi's learning on the formation of Toegye's thought, refer to Yi Sang-eun, *Toegye-ui saeng-ae-wa hangmun* (Toegye's Life and Learning) (Seoul: Yemun seowon, 1999), 83–107.

29. Yi Hwang, "Simgyeong huron" 心經後論 (Postscripts to The Classic of the Heart-Mind), in *Toegye jip*, 30:410b.

30. Ibid., 30:411a–b.

31. Ibid., 30:410b–c. In fact, it is another matter whether or not Zhu Xi was biased toward theoretical study because Zhu Xi, in his debate with Lu Xiangshan (陸象山) emphasized both the cultivation of virtue and theoretical study simultaneously. Scholars like Qian Mu (錢穆) and Chen Lai (陳來) supported Zhu Xi's position. [Refer to Qian Mu, *Zhu Zi xue ti-gang* 朱子學提綱 (The Outline of Master Zhu's Learning), trans. Yi Wan-jae and Baek Do-geun (Daegu: Yimun Publishing Company, 2000), 326–31; and to Chen Lai, *Zhu Zi zhe-xue yan-jiu* 朱子哲學研究 (A Study of Master Zhu's Thought) (Shanghai: Hua-dong Shi-fan University Press, 2000), 326–31]. Nevertheless, at the time of his debate with Lu Xiangshan, Zhu Xi had already displayed more of a predilection toward theoretical study than Lu. And Toegye thought that Zhu Xi's disciples attached too much importance to theoretical study, neglecting the cultivation of virtue.

32. Yi Hwang, "Jeonseumnok nonbyeon" 傳習錄論辯 (A Critique of *The Records of Wang Yang-ming's Teachings*), in *Toegye jip*, 30:418a.

33. Ibid., 30:417c–d.

34. Confucius, "Book 7," in *The Analects*.

35. Bak Se-dang (朴世堂), who was one of the precursors of the *Silhak* (實學, Practical Learning) school of thought in late Joseon, criticized Zhu Xi's view on *gyeongmul chiji / ge-wu zhi-zhi* (格物致知), which requires wide and far-reaching insight through the study of the ultimate *li*, and argued that the purpose of *gyeongmul chiji* is to pursue the principle appropriate to a given thing and to positively transform the thing in accordance with the imperatives of this principle. Concerning the details of Bak Se-dang's *gyeongmul chiji*, refer to Kim Hyoungchan, "Samunnanjeok nollangwa saseo-ui jaehaeseok" (On the Issue of Enemies of Confucianism and the Reinterpretation of the Four Books), *Han-guk sasang-gwa munhwa* 63 (2012): 345–48.

36. Si-ma Wen-gong (司馬溫公) refers to Si-ma Guang (司馬光, 1019–1086). As he was posthumously given the title of "Tai-shi Wen-guo-gong (太師溫國公)," he is also called "Si-ma Wen-gong." He was a representative scholar and politician

of Northern Song, who opposed the new system of law drafted by Wang An-shi (王安石). Yulgok raised questions about some phrases in his "Du-le-yuan-ji (獨樂園記, A Record of the Solitary Enjoyment of Pastoral Life)."

37. Yi I, "The Appended Notes Presented to Master Toegye in 1558," in *Yulgok jeonseo*, 44:179a.

38. Concerning the detailed contents of the relation between "Be and Ought" in Neo-Confucianism, refer to Youn Sasoon, "Jonjaewa dang-wi-e gwanhan Toegye-ui ilchisi" (The Identity of Be and Ought in Toegye's Thought), in *Han-guk yuhak sasan-gnon* (A Study on Korean Confucian Thought) (Seoul: Yemun seowon, 1997), 259–83.

39. Yan-ping was the pseudonym of Li Tong (李侗, 1093–1163), who was a scholar of Southern Song. He was a disciple of Cheng Hao and Cheng Yi and a master of Zhu Xi.

40. Ge-an was the pseudonym of Zhao Shun-sun (趙順孫, 1215–1276), who was a scholar of the classics in the Song Dynasty.

41. Yi I, "The Appended Notes Presented to Master Toegye," in *Yulgok jeonseo*, 44:175b–c.

42. Zhu Xi, "Da Xue huo-wen," in *Si-shu da-quan* I 四書大全 (The Collection of the Four Books I), ed. Hu Guang 胡廣 et al. (Jinju: Suri, 2012), 109.

43. Shang-cai (上蔡) refers to Xie Liang-zuo (謝良佐, 1050–1103), whose home-town was Shang-cai in Henan province (河南省). He was a scholar in the Song Dynasty and studied under Cheng Hao and Cheng Yi.

44. Yi I, "The Appended Notes Presented to Master Toegye," in *Yulgok jeonseo*, 44:179c.

45. Yi Hwang, "The Appended Response to Yi Sukheon," in *Toegye jip*, 29:373c–374c.

46. Si-ma Guang, "Du-le-yuan-ji" 獨樂園記 (A Record of the Solitary Enjoyment of Pastoral Life). "迂叟平日讀書, 上師聖人, 下友群賢, 窺仁義之原, 探禮樂之緒, 自未始有形之前, 暨四達無窮之外. 事物之理, 舉集目前, 可者學之, 未至於可, 何求於人, 何待於外哉."

47. In order to examine his theory of self-cultivation, scholars of Yulgok have paid attention to his systematic division of the stages of study, which consist of *geogyeong* (居敬), *gungni* (窮理), and *yeokhaeng* (力行). Detailed studies of this subject were carried out in the following two works: Jeong Won-jae, "Jigakseol-e ipgakhan Yi I cheorak-ui haeseok" (An Interpretation of Yi I's Philosophy on the Basis of the Theory of Perception) (PhD diss., Seoul National University, 2000), 138–59; and Kim Gyeong-ho, *In-gyeok seongsuk-ui saeroun jipyeong: Yulgok-ui ingannon* (A New Horizon for the Maturation of Personality: Yulgok's Theory of the Human Being) (Goyang: Jeongbo-wa saram, 2008), 280–90.

48. Hu shi (胡氏) refers to Hu Bing-wen (胡炳文, 1250–1333), who was a classi-cal scholar in the Yuan Dynasty. His pseudonym is Yun-feng (雲峰).

49. Zhen shi (陳氏) refers to Zhen Chun (陳淳, 1159–1223), who was a scholar in Southern Song. Bei-xi (北溪, Zhen Chun's pseudonym) and Huang Gan (黃榦) were representative disciples of Zhu Xi.

50. Han Zi (韓子) refers to Han Yu (韓愈, 768–824), who was a scholar in the Tang Dynasty. In "Miscellaneous Writings," which is contained in *The Collected*

Works of Han Yu, Vol. 13, he said, "People dare to adopt the bad attitude of haughtiness because they take their position for granted (夫敖雖凶德, 必有恃而敢行)."

51. Yi I, "The Appended Notes Presented to Master Toegye in 1558," in *Yulgok jeonseo*, 44:179c–d.

52. Zhu Xi, "Chuan (傳) 8," in *Da Xue zhang-ju*.

53. Yi I, "The Appended Notes Presented to Master Toegye in 1558," in *Yulgok jeonseo*, 44:179d–180a.

Chapter 3

The Four Beginnings and Seven Feelings

The Eight-Year Debate between Toegye and Gobong

The year 1558, when Yulgok first visited Toegye, was a notable period in Toegye's career. After Yulgok left Toegye's house in February, he sent a letter and his first *munmok / wen-mu* (問目, a list of questions) to Toegye, who sent a reply to Yulgok in May. From that point on, an exchange of ideas via letters began between the two scholars. In November of the same year, Gi Dae-seung (奇大升, pen name: Gobong 高峯, 1527–1572) called on Toegye, and after a period Toegye heard the news that Gobong had raised a question about "the four beginnings and the seven feelings (the four-seven)," which was recorded in his "Cheonmyeong do (天命圖, The Diagram of the Mandate of Heaven)." Toegye sent a letter to Gobong in January of the following year, and their "controversy on the four-seven (四端七情論)" commenced, during which Toegye, twenty-six years older than Gobong, entertained the latter with courtesy. This controversy, which continued via letters for eight years until July 1566, was one of the representative scholarly debates of the Joseon era. Beginning about 160 years after the foundation of Joseon, it not only showed the Neo-Confucianism of Joseon in full flower but also had decisive influence on the development of the Confucianism of Joseon.

In 1572, two years after Toegye died, Seong Hon (成渾, pen name: Ugye 牛溪, 1535–1598) asked Yulgok about the point of the controversy on the four-seven, and taking this opportunity, started a debate with Yulgok, which developed into a debate on "the human mind and the moral mind (*yinsim dosim / ren-xin dao-xin* 人心道心)."

Toegye's learning expanded from 1558 when Yulgok sent his first *munmok* to him until 1570 when Yulgok sent his second *munmok*, and it was manifested in his controversy with Gobong on "the four-seven." Toegye's position, which he elaborated in the controversy, was expressed in his responses to Yulgok's second and third *munmok*s. For his own part, Yulgok, while adopting a critical view of Toegye's position, consolidated his own standpoint. Later he began to debate with Seong Hon, who adhered to Toegye's position.

Fundamentally, Yulgok supported Gobong's theory. Though he was interested in the controversy between Toegye and Gobong, he seems to have believed that he was too young and too much of a novice in terms of learning to contribute to the debate because he was nine years younger than Gobong. Later, in 1572, he sent a letter to Seong Hon in which he gave his impressions of the controversy.

> Master Toegye is unrivaled in his accuracy, meticulousness, judiciousness, and precision. However, his theory stipulating that "*Li* issues and *gi* follows the issuance of *li* (理發氣隨之)" implies the trifling mistake of giving precedence to *li* over *gi*. Before the old master passed away, I should have asked him about this matter. However, as I was too young and too superficial in my learning at that time, I dared not ask it of the master. Whenever I think about this matter, I feel sorry deep in my heart.[1]

"THE DIAGRAM OF THE MANDATE OF HEAVEN"

The controversy on the four-seven was originally caused by "The Diagram of the Mandate of Heaven," drawn by Jeong Ji-un (鄭之雲, pen name: Chuman 秋巒, 1509–1561). The diagram shows, according to the Neo-Confucian view of the world, the procedures underlying the embodiment in human beings of the principles of the universe and of nature. According to Neo-Confucianism, Heaven endows human beings, at the time of their birth, with the universal principles of nature. These principles are latent in the human mind as the manifestation of the original moral nature and reveal themselves in reality as moral feelings. Therefore a human being as a constituent of nature is aboriginally created to lead a moral life according to the universal principles of nature.

"The Diagram of the Mandate of Heaven" is an illustration that concisely displays the Neo-Confucian metaphysical theories dealing with the ground and principle of the moral life of man. Since Gwon Geun (權近, pen name: Yangchon 陽村, 1352–1409) had drawn "Cheonin simseong habil ji do (天人心性合一之圖, The Diagram of the Unity of Heaven and Man, Mind and Nature)," the style of the diagram showing the relationship between man and nature through a focus on the human mind was considered to effectively represent the characteristics of the Confucianism of Joseon.

The characteristics of the diagrams drawn in the Joseon era are easily distinguished from those produced in China, for example Zhou Dun-yi's (周敦頤, pen name: Lian-gu 濂溪, 1017–1073) "Tai-ji-tu (太極圖, The Diagram of the Supreme Polarity)."

While the Chinese "The Diagram of the Supreme Polarity" regarded man as a constituent in the formative process of the whole universe, the Korean "The Diagram of the Mandate of Heaven," with the universe in the background, placed the human mind, man's original moral nature, and moral feelings in the foreground. The basic composition of "The Diagram of the Unity of Heaven and Man, Mind, and Nature" drawn by Yangchon, with the human mind and original moral nature in the center, found its way into the diagrams

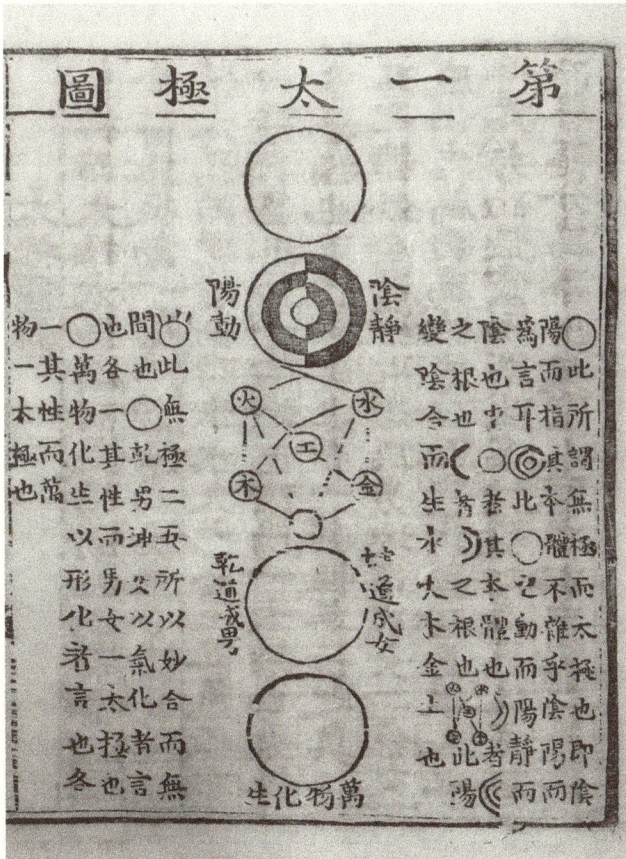

Image 3.1   Zhou Dun-yi's "The Diagram of the Supreme Polarity." *Source*: "Taegeuk do 太極圖" (Vol.7, p. 10) in *Toegye seonsaeng munjip* 退溪先生文集. Author: Yi Hwang 李 滉. Publisher: Dosan seowon 陶山書院, Korea. Date of publication: 1697. Used here with permission from Korea University Library.

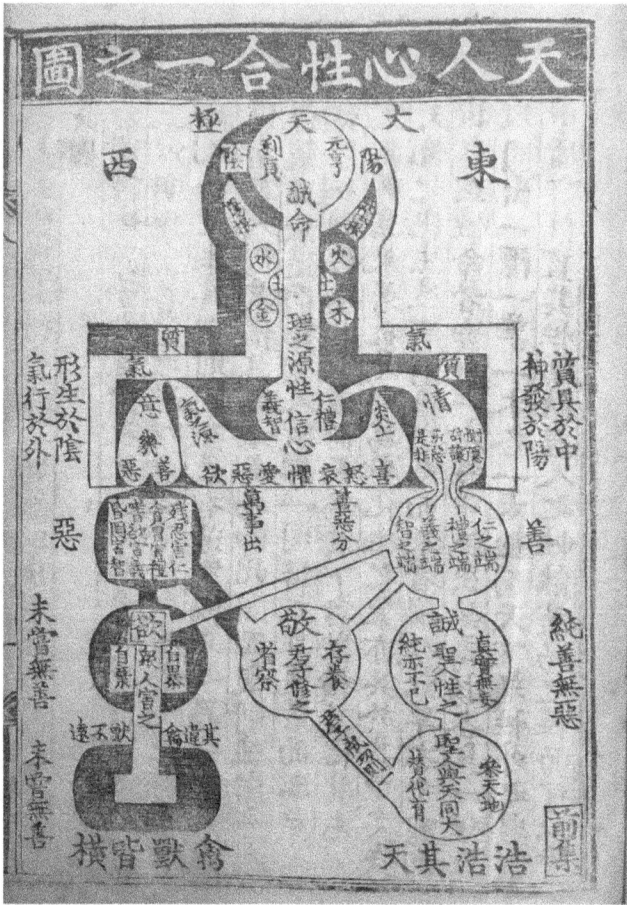

Image 3.2　Gwon Geun's "The Diagram of the Unity of Heaven and Man, Mind and Nature." *Source*: "Cheonin simseong habil jido 天人心性合一之圖" in *Yangchon seonsaeng yiphak doseol* 陽村先生入學圖說. Author: Gwon Geun 權近. Publisher: Yeongcheon 永川, Korea Date of publication: 1547. Used here with permission from Korea University Library.

drawn by Toegye, Chuman, and Kim In-hu (金麟厚, pen name: Haseo 河西, 1510–1560).[2] These diagrams demonstrated the intentions of the intellectuals of Joseon, who attempted to understand and explain the universe on the basis of the human mind and of morality.

Joseon was a dynasty that was established by intellectuals on the basis of Neo-Confucian ideology. They took the initiative in the foundation and governance of Joseon and endeavored to institutionalize and popularize the Neo-Confucian theoretical grounds for the development of the ideal ethical state. "The Diagram of the Mandate of Heaven" was a useful and easy tool in the promotion of such an endeavor because it summarized and clearly

Image 3.3   Kim In-hu's "The Diagram of the Mandate of Heaven." *Source*: "Haseo Kim seonseang Cheonmyeong do 河西金先生天命圖" in *Cheonmyeong dohae* 天命圖解. Author: Jeong Ji-un 鄭之雲. Publisher: Neungseong hyeon 綾城縣, Korea Date of publication: 1578. Used here with permission from Korea University Library.

illustrated Neo-Confucian ideals on a single sheet of paper. For this reason, Neo-Confucian scholars took special note of Chuman's "The Diagram of the Mandate of Heaven" and were especially interested in the composition and delineation of the Neo-Confucian theories included in the diagram. Their special interest in the diagram led to a long-term controversy focused on the composition and explanation of the four beginnings and the seven feelings.

Chuman, on the basis of his studies under Kim Jeong-guk (金正國, pen name: Sajae 思齋, 1485–1541), drew "The Diagram of the Mandate of Heaven I"[3] around 1537. He wanted to arrange a diagram of Neo-Confucian theories on the relationship between the universe and the human mind and nature, and several scholars copied it. In 1553 Toegye, through his nephew, named Gyo (喬), was able to view a copy of "The Diagram of the Mandate of Heaven II," and he wanted to see Chuman's original diagram. Chuman met Toegye, bringing with him his revised diagram "The Diagram of the

Mandate of Heaven III." Toegye gave his opinion of the diagram and Chuman accepted his view. About three months later, Chuman called on Toegye
with his new "The Diagram of the Mandate of Heaven IV," a revised version
that incorporated Toegye's suggestions. Chuman and Teogye made further
revisions and completed "The Diagram of the Mandate of Heaven V." With
this diagram in hand, Chuman met Gobong, who disagreed with some parts
of it. Later, Toegye, through his controversy with Gobong, accepted some
aspects of Gobong's opinion and drew his revised diagram, "The Diagram of
the Mandate of Heaven VI."[4]

There are several extant editions of "Cheonmyeong do (The Diagram of
the Mandate of Heaven)"[5], among which the most famous ones are "Cheonmyeong gudo (天命舊圖, The Old Diagram of the Mandate of Heaven)" and
"Cheongmyeong sindo (天命新圖, The New Diagram of the Mandate of
Heaven)" contained in "Cheonmyeong doseol huseo (天命圖說後敍, Postscripts to the Interpretation of The Diagram of the Mandate of Heaven)" of
Toegye jip.

For a long time it was a kind of idée fixe among scholars that
"The Old Diagram of the Mandate of Heaven" contained in *Toegye jip* was
solely Chuman's work, that "The New Diagram" was the edition revised by
Toegye, and that the controversy on the four-seven began with Gobong's
question to Toegye about "The New Diagram." After Gobong died, some
scholar-officials presented to the king a petition titled "Cheong-hyang so
(請享疏)"[6] in order to request the enshrinement of Gobong's tablet in the
National Shrine of Confucius. In the petition the scholar-officials supported
the conventional wisdom about the beginning of the controversy between
Toegye and Gobong. Therefore not only most of the scholars of Joseon in
the period soon after Gobong died but also those of recent years accepted
this cause of the debate.[7]

However, a new conclusion was drawn recently through close examination of the letters between Toegye and Gobong.[8] According to this reading, "The Old Diagram of the Mandate of Heaven" in *Toegye jip* refers to
"The Diagram of the Mandate of Heaven V," which contains the revisions
of both Chuman and Toegye, which therefore suggests that Gobong posed
a question to Toegye about "The Diagram of the Mandate of Heaven V."
By contrast, "The New Diagram of the Mandate of Heaven" in *Toegye jip* is
commonly presumed to refer to "The Diagram VI," which reflects some con-
clusions of the debate between Toegye and Gobong. So the occasion of the
controversy, according to the new research, was not a question of Gobong's
about the statement in "The Diagram VI" that "the four beginnings are the
issuance of *li* and the seven feelings are that of *gi*" but a query about the

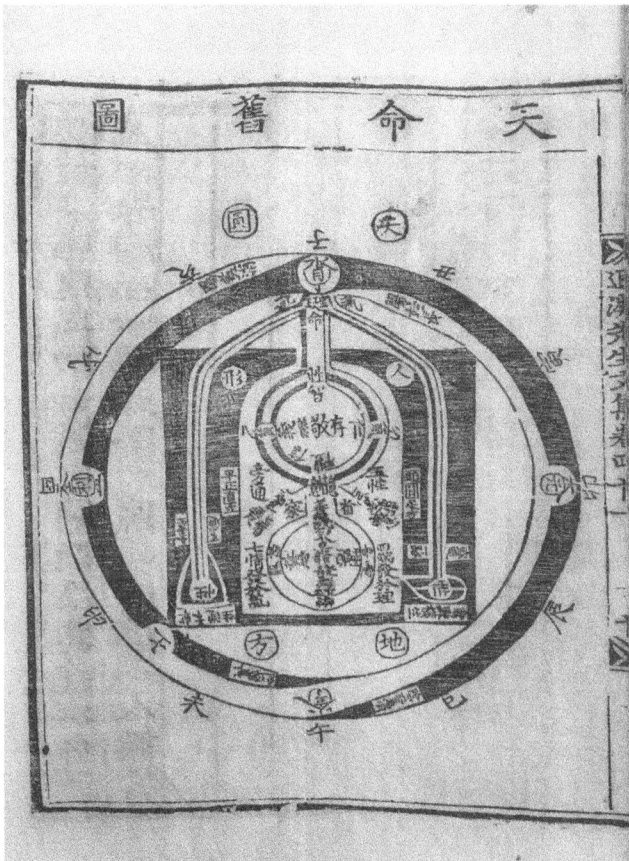

Image 3.4 "The Old Diagram of the Mandate of Heaven." *Source*: "Cheonmyeong gudo 天命舊圖" (Vol.41, p. 10) in *Toegye seonsaeng munjip* 退溪先生文集. Author: Yi Hwang 李滉. Publisher: Dosan seowon 陶山書院, Korea Date of publication: 1697. Used here with permission from Korea University Library.

statements in "The Diagram V," namely that "the four beginnings issue from *li*" and "the seven feelings issue from *gi*."

In October 1558, when Gobong was staying in the capital city of Han-yang to take the state examination, Chuman visited him, bringing with him "The Diagram V." At that time Gobong might have heard that the diagram had been revised jointly by Chuman and Toegye. He posed a question about the layout and explanatory method of the four beginnings and the seven feelings. In January of the following year, Toegye wrote a letter to Gobong and then the historical "controversy on the four-even" commenced.

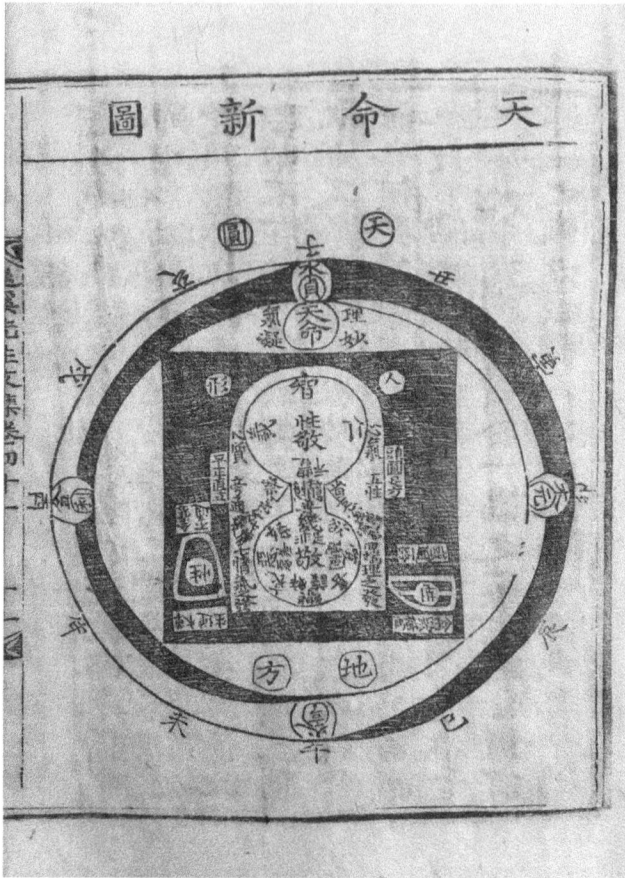

Image 3.5 "The New Diagram of the Mandate of Heaven." *Source*: "Cheonmyeong sindo 天命新圖" (Vol.41, p. 11) in *Toegye seonsaeng munjip* 退溪先生文集. Author: Yi Hwang 李滉. Publisher: Dosan seowon 陶山書院, Korea Date of publication: 1697. Used here with permission from Korea University Library.

MORAL FEELINGS AND THE ORIGINAL MORAL NATURE[9]

Both *sadan / si-duan* (四端, the four beginnings) and *chiljeong / qi-qing* (七情, the seven feelings) referred to human feelings, especially those concerned with morals. However, while *chiljeong* directly referred to the seven feelings of joy (喜), anger (怒), sorrow (哀), fear (懼), love (愛), hatred (惡), and lust (欲), *sadan* was not originally a term denoting feelings because it initially referred to "the four clues" on the basis of which the original moral nature may be inferred.

Mencius, who was the first to use the term *sadan / si-duan* (四端),[10] in order to support his view of "the innate goodness of man," suggested the four clues on the basis of which man's good original nature might be inferred. According to him, as the original moral nature immanent in the mind cannot be identified directly, it must be inferred from empirical facts or from the four feelings concerned with morals, that is, the mind of compassion (惻隱之心), the mind of shame and dislike for evil (羞惡之心), the mind of modesty and deference (辭讓之心), and the mind of moral discernment of right and wrong (是非之心). Mencius regarded these four feelings as the four clues on the basis of which benevolence (仁), righteousness (義), propriety (禮), and wisdom (智), which have been defined in Confucianism as the components of original human nature, can be inferred. Since then, the four clues have been seen as genuinely good moral feelings revealing the good original moral traits of benevolence, righteousness, propriety, and wisdom.

On the other hand, the seven feelings represent the whole gamut of feelings issuing from the original moral nature of man. In Confucianism the characteristics of the original moral nature have been classified as "benevolence, righteousness, propriety, and wisdom." However, the original moral nature may be manifested as a variety of feelings arising in accordance with varying situations. In Neo-Confucianism, on the basis of the explication of "Li yun (禮運, The Circle of Rites)" in *The Book of Rites* (禮記), the whole spectrum of feelings is represented by the seven feelings.

What are man's feelings? Joy, anger, sorrow, fear, love, hatred and lust. These seven feelings are naturally manifested.[11]

What is more widely known concerning the various kinds of feeling is the following statement in "Zhong Yong (中庸, The Doctrine of the Mean)," which was originally a chapter of *The Book of Rites* and later became a book in its own right.

The state of mind before the issuance of joy, anger, sorrow, and pleasure is called "equilibrium (中)," and the state of mind after which they have issued and "act in their due degree (中節)" is called "harmony (和)." This "equilibrium" is the great source of Heaven and Earth and this "harmony" is the way pervading Heaven and Earth.[12]

Both the seven feelings suggested in "Li yun" and the four feelings discussed in "Zhong Yong" represent moral feelings. Even though it is difficult to adequately categorize such feelings,[13] in Confucianism they are generally classified into the seven feelings, following the proposal in "Li yun."

According to "Li yun," man's feelings are naturally manifested. However, "Li yun" excluded the feelings of hunger and sickness because they are feelings that are experienced passively through physiological functions, not moral feelings through which conscious or unconscious judgments on certain phenomena are exercised. As explained in "Zhong Yong," the state of mind before the issuance of moral feelings is called equilibrium, while the state of mind after which they have issued and manifested themselves to their proper extent is called harmony. In addition, the "equilibrium" that conforms to natural principles is said to be the great source of Heaven and Earth and the "harmony" in this formulation is said to be the way pervading Heaven and Earth. Later, Neo-Confucian scholars clearly defined the "origin" of moral feelings conforming to natural principles as "the original moral nature" or as "the essence of mind before issuance (未發心體)," which was distinguished from moral feelings. However, in "Zhong Yong" in *The Book of Rites*, the original moral nature or the essence of mind before issuance was considered to be constituted of the various aspects of moral feelings, perhaps because at the time when *The Book of Rites* was written, the division of the concepts of feeling and of the original nature was still ill-defined.

The ordinary moral feelings that the seven feelings refer to inevitably issue forth and their conformity to natural principles after their issuance can be recognized by people. However, their conformity to natural principles before their issuance and to "the original moral nature" or "the essence of mind before issuance" cannot be confirmed.

Originally, the term "the four beginnings" did not refer to feelings because it was used to denote the elements of the original moral nature. Therefore the discussion of the four beginnings in isolation from the original moral nature is meaningless. Mencius talked about the origin of the term "the four beginnings (四端)" as follows:

All people have a mind that cannot endure the pain of others. In ancient times kings ruled the people with a mind that could not endure the sufferings of people. If a king ruled people with such a disposition, he could reign over the country as easily as he could turn his hand over.

It may be said that all men have a mind that cannot bear to see the pain of others, as is shown by the following instance. Anyone who sees a child on the verge of falling into a well will be shocked and immediately evince a compassionate mind. They feel this way not to make friends with the child's parents, and not to be praised by friends or neighbors, but in order not to hear the screams of the child any longer.

In light of this instance, a man who does not feel compassion, who is not ashamed of his misdeeds, who does not have a modest and deferential mind, and who cannot judge right from wrong, cannot be said to be a human being. A compassionate mind is the clue to benevolence, the capacity to feel ashamed of misdeeds or to hate them is the clue to righteousness, a modest and deferential mind is the clue to propriety, and the capacity to distinguish between right and wrong is the clue to wisdom.

One has these four clues (beginnings) just as one has four limbs. The person who says that he cannot engage in good deeds undermines himself, and the person who says that his king cannot carry out good deeds weakens his king.

Generally speaking, when one knows how to build upon the four clues, one may feel as if one sees a fire beginning to flare up, or a fountain beginning to gush. So if one can enrich oneself through these clues, one can sustain the whole world, and if not, one cannot even attend upon one's parents.[14]

According to Mencius, the minds of compassion, shame, modesty, and moral judgment, which can be experienced by anyone, are the four clues that enable one to infer "the four virtues (四德)." He compared the four clues that are innate in man to the four limbs of man in order to emphasize the four original natural traits or virtues of benevolence, righteousness, propriety, and wisdom. According to Mencius, if one cultivates these latent clues and learns to display them, the four virtues will begin to issue like tongues of flame from kindling or like drops of water from a fountain. As the four virtues spontaneously issue from the mind, soon they will grow like a blazing field of fire or like drops of water forming a pond. Therefore as Mencius says, if one can cultivate and display them, one can sustain the whole world, and if not, one cannot even take care of one's parents.

Here, the phenomena to be cultivated and displayed are "the four clues." The four virtues that can be inferred from these clues are still latent. According to Mencius, the four virtues are the sources of the four clues. Therefore is it possible to derive the power of the sources of the clues, like a blazing field of fire or water drops forming a pond, only through the cultivation of the clues? And what is the connection of the four clues within the realm of cognition with the four virtues external to this realm?[15]

Zhu Xi conceptually divided the clues and "their sources (the four virtues)" and clarified their relationship. He regarded "the four clues" discussed by Mencius as feelings and their sources as the original nature of man, and explained that "the original nature issues to become feelings (性發爲情)"[16] and "the mind combines and governs nature and the feelings (心統性情)."[17] However, how can the original nature that refers to latent attributes become feelings, and how can the mind administer feelings that refer to the phenomenal manifestation of latent attributes? In light of these questions it was necessary to suggest a method of bridging the gap between the cognizable and incognizable realms and of consistently explicating the structure and function of the two realms. The theory of *li-gi* (理氣論) was the precise method of achieving this.

LI AND *GI*

Even before Gobong raised the question, Toegye thought that Chuman's explanation of the four beginnings and the seven feelings in "The Diagram of the Mandate of Heaven," namely that "the four beginnings issue from *li* (理) and the seven feelings issue from *gi* (氣)," was somewhat implausible.[18] So Toegye proposed his first amendment[19] as a response to Gobong's criticism. Toegye thought that Chuman's explanation was fanciful in that it distinguishes the four beginnings and the seven feelings on the basis of *li* and *gi*. In view of the Neo-Confucian theory of *li-gi*, Toegye's thinking was quite reasonable.

In Neo-Confucianism, *li* means principle or norm and *gi* means matter or energy. All beings are a combination of *li* and *gi*, and the movement or function of things and of spirit are the act of *li* and *gi* combining. *Gi* moves and functions while *li* is the rule that maintains the parameters of the functioning and movement of *gi*. The statement "*li* superintends *gi*" is often introduced to emphasize this role of *li*.

Li is the principle of all beings and functions. As it is the universal principle of the universe and nature, it is considered to be authentic and perfect. On the other hand, *gi* has the attributes of *eum / yin* (陰) and *yang / yang* (陽), which symbolize light and shadow or dark. *Gi*, with its fundamentally contrasting attributes, is subject to functioning and change, and when it is manifested it displays various aspects such as clarity, turbidity, purity, and impurity. Genuine and perfect *li* combines with clear, turbid, pure, and impure *gi* to manifest its latent characteristics, which are transformed into various concrete attributes in the phenomenal world.

Of course, *li* and *gi* are abstract concepts that were introduced to further the inquiry into the universe and nature. Any being or function in the universe and nature is not composed of either *li* or *gi* because they cannot actually be separated from each other (理氣不相離). However, it is evident that they are conceptually distinguishable. Though they perpetually coexist, the two cannot be conceptually intermingled in any circumstance (理氣不相雜). Owing to their subtle relationship—de facto inseparable but conceptually separable—*li* and *gi* are said to be both "one but two and two but one (一而二, 二而一)." Therefore their relationship has been explained somewhat inconsistently as one of monistic dualism or conversely of dualistic monism.[20]

Nevertheless, the introduction of the concepts of *li* and *gi* in Neo-Confucianism provided an innovative source of momentum because through the theory of *li-gi* the interrelation of mind and original nature or feeling could be elucidated with consistency. So both feeling that is cognizable through sensory organs and the original nature that is outside the realm of cognition could be rendered conceptually and theoretically compatible. In addition, the mind, the original nature and feeling, which had been difficult to explain without relying on subjective experience, could be interpreted objectively as if they were actual entities. This is because the theory of *li-gi* originally derived from the sphere of ontology.

According to the theory of *li-gi*, the mind, the original nature and feeling can be elucidated as follows. Man is endowed with *li*, which is the general principle of the universe and nature and which becomes man's fundamental attribute or original nature.[21] So human nature (性) is identified with the *li* or principle (理) of nature (性卽理), and the mind (心), where the original nature is harbored, is composed of *gi* (心是氣). Because of the original nature or the universal principle harbored in the mind (性卽理), the mind develops the capabilities of cognition and judgment. Therefore it would be meaningless to discuss the mind in isolation from the original nature. In this context the mind may be said to be the combination of *li* and *gi* (心合理氣). Some people even maintain that the mind should be regarded as *li* (心是理).[22]

The original nature, stimulated by a certain object or situation, responds to it and in this way is manifested as feeling. To put it more concretely, the original nature latent in the mind (性卽理), stimulated by outside phenomena, is manifested as feeling with the assistance of *gi* (matter or energy). As *li* itself, which is the universal principle or norm, does not have a physical function, it needs the assistance of *gi* (matter or energy) in order to be manifested in phenomenal form. *Gi* has a variety of qualities such as clarity, turbidity, purity, and impurity. If *gi* is clear and pure, the original moral attributes of *li* may be completely manifested as authentic feelings, but if *gi* is turbid and impure, the original characteristics of *li* are liable to be manifested as distorted feelings.

Through the introduction of the concepts of *li* and *gi*, the mind, the original nature, feeling, and the moral virtues related to them are explained as if they are objective entities in the physical world. Neo-Confucianism, through such an explanation, consistently elucidates the interrelationship of the mind, the original moral nature and moral feeling, and advances the notion that the moral life is as evident a need and as inevitable an outcome as living in accordance with the physical laws of the universe and nature.

Confucianism, originally established by Confucius and built on by Mencius, explained, on the basis of empirical facts accumulated from history and practical reality, moral norms and their practice through terms such as benevolence (仁), righteousness (義), the rectification of names (正名), the four beginnings (四端), and the seven feelings (七情). Neo-Confucianism, in supplementing Confucius's and Mencius's thought with the theory of *li-gi*, elevated Confucian moral norms from the level of "*sollen* (當爲)" to that of "*sein* (存在)." That is, by explaining the principles of moral norms and the modes of their embodiment on the basis of the ontological theory of *li-gi*,

Neo-Confucian scholars made it possible to understand moral norms as fundamental ontological principles.[23]

Neo-Confucian scholars did not distinguish the realm of natural laws from that of moral norms. Neither did they distinguish the ethics of nature from those of man. Regarding the theory of *li-gi*, which proposed that fundamental ontological characteristics were the basis of the mind, the original nature, and the feelings that embody moral norms, they established a theoretical system in which nature, society, and the individual were directed toward the same moral norms through an ontological imperative. Consequently, they could declare the ineluctability of moral norms to be as firm as that of natural law.[24] In this way, they could equip themselves with a firm theoretical system that enabled them to direct their energies toward the establishment and management of an ideal moral society. However, because of their view of moral norms, which were subject to the demands or dictates of the established social order as eternal and universal principles, the Neo-Confucian intelligentsia sometimes functioned as an obstacle to social reform.

When we try to interpret the theory of the heart-mind and nature (心性論) on the basis of the theory of *li-gi*, which was concerned with ontological subjects, we may be confronted with an incompatibility resulting from a category error. The interpretation of a moral problem through the use of the theoretical tool of *li-gi* may lead us to explain the realm of value judgment or of the moral life as if it were an ontological realm, just as nature is. However, we may have difficulty in eliminating the resulting discord because we are applying concepts appropriate to the evaluation of the empirical facts of the physical world to the abstract realm of value judgment. This is also an aporia that has to be coped with when we engage in philosophical and conceptual discourse through the medium of language.

PERSPECTIVES ON CAUSE AND EFFECT

The statement in "The Diagram of the Mandate of Heaven V" that "the four beginnings issue from *li* and the seven feelings issue from *gi*," which originated the controversy on the four-seven, was a typical example of the Neo-Confucian method of expounding a theory on the basis of views on mind-nature and *li-gi*. So the statement refers, on the basis of mind-nature, to the relation of moral feelings to the original moral nature on the one hand and, on the basis of *li-gi*, to the ontological structure of moral feelings on the other. Because of these dual implications of the statement, Gobong asked Chuman about the positioning and the explanation of the four-seven in "The Diagram of the Mandate of Heaven V." Because Gobong asked the question for the first time when he met face-to-face with Chuman and left no record of their meeting, we do not have a firsthand account of his question, but it could be inferred later from the letters exchanged between Toegye and Gobong. Toegye's letter to Gobong was as follows:

> Some scholars I know told me about your critical view on Chuman's statement about the four-seven. I've already discerned something misguided about the statement. Your criticism of it made me further aware of its crudeness and error. So I revised it as follows: "The issuance of the four beginnings refers to genuine *li* and the issued beginnings are all good; the issuance of the seven feelings accompanies *gi* and the issued feelings may be good or evil." I am curious as to whether this revision might be seen as correct.[25]

Soon after Gobong called on Toegye in November 1558 to tell him the news that he had passed the state examination, Toegye seems to have heard of his critical view on "The Diagram of the Mandate of Heaven" and the four-seven. In January 1559, Toegye suggested his first revision in his letter to Gobong.

After two months Gobong answered Toegye as follows:

> If we say, "The four beginnings issue from *li* and the issued beginnings are all good; the seven feelings issue from *gi* and the issued feelings may be good or evil," it means that *li* and *gi* are two independent entities, and that the seven feelings do not issue from the original nature and the four beginnings do not ride on *gi*. . . . On the other hand, the revision of the above statement, that is, "The issuance of the four beginnings refers to genuine *li* and the issued beginnings are all good; the issuance of the seven feelings accompanies *gi* and the issued feelings may be good or evil," is a little better than the former statement. But I think it is still untenable.[26]

According to this letter, Gobong seems to have raised a question about the statement "The four beginnings issue from *li* and the issued beginnings are all good; the seven feelings issue from *gi* and the issued feelings may be good or evil." Later, however, Gobong, ascribing his mistake to his vague memory, acknowledged that what he had actually read in "The Diagram of the Mandate of Heaven" was not this statement but the proposition "The four beginnings issue from *li* and the seven feelings issue from *gi*."[27]

In this light, we can delineate the controversy between the two as follows:

【The statement on the four-seven Gobong read in "The Diagram of the Mandate of Heaven V" (Chuman's statement)】

"The four beginnings issue from *li* and the seven feelings issue from *gi*."

"四端, 發於理; 七情, 發於氣."

【Toegye's first revision】

"The issuance of the four beginnings refers to genuine *li* and the issued beginnings are all good; the issuance of the seven feelings accompanies *gi* and the issued feelings may be good or evil."

"四端之發純理, 故無不善; 七情之發兼氣, 故有善惡.."

Toegye's first revision may be interpreted as follows:

1. Toegye softened the strict division of *li* and *gi* as the origin of the four beginnings and of the seven feelings, respectively. He acknowledged Gobong's criticism of this schematization of *li* and *gi*.
2. In the case of the four beginnings Toegye amended *li*, rendering it as "genuine *li*," and in the case of the seven feelings he adopted the word "accompany" to describe their relationship with *gi*. In his controversy with Toegye Gobong argued that the origin of the four beginnings may be said to be *li* but that the origin of the seven feelings is also *li*, though they may be influenced by *gi*. Toegye accepted this argument and said that the issuance of the seven feelings accompanies *gi*. However, Toegye still adhered to his position that the four beginnings and the seven feelings should be explained mainly in terms of their relationship with *li* and *gi*, respectively.
3. Toegye clearly showed that the division of the four beginnings and the seven feelings is related to the problem of good and evil. Gobong mistook the statement "The four beginnings issue from *li* and the issued beginnings are all good; the seven feelings issue from *gi* and the issued feelings may be good or evil" for the first statement that he had read in "The Diagram of the Mandate of Heaven." We may presume that Gobong's mistake was a consequence of the fact that he had repeatedly heard of Toegye's main argument that the division of the four-seven is related to the problem of good and evil when he had talked with Chuman and Toegye.

Ultimately, Toegye, in his first revision, reinforced his axiological position while partly acknowledging Gobong's view, which was based on the theory of *li-gi*.

However, Gobong still raised two questions about Toegye's first revision:

1. As the four beginnings refer to several kinds of the seven feelings, the four and the seven cannot be divided. That is, of the moral feelings implied in the seven feelings, only those coinciding with righteous principle are called the four beginnings.
2. Though Toegye adopted the phrases "genuine *li*" and "accompany *gi*" and somewhat softened Chuman's strict division of *li* and *gi*, his first revision

was still unclear and may have caused misunderstanding. Gobong pointed out that though it is true that *li* superintends *gi* and *gi* is the matter or stuff of *li*, they should not be divided because they in fact coexist with each other.[28]

According to Gobong, as both the four beginnings and the seven feelings issue from the original nature of man, their basis is *li*. The seven feelings refer to *li* that has been revealed as feelings, and the four beginnings refer to those feelings that are "in accord with principles (中節)." That is to say, according to Gobong, the four beginnings are included in the seven feelings and the division of the four and the seven are determined by the effect of issuance of the feelings in question.[29] In addition, Gobong maintained, in spite of the role of *li* as the superintendence of *gi* and that of *gi* as the matter or stuff of *li*, that *li* and *gi* "cannot be separated from each other (不相離)."

Contrary to Gobong's view, Toegye emphasized that the four and the seven can be divided. What mattered to Toegye was not the conclusion that the four beginnings are genuinely good and the seven feelings may be good or bad but the grounds for such a conclusion. It was not important to Toegye how to classify the effects of already manifested feelings. What mattered to him was the method of studying and cultivating the self in order to live while experiencing purely good feelings such as the four beginnings, and in this context he maintained that "the genuinely good original moral nature (性卽理)" is implied in the basis of moral feelings.

However, Toegye did not criticize Gobong's insistence that the four beginnings are included in the seven feelings.

A scholar pursuing a just form of learning and nuanced principles, with broad-mindedness and lofty insight, should not prematurely adhere to one doctrine but try to disinterestedly and patiently interpret its meaning. And then he can grasp the difference in sameness (同中有異) and the sameness in difference (異中有同). If he concludes that, although *li* and *gi* are divided into two, they are actually inseparable from each other and that, although *li* and *gi* are one, they are not intermingled with each other, he may be said to have attained the unprejudiced and profound stage of learning.[30]

When we examine certain objects, we may observe their difference in their sameness and vice versa. Then we judge that they are the same or different. Our judgment in this case is not a matter of truth or falsity but of varying viewpoints. However, it is important to keep in mind both their sameness and their difference. Likewise, in the arguments between Gobong and Toegye the former emphasized the sameness of the four and the seven while the latter emphasized the difference between them. The attitude that should be avoided is to cling to one's own viewpoint, and Toegye warned against such a blinkered attitude. The reason he observed "the difference in sameness (同中有異)" was that such a viewpoint agreed with the intentions of the sages who pondered over the four beginnings and the seven feelings. The sages' intentions here refer to the desired educational and practical effects of the theory of the four-seven.

THE SAGES' INTENTIONS

The structure and the function of the mind, the original nature or feelings can be explained by the conception of *li* and *gi*, which cannot be separated and intermingled. However, the ultimate goal of Neo-Confucianism does not lie in theoretical pursuits such as the interpretation of good or bad feelings. Instead it aims at judging and acting with genuinely good feelings in the face of the temptations of a corrupted reality. As Mencius once said, one should pursue a form of learning that embraces and helps to preserve the whole world through practical effort and tenacious will, like a spark turning into a conflagration and burning a whole field and drops of water agglomerating into a wide lake. They cannot be explained with a prosaic theory of *li-gi* such as one that characterizes *li* as superintendent and *gi* as matter.

Toegye tried to derive the real grounds of the four beginnings and the seven feelings from *li* and *gi*. According to him, the genuinely good moral feelings of the four beginnings originate from the perfection of *li*, while the seven feelings that are prone to fall into evil originate from the influence of *gi*. In other words, without *li* genuinely good moral feelings cannot be manifested and without *gi* genuinely good moral feelings do not fall into evil. Toegye reflected on the reason why the old sages coined the phrase "the four beginnings" instead of employing only the phrase "the seven feelings." By saying, "Mencius's intention was to emphasize the good original nature and to stipulate that the four beginnings genuinely issue from benevolence, righteousness, propriety, and wisdom,"[31] he called attention to the intention of sages who had differing conceptions of the four and the seven.

To be sure, Toegye did not neglect Gobong's opinion, but his viewpoint on the four-seven was different from Gobong's. On the basis of moral feelings, Gobong pointed out, both the four and the seven originate from *li* or the original moral nature. In light of the ensuing moral feelings, the four and the seven are divided because the four are in accord with principles and the seven are not. Nevertheless, Gobong maintained that the seven include the four because both of them originate from *li*. However, Toegye observed that the four refers to genuinely good feelings, while the seven are the feelings that are prone to fall into evil.[32] Considering the reason why the old sages coined the phrase "the four beginnings" in spite of the existing phrase "the seven feelings," which generally refer to moral feelings, he said that it is more accurate to divide feelings into the four and the seven.

This division is not based on the existence of the four and the seven but on their implications.[33] Though *li* and *gi*, which are neither separable nor unifiable, cannot actually function independently, Toegye believed that the origins of the four and the seven can be explained by *li* and *gi*, respectively, if we focus our attention on the cause of the distinction between the four as genuinely good feelings and the seven as the originally good feelings that are prone to fall into evil.[34]

When Toegye first read Chuman's statement that the four beginnings issue from *li* and the seven feelings issue from *gi*, he thought that it was an over-reaching proposition. When Gobong argued against this statement, Toegye accepted, on the basis of the theory of *li-gi*, his opinion and drew up his first revision. However, after Toegye read in *Zhu Zi yu-lei* (朱子語類, *The Classified Conversations of Master Zhu*) Zhu Xi's clear division of the four beginnings as the issuance of *li* and the seven feelings as the issuance of *gi*, Toegye mentioned to Gobong Zhu Xi's remark as the basis of his second revision.

【Toegye's second revision】

"The four beginnings are the issuance of *li* and the seven feelings are the issuance of *gi*."
"四端是理之發, 七情是氣之發."[35]

THE BASIS OF MORAL FEELINGS

Gobong, in accordance with the implications of the four beginnings and the seven feelings, could readily accept the division of the four and the seven on the basis of the *li*-principal (主理) and the *gi*-principal (主氣). More-over, as Toegye supported his view with Zhu Xi's statement, it might have been difficult for Gobong to refute Toegye's stance. Later, Namdang (南塘) Han Won-jin (韓元震, 1682–1751) tenaciously protested that Zhu Xi's state-ment quoted by Toegye might have been the result of some editorial errors or a temporary view of Zhu Xi and not his core perspective.[36] But Gobong's attitude was not as committed as Namdang's. He only said ambiguously that Zhu Xi's view might have been the consequence of some unavoidable cir-cumstances.[37] Nevertheless, he did not admit the view that the bases of the four and the seven are different. He thought that they are the same because both the four and the seven are feelings. So it was difficult to reconcile the antithetical attitudes of Toegye and Gobong.

While Gobong thought that the four beginnings are encompassed by the seven feelings and distinguished the four and the seven on the basis of whether they are ultimately "in accord with principles (中節)" or not (不中節), Toegye, regarding the essential difference between the four and the seven as that of good and evil, paid attention to their foundations and said that their difference derives from their respective bases of *li* and *gi*. In addition, Gobong paid attention to the fact that all moral feelings issue from the original moral nature and argued that the four and the seven are not different because both of them issue from *li* or from the original nature.

On careful examination of their views, it seems clear that they used the term "issuance (發現)" with different meanings. In the discussion of "what the four-seven refer to (所指)" and "what they further imply (所就而言)," though Gobong admitted that the four and the seven can be divided according to the *li*-principal (主理) and the *gi*-principal (主氣) or by the issuance of *li* (理發) and *gi* (氣發), he maintained that "the basis or origin (所從來)" of both the four and the seven is *li*. On the other hand, Toegye maintained that if the difference of the four and the seven is admitted, quite naturally the bases of the four-seven can also be divided according to the *li*-principal and the *gi*-principal. Gobong understood what the four-seven refer to and what they further imply in semantic terms, while he understood the basis of the four-seven ontologically. However, Toegye did not have to resolve the basis of the four and the seven separately because he axiologically understood their basis as well as what they refer to and what they further imply.

According to Gobong's position, as we call only the *li* of "physical nature (氣質之性)" "the innate/original nature (本然之性)," of the seven feelings only the four beginnings that are in accord with principles may be said to have originated from *li* or to have issued from *li*. However, Gobong argued that though the seven are subject to the influence of *gi*, the four and the seven cannot be divided on the basis of their origin because both originate ontologically from *li* or the original nature.[38]

However, as the original nature and physical nature are divided on the basis of *li* and *gi*, Toegye thought that the four and the seven are divided on the basis of good *li* and bad *gi*. The original nature and physical nature are the concepts necessary for the explanation of good and evil in connection with the original moral nature. That is, physical nature implies that the original nature located in the *gi* of the mind may have various dispositions toward good and evil under the influence of a given temperament. The original nature is the basis of genuinely good feelings or the human nature corresponding to *li*. From the standpoint of good and evil, as the original nature and physical nature are interpreted according to the *li*-principal and the *gi*-principal, respectively, the four and the seven can also be interpreted respectively according to these principles. In this connection Toegye tried to understand axiologically the basis of the four-seven as well as what they refer to and what they further imply. However, he could not have confidence in his understanding of the four-seven because Zhu Xi's understanding of the four as the issuance of *li* and the seven as that of *gi*, as Gobong pointed out, does not agree with the theory of *li-gi*, which is based on the inseparability of *li* and *gi*.

As a result, Toegye labored over his third revision.

【Toegye's third revision】

"The four beginnings are the issuance of *li* followed by *gi* and the seven feelings are the issuance of *gi* on which *li* rides."
"四則理發而氣隨之, 七則氣發而理乘之."[39]

THE FUNCTIONING OF *LI* AS A METAPHOR[40]

To the extent that the meaning of the four beginnings was at issue, Gobong agreed with Toegye's view that they are the issuance of *li*. However, the statement that *li*, which refers to an unvarying principle or a norm, functions through its issuance was subject to incessant criticisms. In particular, because Yulgok criticized the concept of the functioning of what was seen as immobile *li*, Toegye's view on *li-gi* became one of the main objects of criticism on the part of scholars of the Yulgok School.

In fact, the widespread notion that the philosophy of Toegye was strongly biased toward the *li*-principal is ascribed to his advocacy of "the issuance of *li*." No doubt there were Confucian scholars in the Joseon Dynasty who attached as much importance to *li* as Toegye had, such as Hwaseo (華西) Yi Hang-no (李恒老, 1792–1868), Hanju (寒洲) Yi Jin-sang (李震相, 1818–1886), and Nosa (蘆沙) Gi Jeong-jin (奇正鎭, 1798–1879). But Toegye, who used to be compared with the renowned Yulgok, was considered a representative advocate of the *li*-principal.

Toegye, even before the beginning of his controversy with Gobong about the four-seven, emphasized the role of *li*. Nevertheless, when he first read Chuman's statement "The four beginnings issue from *li* and the seven feelings issue from *gi*," he hesitated to accept it. Moreover, during his controversy with Gobong, he warned that Gobong sometimes overemphasized the role of *li*.[41] Actually, however, Gobong's emphasis in this respect evidently did not go further than saying, "Seen semantically, the role of *li* is confined to the possibility of its issuance." Gobong understood the term "origin (所從來)" ontologically and determined that it is ontologically impossible for *li* to issue. However, he admitted the semantic role of *li*. With regard to its ontological or physical sense, he proposed that the function of issuance is not the role of *li* but that of *gi*. Gobong's thinking was reasonable in view of the general understanding and the ordinary usage of the concept of *li*.

On the other hand, Toegye pondered on the role of *li* from the time of his controversy with Gobong about the four-seven until his later years and took pains to express the role of *li* that might be neglected by scholars like Gobong. Consequently, he made the propositions that "*li* issues (理發)," "*li* moves (理動)," and "*li* arrives of its own accord (理自到)."[42] The proposition "*li* issues," which was made during the controversy of the four-seven, is similar in content to the other two propositions. During his lifetime and since his death, not only scholars in the Joseon Dynasty but also those of today have argued about this issue.[43] This is because the propositions that "*li* issues," "*li* moves," and "*li* arrives of its own accord" are contrary to the ordinary usage of the Neo-Confucian concept of *li* and because they are considered to be the key to the in-depth illumination of the characteristics of Toegye's philosophy. His controversy with Gobong was a decisive moment in his formulation of his theory of *li*.

The theory of *li-gi* is a dualistic theoretical system that explains through *li* and *gi* the formation, movement, change, and extinction of all things in the universe.[44] Dualistic theories are familiar both in the East and the West because people often adopt dualism to explain the boundless universe, which maintains orderliness among diversity. In the history of Western philosophy, dualistic theory is most iconically represented by Aristotle's "form (形相)" and "matter (質料)," and in the history of Eastern philosophy it is best represented by *li* and *gi*.

In the dualistic theory of *li-gi*, the meaning of and relation between *li* and *gi* may be arguable, but their roles are clearly distinguished from each other. *Li* refers to the principle, rule, or norm that enables *gi* to move and function with a certain tendency. According to this distinction, Toegye's propositions that "*li* issues (發)," "*li* moves (動)," and "*li* arrives of its own accord (自到)" are evidently contrary to the usage of the concepts of *li* and *gi*. During the controversy with Toegye, Gobong pointed out that a phrase like "the issuance of *li*" could be used restrictively, as in the case when such a statement was required for the explanation of a writer's intention. Many scholars of the Joseon Dynasty criticized such seemingly inconsistent positions. However, it cannot be concluded that such a statement by Toegye was the consequence of his ignorance because he was a representative Neo-Confucian scholar in the Joseon Dynasty. No one can underestimate his scholarly achievements in view of his profound knowledge, revealed in his answers to Yulgok's lists of questions and in his logical criticism of Gobong's opinion. Neither can we simply conclude that Toegye engaged in arbitrary arguments when deviating from the fundamental tenets of Neo-Confucianism because his writings usually implied his profound thoughts and nuanced opinions. Therefore it is necessary for us to carefully examine the context in which he suggested such arguable propositions.

First, Toegye suggested the statement "*li* issues" in the context of explaining the moral feelings that derive from the four beginnings and the seven feelings. In his second revision sent to Gobong, he said, "The four beginnings are the issuance of *li* and the seven feelings are the issuance of *gi*," and in his third revision he argued, "The four beginnings are the issuance of *li* followed by *gi* and the seven feelings are the issuance of *gi* on which *li* rides." The main reason that he distinguished the four from the seven in this way was that the theory of *li-gi* is fundamentally ontological in character, but semantically its implication is axiological. When the issuance of *li* is not hindered by *gi*, the genuinely good and perfect *li* is revealed in its entirety, and when its issuance is obstructed by the impure and rough *gi*, a defective form of *li* is prone to be revealed. With respect to the feelings of a human being, as "the four beginnings that are not hindered by *gi* are genuinely good and the seven feelings that are hindered by *gi* are prone to be evil (本善而易流於惡)," axiologically, on the basis of "the origin (所從來)" of the four-seven, it may be said that the pure good of the four is the issuance of *li* and the inclination toward evil of the seven is the issuance of *gi*. Therefore, in accordance with what the four-seven refer to (所指), Toegye clearly explained the difference between the four and the seven.[45]

Of course, Toegye's explanation does not imply that *li* has physical or chemical functions, which directly cause some phenomena. After all, it may be said that the function of *gi* that is completely in accord with *li* should be called the function of *li*. Actually, Gobong also understood this to be the case. However, when he explained, "The issuance of *li* refers to the issuance of *gi* in conformity with the unobstructed dictates of *li*,"[46] Toegye criticized Gobong's explanation for not avoiding the mistake of regarding *gi* as *li*.[47] Though Gobong's intention was to agree, in his own way, with Toegye's view on the issuance of *li*, Toegye pointed out that what he meant by the issuance of *li* was at odds with what Gobong meant.

What Toegye intended by the issuance of *li* can be realized with the assistance of *gi*. However, he thought that the issuance of *li* refers to the emergence of latent faculties or the manifestation in natural phenomena of the genuinely good original moral nature of the mind. Like Mencius's discussion of the issuance of compassion, the issuance of *li* refers to the spontaneous issuance of the latent original moral nature. Though its physical manifestation is ascribed to the role of *gi*, Toegye's conception of the issuance of latent faculties does not refer to the physical function of *li*. However, until the conclusion of the controversy with Gobong on the four-seven, he could not elaborate further in explaining the issuance of *li*. It is possible that he pondered over this matter until the end of his life.

THE CONCLUSION OF THE CONTROVERSY

After receiving Toegye's third revision and long letter in which he criticized Gobong's views in detail, Gobong sent to Toegye a similarly lengthy letter in which he elaborated on his perspective in the argument. Their debate became more complex and profound, and the difference in their stances became more obvious. On receipt of Gobong's letter, Toegye outlined some points that were in dispute, but he did not send them to Gobong, and the debate between them ceased in 1562.

During the intervals of his debate with Toegye, Gobong also debated the theory of *li-gi* with Sojae (蘇齋) No Su-sin (盧守愼, 1515–1590) and Chodang (草堂) Heo Yeop (許曄, 1515–1580). As he could not persuade them of his position, Gobong sent a letter to Toegye in July 1566 in which he worried about their misunderstanding of the theory of *li-gi*.[48] To this letter he attached "Postscripts to the Four-Seven (四端七情後說)" and "General Remarks on the Four-Seven (四端七情總論)." In "Postscripts to the Four-Seven"[49] Gobong wrote that some of his views on the four-seven had changed. In the "General Remarks on the Four-Seven"[50] he suggested that he would like to end his debate with Toegye by systematizing the points at issue on the basis of Toegye's second revision, which was compatible with Zhu Xi's view.

Toegye generally accepted the contents of the postscripts[51] in which the points under discussion were dealt with from Gobong's perspective. As a result, their eight-year controversy effectively ended. Ostensibly it seemed to conclude by mutual consent, but in fact some of the tensions between their positions remained unresolved.

In his postscripts Gobong abandoned his opposition to the view of the seven feelings as the issuance of *gi* and accepted Toegye's second revision, encapsulated in the dictum "The four beginnings are the issuance of *li* and the seven feelings are the issuance of *gi*." Gobong thought that as the four beginnings presuppose the cultivation of genuinely good feelings until they become perfect, they may be called the issuance of *li*, and as the seven feelings presuppose the curbing of exorbitant feelings until they become moderate, they may be called the issuance of *gi*. In other words, Gobong accepted, on the basis of the theory of self-cultivation, the four beginnings as the issuance of *li* and the seven feelings as the issuance of *gi*.

However, Gobong's ensuing explanation showed that he accepted the view of the seven feelings as the issuance of *gi* only when they are subject to the theory of self-cultivation. He adhered to his theory of *li-gi* and said that the seven feelings comprise the four beginnings, and in this sense he maintained that the seven feelings are not the issuance of *gi* but instead structurally comprise both *li* and *gi*. However, according to Gobong, though the seven feelings possess both *li* and *gi* because they are feelings mingled with turbid "physical matter (氣質)," they must be made to overcome and control this natural turbidity through the individual's self-cultivation. Only in this sense the seven may be called the issuance of *gi*. However, he also maintained that the seven, in accord with the principle (*li*), may be considered to constitute the four beginnings.

In short, Gobong admitted that the four beginnings are the issuance of *li* in the sense that they should be extended through "recognition and mastery (體認)" and that the seven feelings are the issuance of *gi* in the sense that they are subject to introspection, "refinement, and control (克治)." He also maintained that at their core the seven feelings combined with *li-gi* originally constitute the issuance of *li*.

For his part, Toegye was not opposed to Gobong's views suggested in his postscripts and general remarks, merely saying that he needed to review his position. So we may presume that Toegye ultimately accepted Gobong's views that the four are the issuance of *li* and the seven are the issuance of *gi*.

However, the fact that neither Toegye nor Gobong elucidated their different understandings of the issuance of *li* and of *gi*, that Toegye did not clearly describe the sages' seven feelings and their origin, and that he wrote in his "The Diagram of the Saying 'The Mind Combines and Governs Nature and the Feelings' (心統性情圖)" in *Ten Diagrams of Sage Learning* (聖學十圖), his third revision that is considered to be his final view on the four-seven, "The four beginnings are the issuance of *li* followed by *gi* and the seven feelings are the issuance of *gi* on which *li* rides," all suggest that there were still several differences between Toegye's and Gobong's views.

AFTER THE CONTROVERSY I: "ONE'S SPEECH THROUGH WHICH *LI* ARRIVES"

After the conclusion of their debates, Toegye and Gobong began to develop their respective views on the issuance of *li*. In arguing against Gobong's statement "The issuance of *li* refers to the issuance of *gi* in conformity with the unobstructed dictates of *li*," Toegye maintained that Gobong mistook the issuance of *gi* for that of *li*. However, Toegye himself could not definitively explain the issuance of *li*. Only in his later years did he sum up his thinking with the proposition "*li* arrives of its own accord," at which time the full-fledged debate on the role of *li* began to develop.

The proposition "*li* arrives of its own accord" arose in light of the need to explain the role of *li* in the relationship between the subject and the object when a person (subject) recognizes a thing (object). Originally, Gobong suggested earlier than Toegye that the statement that "*li* arrives" is tenable in the context of the interpretation of *mulgyeok / wu-ge* (物格), which was discussed in Zhu Xi's *Da Xue zhang-ju* (大學章句, *The Great Learning in Chapters and Verses*). In this context Zhu Xi interpreted *mul / wu* (物) as "the principle (*li*) of things (事物之理)" and *gyeok / ge* (格) as "arrival (到)" and added the note, "The perfect 'principle (*li*)' of things arrives anywhere (物理之極處無不到)."[52] Gobong adopted Zhu Xi's note as his interpretation of *mulgyeok*. However, Toegye thought that Gobong's interpretation was too overarching. According to Toegye, as the subject of cognition is the mind of a person and the *li* of a thing is the object of cognition, to regard the object of cognition as the subject is unreasonable.[53] However, after due consideration, Toegye suggested the proposition that "*li* arrives of its own accord (理自到)" in his letter to Gobong, written fifty days before he died.

First, let's review the origin of this debate, that is, Zhu Xi's concept of *gyeongmul chiji* (物格致知) in his "A Supplementary Chapter (補亡章)."

The meaning of the expression "The perfection of knowledge (致知)" depends on "the investigation of things (格物)," is this: If we wish to extend our knowledge to the utmost, we must investigate the principles of all things we come into contact with, for the intelligent mind of man is certainly formed to perform the act of knowing, and there is not a single thing in which universal principles do not inhere. It is only because all principles have not been investigated that man's knowledge is incomplete. For this reason, the first step in the education of an adult is to instruct the learner, in regard to all things in the world, to proceed from what knowledge he has of their principles, and to investigate further until he reaches the limit of his capacities. After exerting himself in this way for a long time, he will one day achieve a wide and far-reaching insight (*hwaryeon gwantong / huo-ran-guan-tong* 豁然貫通) into the principles of things. Then the qualities of all things, whether internal or external, refined or coarse, will be apprehended, and the mind, in its total essence and great functioning, will be perfectly intelligent. This is called "the investigation of things (*mulgyeok / wu-ge* 物格)." This is called "the perfection of knowledge (*jijiji / zhi-zhi-zhi* 知之至)."[54]

Ultimately, the meaning of *gyeongmul chiji* is to investigate things or phenomena one by one and ultimately to acquire knowledge of the universal principles of the whole world. According to Zhu Xi, the subject of cognition is man's mind and its object is the *li* of things. What should be recognized through *gyeongmul* is not the state or the physical characteristics of a thing but the *li* inherent in it.[55] As man's mind has the capacity to investigate the *li* of a thing and everything has its own *li*, man can recognize the *li* of a thing. Simply put, *li* refers to the universal principle or norm inherent in any human being and thing. Therefore, starting from the recognition of an individual thing, one day one will achieve "a wide and far-reaching insight" into the principles of things. Zhu Xi regarded the universal principle as the perfect principle grasped by such intellectual insight.

Man's capacity of intellectually penetrating into the universal principle refers to the process of gaining an insight into the universality of the *li* of each thing through their investigation. In this state of insight man grasps every aspect of a thing: its inside and outside and its refinement and coarseness. In this state man can also maintain and display his mental capacity most adequately and apply it to the practical affairs of the world.

However, Zhu Xi did not explain in detail the concept of "a wide and far-reaching insight." He wrote only about the process of study necessary for the attainment of insight and about the state of being after this has been achieved. The insight, that is, the gaining of ultimate knowledge is merely a symbolic expression depicting the state in which the universal principles or norms, which are inherent in objects of cognition such as things, nature, and society, are recognized and experienced by the subject of cognition. Zhu Xi thought that in the state of ultimate insight "things are investigated (物格)" and "knowledge of *li* (principle) becomes perfect (知之至)." However, *mulgyeok* (物格) became an object of dispute among the scholars of Joseon because the word may be interpreted in Korean as "[something] arrives at the *li* of things" or "the *li* of things arrives [at something]."

Zhu Xi explained *gyeongmul* (格物) as the process of "investigating the *li* of things to the ultimate conclusion and attempting to arrive at the perfection of *li* (窮至事物之理, 欲其極處無不到也)."[56] On the other hand, Zhu Xi explained *mulgyeok* (物格), which is the consequence of "investigating the *li* (principles) of things to the ultimate conclusion (格物)," as "物理之極處無不到也."[57] This Chinese explanation of *mulgyeok* was interpreted in two ways: first, "In all cases the *li* of things arrives at its perfection," and second, "In all cases [something] arrives at the perfection of the *li* of things."

As for the explanation of *gyeongmul*, we may presume that the subject of cognition such as a man or the human mind is implicit in the concept and interpret it as "[man or the human mind] investigates the *li* of things to the ultimate conclusion and arrives at the perfection of *li*." However, in the case of the first interpretation of *mulgyeok*, many objections can be raised because the subject *li*, denoting a principle or norm, is understood as having mobility as it has the characteristic of "'arriving" or, in short, because the object of cognition, *li*, is conceptualized as the subject of cognition. In addition, the second interpretation of *mulgyeok* is almost the same as that of *gyeongmul* because the omitted subject is obviously man or the human mind.

The interpretation of *mulgyeok*, even before Toegye's era, had been contentious among the Confucian scholars of Joseon because it was concerned with the recognition of *li*, the existence of which was one of the main tenets of Neo-Confucianism. At first, Toegye thought that *mulgyeok* should be interpreted as "arriving in all cases at the perfection of the *li* of things."

Gobong, however, interpreted *mulgyeok* as "the *li* of things arriving in all cases at its perfection." In a letter to Toegye he quoted three instances of the use of *li* that supported his interpretation.

Concerning *mulgyeok*:

I found "One's speech through which *li* arrives" in Zhu-xi's memorial to the King in 1188; "*Li* arrives at whatever it meets" in the annotation under the item "Too minute to be revealed (發微不可見)" in *Tong-shu* (通書); and "[the highest goodness or the righteous *li*] arriving anywhere" in an annotation to *Questions and Answers on The Great Learning* (大學或問). After pondering these instances, I think I can interpret the following two statements as follows: "理詣其極" discussed in *Questions and Answers of The Great Learning* as "*Li* arrives at its perfection" and "極處無不到" discussed in *The Great Learning in Chapters and Verses* (大學章句) as "In all cases *li* arrives at its perfection."[58]

Gobong referred to these three quotations in order to show that a sentence with *li* (理) as its subject and "arrive (到)" as its predicate was plausible. The first quotation from Zhu Xi was originally a statement admiring Cheng Ming-dao's (程明道) criticism of Buddhism. This statement ("理到之言") can be roughly translated as "How truly reasonable his speech is!"[59] Literally, however, it is translated either as "his speech that arrives at *li*" or "his speech through which *li* arrives,"[60] which is commensurate with the case of interpreting *mulgyeok* as "the arrival [of something] at the *li* of things" or "the *li* of things arrives [at something]." Unlike Chinese, Korean uses postpositions in a thoroughgoing way in order to classify a word preceding a postposition as a subject, object, or complement. So when a Chinese sentence lacking postpositions is translated into Korean, the first step to logically take is to evaluate the part of speech of each Chinese letter. This is not always straightforward, and the confusion concerning the various interpretations of *mulgyeok* was caused by the difficulty of determining the parts of speech involved. Considering the context of his quoting of "理到之言," Gobong might have intended to interpret *mulgyeok* as "the *li* of things arriving at the statement."

The second quotation from the annotation in *Tong-shu* means "*li* arrives at whatever it meets and penetrates through all things."[61] And the third quotation from *Questions and Answers on The Great Learning* means "not a scintilla of 'the highest good' (mentioned in the phrase 'to rest in the highest goodness [止於至善]') is to accept imperfection and to not arrive anywhere."[62] Here the highest goodness refers to the extremely elaborate "righteous *li* (義理)" or "the Supreme Polarity (太極),"[63] not a scintilla of which does not arrive anywhere. Though the third quotation is open to various interpretations, in the context of the preceding two quotations, the subject of this quotation is "the highest good" (the righteous *li* or the Supreme Polarity) and its predicate is "arrive."

Gobong referred to these three quotations in order to support the interpretation of *mulgyeok* as "the *li* of things arriving at its perfect state." According to Zhu Xi, because "the perfect state of *li* of things (物理之極處)" refers to "the universal *li*" recognized at the moment of its "penetration (豁然貫通)" of all things, in the final analysis, it means "the arrival of the *li* of things at its universal state." As views similar to those suggested in these three quotations are common in Chinese texts, according to Gobong, *mulgyeok* can be interpreted as "the arrival of the *li* of things."

Nevertheless, it seems that he did not accept the physical "arrival" or the mobility of *li*. He pointed out that in the interpretation of *mulgyeok*, the *li* of things can be seen as the subject so long as it is conceived of syntactically and semantically. We have seen that Gobong had a similar view on the four beginnings. That is, according to Gobong, the four beginnings can be said to be the issuance of *li* on the basis of semantics but cannot be seen as such on the basis of ontology. Likewise, though *li* does not have the function of arrival "ontologically and physically" (in actuality), it can be said "semantically" (in view of its implication) that *li* arrives. Gobong wanted to show Toegye that such examples are frequently found in the interpretations of Chinese scholars.

The most representative example is Gobong's first quotation concerning "理到之言," which can be interpreted either as "one's speech that arrives at *li*" or "one's speech through which *li* arrives." However, in view of the other two quotations, the latter interpretation was what Gobong had in mind. So his intention in referring to the three similar quotations was to support the proposition "*li* arrives [at something]." Though Toegye did not wholly agree with Gobong's view, it proved to be an important impetus to the development of his thinking on the role of *li*.

AFTER THE CONTROVERSY II:
"*LI* ARRIVES OF ITS OWN ACCORD"

When Gobong said that *mulgyeok* can be interpreted as "the *li* of things necessarily arriving at perfection," Toegye clearly stated that the subject of interpretation must logically be the human mind, not *li*. According to Toegye, as the subject that recognizes the object of *li* (of things) is the human mind, the subject of the predicate "investigate and arrive (格)" is the mind of man. However, Toegye took pains to devise an appropriate interpretation of *mulgyeok* while reviewing Gobong's thoughts and other literature. Finally, about fifty days before his death on October 15, 1570, he sent a letter to Gobong that contained his new view on this matter, excerpted here:

The reason I maintained an incorrect view was that I adhered only to Zhu Xi's assertion, "*Li* has 'no feeling or intention (無情意),' 'no capacity for calculation or estimation (無計度),' and 'no capacity for operation (無造作).'" So I thought, "How can the *li* of things, which can be discovered through my investigation of ultimate principles, arrive at its perfection of its own accord?" So I interpreted the *gyeok* (格, investigate or arrive) of *mulgyeok* and *do / dao* (到, arrive) of *mubudo / wu-bu-dao* (無不到, arriving in all cases) solely as "what 'I' arrive." . . . However, Zhu Xi also said, "As *li* inevitably has its own function (用), it is not necessary to also mention the function of mind." So, according to Zhu Xi, *li* does not function outside the human mind, and through its abstruse functioning it issues and arrives wherever the human mind arrives. Thus, I only worry that my investigation may fail to arrive at the perfection of the *li* of things (格物), not that *li* does not arrive of its own accord. Therefore, as *gyeongmul* indeed means "to investigate and ultimately arrive at the perfection of the *li* of things," we should interpret *mulgyeok* (物格) as "the *li* of things arriving at its perfection in accordance with the results of our investigation." In the last analysis, to say that *li* has no feeling, no intention, and no operation refers to the "essence (體)" of *li*, and to argue that the *li* of things issues and arrives in accordance with the results of one's investigation refers to the "extremely abstruse functioning" of *li*. In the past I merely thought that the essence of *li* has no function, not knowing that the abstruse functioning of *li* may be manifested as a phenomenon. So how remote from truth it was that I regarded *li* like a dead thing![64]

Toegye said that in the past he had interpreted *mulgyeok* as arriving at the *li* of things in accordance with Zhu Xi's remark "*li* has no feeling or intention, no capacity for calculation or estimation, and no capacity for operation." At this point, however, he admitted after due consideration that it is right to interpret *mulgyeok* as the arriving of the *li* of things. It was reasonable for Zhu Xi to say that as *li* is a concept that implies a principle or norm, it has "no feeling or intention," "no capacity for calculation or estimation," and "no capacity for operation." So in the past Toegye, on the basis of Zhu Xi's "explanation of *mulgyeok* (物理至極處無不到也)," had interpreted it as entailing that "[someone] definitely arrives at the perfection of *li*," but now he revised his interpretation and said, "The *li* of things arrives at its perfection in all cases."

As one's mind or the subject of cognition investigates the *li* of a thing or the object of cognition, the *li* of things is gradually recognized not as individual instantiations of *li* but as the universal *li* or the original nature inherent in the mind of the subject of cognition. This is the process of one's mind recognizing the universal *li*. Conversely, it is also the process of the universal *li* revealing itself to one's mind. In other words, as one's mind exerts itself in order to recognize the *li* of things, there comes a moment when the *li* of things reveals the ultimate aspect of the universal *li* and is recognized as such.

Ultimately, the perfection of the *li* of things refers to the ultimate and univer- sal *li*. In this context Zhu Xi explained *mulgyeok* in *Questions and Answers on The Great Learning*, as follows:

> *Mulgyeok* refers to the arrival of the *li* of things at its perfection. If the *li* of things arrives at its perfection, my knowledge also becomes perfect in accor- dance with the arrival of *li*.[65]

The arrival of the *li* of things at its perfection means that the *li* of each thing is finally revealed in instantiations of the ultimate and universal *li*. In such a state one can display one's perfect capacity for cognition and achieve "a wide and far-reaching insight" into the ultimate and universal *li*. In this quotation Zhu Xi explains that *mulgyeok* is expressed on the basis of the role of the *li* of things rather than of the subject of cognition. In accordance with this explanation, Toegye thought that if the revelation of the *li* of each thing as the universal *li* is attributed only to the role of one's mind, it would be akin to regarding *li* as a "dead thing." Nevertheless, Toegye emphasized the role of the human mind by explaining that *li* ultimately arrives at its perfection in the mind and that *li* or the object of cognition reveals itself as the mind or the subject of cognition approaches it. And Toegye explained "the function without function," in which *li* reveals its universal principle in accordance with the effort of one's mind, as "the arrival of *li* of its own accord (理自到)."

What is important here is that the concept of *li*, meaning a principle or norm, can have the predicate "arrive (到)" or "arrive anywhere (無不到)." Toegye seems to have taken pains after reading Gobong's thoughts to show that the sentence "*li* arrives" is possible. Consequently, he suggested the proposition "*li* arrives of its own accord" together with the following two reasons for its validity.

First, *li* can be explained by dividing it into "essence (體)" and "function (用)." As is well known, the method of explicating an entity in terms of its essence and function was derived from Buddhism. Though *li*, insofar as it means a principle or norm, was generally understood as a metaphysical con- cept without the dimension of function, the theory of essence and function in Buddhist thinking admits the functioning of a metaphysical concept like *li*. Function is an aspect of essence. So though the physical function of *li* must be achieved through the assistance of *gi*, the essence of *li* has its own function other than the purely physical. Here the function of *li* does not refer to that of the phenomenal world but to that of the supra-phenomenal. In other words, the function of *li*, unlike the physical function of *gi*, is to reveal its essence. Those who do not understand the function of *li* attribute all functions to *gi* and regard *li* as lifeless. Toegye confessed that he had once made such an error.

Second, the function of *li* is not outside the human mind. In accordance with the manifestation of the human mind, *li* exerts itself and arrives anywhere. *Gyeongmul* means the recognition and experience of the *li* of external things through the faculty of cognition of the human mind, and *mulgyeok* means the revelation, in accordance with the investigation of the human mind into the *li* of things, of every aspect of the ultimate and universal essence of the *li* of things in the mind of the subject of cognition. Toegye added that the function of *li* is not exercised outside the human mind. That is, though the essence of the *li* of things lies in external objects, the function of *li* that reveals the universal principle at the moment of *mulgyeok* is performed inside the mind of the subject of cognition. Compared with Zhu Xi's statement "When the *li* of things arrives at its perfection, one's capacity for cognition exerts itself in accordance with the arrival of *li*," Toegye laid more emphasis on the role of the mind of man or the subject of cognition. In this context he also said, "I only worry that I may not investigate the principles of things thoroughly; I don't fret that *li* may not arrive of its own accord." Toegye's statement implies that the moment when one wholeheartedly investigates the *li* of things and achieves a wide and far-reaching insight into *li*, it reveals its essence of its own accord. In other words, as one cannot affect the workings of *li*, one merely strives to understand and then *li* will naturally reveal itself.

The proposition "*li* arrives of its own accord" means that the universal principle or norm is recognized and experienced in the human mind. Of course, this does not mean that a mass of *li* squeezes itself into one's mind or body to occupy a physical space. Things (or the *li* of things) maintain their existence outside one's mind, but originally the *li* of things, which is the universal principle or norm, refers to the original moral nature latent in one's mind. Therefore the moment one recognizes and experiences, with the capacity for cognition based on the original nature of one's mind, that both one's individual *li* (性卽理) and the *li* of external things refer to the same universal principle or norm, is expressed as "*li* arrives of its own accord." This expression means that when one approaches the *li* of things, this *li* is recognized and accepted as the principle or norm of the universe or nature, not as the *li* of an individual thing.

Of course, this expression implies a more radical attitude than that of Gobong, who said, "*li* arrives." However, Toegye's expression is also a kind of metaphor.[66] *Li* was originally an abstract concept. *Li*, like "the Way" in Lao Zi's dictum "The Way that can be told of is not the unvarying Way (道可道非常道)," is something that cannot be told of except in a figure of speech.[67] Toegye regretted that he had thought that not *li* but one's mind arrives at the ultimate meaning of *li* because he adhered to a belief in the attributes of *li* that have "no feeling or intention," "no capacity for calculation or estimation," and "no capacity for operation." However, in spite of such attributes, the universal *li* must someday be recognized and experienced as a principle like an individual's *li* or original nature. Zhu Xi emphasized *gyeongmul chiji* (格物致知) as the first step in one's course of study because he thought that it was a prerequisite for his appropriate study and praxis. "A wide and far-reaching insight (豁然貫通)" refers to the very moment when the universal *li* (principle or norm) naturally reveals its essence to an individual. Toegye metaphorically described the moment of recognition and experience of the universal *li* in the statement "*li* arrives of its own accord."

To our discussion of metaphysical subjects we usually apply concepts borrowed from everyday language. There may also be some occasions when we coin metaphysical neologisms. However, these words are sooner or later introduced into everyday language and explained and understood in terms of quotidian concepts and logic. In the milieu of everyday language, words mainly describe physical phenomena recognized and felt by sensory organs. That is, most words contained in everyday language are coined in order to represent such phenomena. In the elaboration of abstract philosophy and metaphysics, metaphorical expressions composed of words borrowed from everyday language are adopted. When these metaphorical expressions are understood as descriptions of the phenomenal world, there may arise differences of interpretation or disputes between the speaker and the listener. If the listener does not understand a metaphor of the speaker, the former may criticize the latter for his or her incorrect usage and their dispute may reach an impasse. However, ultimately philosophical expression that transcends the phenomenal world may surmount or bypass the limitation of language and develop through a metaphorical apparatus in the context of everyday language. Those who understand this metaphorical apparatus participate in the elaboration of philosophical thought and advance their discussion incrementally.

However, in the frame of thought in which predicative words implying functions must necessarily accompany a subject representing an entity in the phenomenal world, "*li* arrives of its own accord" is liable to be considered a proposition that is contrary to the fundamental principle or usage of the theory of *li-gi*. Toegye thought as much when he first read the view of Chuman that "The four beginnings issue from *li* and the seven feelings issue from *gi*." However, the concept of *li* had already been put to use outside of its formal parameters in everyday language. For this reason Gobong could interpret "理到之言" as "one's speech through which *li* arrives."

In fact, such a usage is commonly found in the modern Korean language. When we come to genuinely understand a claim or concept that we have not previously had an affinity for or grasped, we say, "The statement touches (arrives at) my mind" or "The real meaning of the statement makes an impact on my mind." For example, we usually say that the real intention of one's father, who sternly rejected one's request ten years before, "now hits home" or that "the (joy of) democracy pierces my heart like a dagger" only after one's government is overthrown by a military coup d'état. These idioms show that an abstract statement or concept eventually reveals its meaning to one's mind in changing conditions or circumstances.

While Gobong maintained that the proposition "*li* arrives" is not contrary to the usage employed by the Chinese language, he believed that the proposition can be stated only in view of its implication and the intention of the speaker. Toegye, who had initially been opposed to Gobong's view, seems to have adopted and indeed developed it gradually. In their debate on the four-seven, while Gobong thought that the proposition of the issuance of *li* is tenable only in view of its implication or in terms of the theory of self-cultivation, not in terms of its ontological meaning, Toegye believed that it was not necessary for even the ontological meaning to be excluded from the explanation of the issuance of *li*. Though he had not been able to clearly elaborate his position at first, he gradually found it possible to explain the issuance of *li* on the basis of essence (體) and function (用).

To understand the process of recognizing the universal *li* solely in terms of the role of the human mind or the subject of cognition is to consider *li* as a dead thing. And to understand the function of the issuance of moral feelings only in terms of *gi* is also to see *li* in this way. The original moral nature is manifested as moral feelings. To consider this manifestation only as the function of *gi* is to regard it merely as a given phenomenon. To fail to observe and explain the role of *li*, which enables *gi* to function, is merely to superficially explain *gi*. A compassionate mind or a metaphysical impulse that arouses a moral feeling at the moment when a child is about to fall into a well is truly the function of the essence of *li*, the issuance of *li*, the mobility of *li*, and the arrival of *li* of its own accord.

AFTER THE CONTROVERSY III:
METAPHYSICAL IMPULSES

If Gobong had clearly suggested his view after receiving Toegye's letter, their debate might have developed further. However, no materials that can illuminate any further controversy have been found. As Toegye sent a letter to Gobong about fifty days before he died (on October 15), Gobong could not have had the opportunity to contribute further to the debate. However, on November 15, one month after receiving Toegye's letter, he composed a short response.

Your statements about "the essence without function (無爲之體)" and "the extremely mysterious function (至神之用)" precisely illuminated the abstruse "principle (道理)." As I ruminated on your statements, I felt like I was learning from you face to face and my respect for you deepened. However, under scrutiny, I think that your statements betray the flaw of neglecting the "naturalness (自在)" of principle. I am curious as to what you think about this matter.[68]

After Gobong died, his disciples quoted Toegye's interpretation of *mulgyeok* (物格) and Gobong's letter in their petition to the king, titled "Cheong-hyang so (請享疏),"[69] which was written in order to obtain permission to enshrine Gobong's tablet in the National Shrine of Confucius. In the petition they quoted the letter as evidence of Gobong's critical view on Toegye's theory of the essence and function of *li* (理體用說) or the theory of *li* arriving of its own accord (理自到說) and maintained that Gobong, by employing the plain word "naturalness (自在)," illuminated the phrase "*li* arriving at its perfection (理詣其極)," which was contained in *Questions and Answers on The Great Learning*. So they argued that Gobong's precise and obvious opinion in the letter should be regarded as an orthodox theory.[70] As the phrase "neglecting the naturalness of principle" may be interpreted as "there is something unnatural in Toegye's view of principle," Gobong seems to have considered that Toegye's view was unsatisfactory. In "Cheong-hyang so" Gobong's disciples, by emphasizing that Gobong was a scholar as great as Toegye, despite being a successor to the latter, asked the king to permit the enshrinement of Gobong's tablet in the National Shrine of Confucius. However, the petition to the king to some degree seems to have exaggerated the extent of Gobong's learning. Moreover, it was not convincing that Gobong's few words in his letter were proof of his scholarly achievement. Though there is no extant record in which Gobong's views are clearly set forth, fortunately his thought can be inferred from his debates with Toegye on the four beginnings and the seven feelings.

As has been discussed, Gobong agreed that the four beginnings are the issuance of *li* and the seven feelings are the issuance of *gi* with respect to "what the four-seven refer to (所指)" and "what the four-seven further imply (所就而言)" but not with respect to "the origin (所從來)" of the four-seven. On the other hand, Toegye accepted the four as the issuance of *li* and the seven as the issuance of *gi*, regardless of these three qualifications. According to Gobong, as the four are genuinely good moral feelings, they can be said to be the issuance of *li* with respect to their implications. However, he maintained that though the four issue from *li*, in fact they issue with the assistance of *gi*, just as the seven do. On the other hand, Toegye said that the four are the issuance of *li* and the seven are the issuance of *gi* in any circumstances, keeping in mind the power of *li* latent in the original moral nature of man or the metaphysical moral impulses of man. What Toegye took into account was the latent power of man's good original nature, which Mencius had tried to explain through the interpretation of the four. As mentioned earlier, Toegye interpreted the four with respect to the essence and function of *li*.

Gobong played a decisive role in the development of Toegye's thought. However, Gobong understood the meaning and role of *li* differently, on the basis of either axiology or ontology. On the basis of axiology, in view of the tenets of the theory of cultivation, he accepted the four as the issuance of *li* and the seven as the issuance of *gi*. However, Gobong was still faced with the deep chasm or aporia between axiology and ontology. So long as Toegye's conceptions of the issuance of *li* and the arrival of *li* of its own accord, which remain the foci of debates among modern scholars, are understood on the basis of ontology, the deep chasm Gobong experienced cannot be bridged. Toegye, after assiduously examining the usages Gobong quoted in his letter, could understand the metaphor of "*li* touches (arrives at something)," imagine *li* transforming itself from the basis of original moral nature into moral feelings through the concept of essence and function and finally bridging the conceptual chasm Gobong experienced. Though ontology and axiology are still divided in the mind of man, Toegye could nimbly cross the chasm between them through the adoption of the concept of the essence and function of *li*. The traces of Toegye's crossing of the chasm disappeared, and ontology remains ontology and axiology remains axiology. However, he explained, on the basis of the theory of *li*, *gi*, and the heart-mind and nature (理氣心性論), the process of metaphysical impulses through which moral nature springs forth from the original nature that is rooted in the universal principles of the natural world and suggested the ideal of the moral life that man should pursue. Whether or not they agreed with the core of Toegye's thought, scholars of the Joseon Dynasty, including Gobong and Yulgok, repeatedly engaged in debates on Toegye's propositions concerning the relation of the original moral nature and moral feelings and about the optimal method of living a life replete with only good moral feelings. Their debates determined the thrust of the Neo-Confucianism of the Joseon Dynasty.

NOTES

1. Yi I, "Response to Seong Howon 成浩原," in *Yulgok jeonseo*, 44:202b.
2. Concerning the various detailed analyses of the characteristics of "The Diagram of the Mandate of Heaven (天命圖)," which were elaborated by scholars of the Joseon Dynasty, refer to Yu Jeong-dong, "5. Cheonmyeong doseol" (Chapter 5. Diagrams and Explanations on the "Mandate of Heaven"), in *Yugyo-ui geunbon jeongsin-gwa han-guk yuhak* (The Basic Spirit of Confucianism and Korean Confucianism) (Seoul: Yugyo munhwa yeon-guso at Sungkyunkwan University, 2014), 559–658.

3. As Chuman's first edition of "The Diagram of the Mandate of Heaven" had been subject to several revisions, some confusion arose in the attempt to define the relationship of "The Diagram" with the controversies on the four beginnings and the seven feelings. In order to avoid such confusion, I have numbered each revision of "The Diagram."

4. Concerning the process of drawing and revising "The Diagram of the Mandate of Heaven," refer to Jeong Ji-un, "Jeong Chuman Cheonmyeong doseol seo" 鄭秋巒天命圖說序 (Preface to Jeong Chuman's Diagram and Explanation of the Mandate of Heaven), in *Gobong jeonjip* 高峯全集 (The Complete Works of Gobong) (Seoul: Daedong munhwa yeon-guwon at Sungkyunkwan University, 1979), 289; Yi Hwang, "Cheonmyeong doseol huseo" 天命圖說後敍 (Postscript to the Diagram and Explanation of the Mandate of Heaven), in *Toegye jip*, 30:405a–410a; Kim Yong-heon, "Gobong Gi Dae-seung-ui sachil nonbyeon-gwa 'Cheonmyeong do'" (Gobong Gi Dae-seung's Involvement in the Controversy on the Four-Seven and the "Diagram of the Mandate of Heaven"), *Jeontong-gwa hyeonsil* 8 (1996).

5. The extant editions of "The Diagram of the Mandate of Heaven" are the illustration contained in "Cheonmyeong dohae (天命圖解, An Explanatory Diagram of the Mandate of Heaven)" (1578), ed. Chuman; "Cheonmyeong gudo" and "Cheongmyeong sindo" (1553), which are contained in *Toegye jip*; and the edition contained in "Cheonmyeong doseol (天命圖說, A Diagram and Interpretation of the Mandate of Heaven)" (1651), ed. Taekdang (澤堂) Yi Sik (李植, 1584–1647). For more detailed information on this matter, refer to Yu Jeong-dong, *Yugyo-ui geunbon jeongsin-gwa han-guk yuhak* (The Basic Spirit of Confucianism and Korean Confucianism) (Seoul: Yugyo munhwa yeon-guso at Sungkyunkwan University, 2014), 559–658.

6. "Cheong-hyang so," in *Gobong jeonjip* (Seoul: Daedong munhwa yeon-guwon at Sungkyunkwan University, 1979), 576d–588a.

7. Jang Ji-yeon, *Joseon yugyo yeonwon* (The Origin of Confucianism in the Joseon Dynasty) (Seoul: Myeongmundang, 2009 [1922]), 107–9; Hyeon Sang-yun, *Joseon yuhaksa* (A History of Joseon Confucianism) (Seoul: Simsan, 2010 [1949]), 118; Youn Sasoon, *Toegye cheorak-ui yeon-gu* (A Study of Toegye's Philosophy) (Seoul: Korea University Press, 1980), 91–92; Michael C. Kalton, *The Four-Seven Debate* (Albany: State University of New York Press, 1994), xxviii–xxix, 1; Han-guk cheorak sasang yeon-guhoe, *Non-jaeng-euro boneun han-guk cheorak* (Korean Strands of Philosophy in View of the Salient Debates) (Seoul: Yemun seowon, 1995), 155; *Gangjwa han-guk cheorak* (Lectures on Korean Philosophy) (Seoul: Yemun seowon, 1995), 365; Youn Sasoon, *Han-guk yuhaksa* (A History of Korean Confucianism), Vol. 1 (Seoul: Jisik Sanup sa, 2012), 306–7.

8. I have conceived of the relationship of the old diagram with the new one in accordance with the following two theses: Yu Jeong-dong, "Cheonmyeong doseol-e gwanhan yeon-gu" (A Study on the Diagram and Interpretations of the Mandate of Heaven), *Yugyo-ui geunbon jeongsin-gwa han-guk yuhak* (The Basic Spirit of Confucianism and Korean Confucianism) (2014), 559–608; Kim Yong-heon, "Gobong Gi Dae-seung-ui sachil nonbyeon-gwa 'cheonmyeong do'" (Gobong Gi Dae-seung's Involvement in the Controversy on the Four-Seven and the "Diagram of the Mandate of Heaven"), *Jeontong-gwa hyeonsil* 8 (1996).

9. Discussions on moral emotions, moral nature, and the debate between Toegye and Gobong regarding the four beginnings and the seven feelings are developed from my article: Kim Hyoungchan, "The Relation between Moral Emotions and Moral Nature: A Review of Toegye's Philosophical Quest for Moral Spontaniety," *Korean Cultural Studies* 74 (Seoul: Minjok munhwa yoen-guwon at Korea University, 2017).

10. Mencius, "Gong-sun-chou I" 公孫丑 上, in *Mencius*.

11. "Li yun" 禮運 (The Circle of Rites), in *Li Ji* 禮記 (*The Book of Rites*). "何謂人情? 喜怒哀懼愛惡欲, 七子弗學而能."

12. "Zhong Yong" 中庸, in *Li Ji*. "喜怒哀樂之未發謂之中, 發而皆中節謂之和, 中也者, 天下之大本也, 和也者, 天下之達道也."

13. Owen Flanagan shows the diverse possibilities offered by the classification of feelings on the basis of Mencius's four beginnings. However, as his study is empirically based, he does not regard the original nature as the source of feelings. Owen Flanagan, *Moral Sprouts and Natural Teleologies* (Milwaukee: Marquette University Press, 2014).

14. Mencius, "Gong-sun-chou I," in *Mencius*.

15. Tu Weiming pointed out that Toegye's dilemma was ascribed to his attempt to interpret the dynamic implied in Mencius's four virtues within the parameters of Zhu Xi's system, which stipulated that "the mind combines and governs nature and the feelings (心統性情)." Tu Wei-ming, "Yi T'oegye's Perception of Human Nature," in *The Rise of Neo-Confucianism in Korea* (New York: Columbia University Press, 1985), 268.

16. Zhu Xi, "You lun ren shuo" 又論仁說 (A Reconsideration of the View on Benevolence), in *Zhu Zi chuan-shu* 朱子全書 (The Complete Works of Master Zhu), Vol. 21 (Shanghai: Shanghai guji chubanshe, 2002), 1411.

17. Zhu Xi borrowed the expression "the mind combines and governs nature and the feelings (心通性情)" from Zhang Zai (張載) and adopted it as his own position. Zhang Zai, "Xing li shi yi" 性理拾遺 (Materials on Xing and Li), in *Zhang Zai Ji* 張載集 (The Collected Works of Zhang Zai) (Beijing: Zhonghua shuju, 1978), 374; Zhu Xi, "Xing and Li II" 性理 二 (Human Nature and Principle), in *Zhu Zi chuan-shu* 14, 226.

18. Yi Hwang, "Toegye dap Gobong sadan chiljeong bun ligi byeon" 退溪答高峯四端七情分理氣辯 (Toegye's Response to Gobong on the Schematization of the Four and the Seven as *Li* and *Gi*), in "Yang seonsaeng sachil ligi wangbok seo" 兩先生四七理氣往復書 (The Views on the Four-Seven and *Li-Gi* Exchanged between the Two Scholars), in *Gobong jeonjip* I, Vol. 1, the right side of page 3.

19. Yi Hwang, "The Views on the Four-Seven and *Li-Gi* Exchanged between the Two Scholars—Toegye's Response to Gobong," in *Gobong jeonjip* I, Vol. 1, the right side of page 1. "The issuance of the four beginnings refers to the genuine *li* and the issued beginnings are all good; the issuance of the seven feelings accompanies *gi* and the issued feelings may be good or evil (四端之發純理, 故無不善; 七情之發 兼氣, 故有善惡)."

20. For a detailed discussion of the definition of the theory of *li-gi* on the basis of monism or dualism, refer to Kim Hyoungchan's "Igironui irwonnonhwa yeon-gu"

(A Study on the Monistic Tendency of the Theory of *Li-Gi*) (PhD diss., Korea University, 1996), 1–10.

21. In Neo-Confucianism, the explanation of the mind, the original nature, and feelings on the basis of the theory of *li-gi* is pertinent not only to human beings but also to animals. This is because all beings in the universe and nature, including human beings, are composed of the combination of *li* and *gi*, and animals, like human beings, have mind, the original nature, and feelings. However, the objective of the theory of *li-gi* or "the theory of the heart-mind and nature (心性論)" in Confucianism and Neo-Confucianism is essentially the interpretation of human beings and their society. For the sake of convenience, my interpretation is focused on human beings.

22. This was also the main theme of the debate on the theory of the mind in the nineteenth-century Joseon Dynasty.

23. Professor Youn Sasoon illuminated Toegye's philosophy on the basis of "be" and "ought." Youn Sasoon, "Jonjaewa dang-wi-e gwanhan Toegye-ui ilchisi" (The Identity of Be and Ought in Toegye's Thought), in *Han-guk yuhak sasangnon* (A Study on Korean Confucian Thought) (Seoul: Yemun seowon, 1997), 259–83.

24. For a detailed discussion on this matter, refer to Kim Hyoungchan, "The *Li-Ki* Structure of the Four Beginnings and the Seven Emotions and the Intent of the Four-Seven Debate," *Acta Koreana* 18, no. 2 (2015): 568.

25. Yi, "The Views on the Four-Seven and *Li-Gi* Exchanged between the Two Scholars," the right side of page 1.

26. Gi Dae-seung, "The Views on the Four-Seven and *Li-Gi* Exchanged between the Two Scholars—Gobong's Response on the Issue of the Four-Seven Presented to Toegye," in *Gobong jeonjip* I, Vol. 1, the left side of page 1 and the right side of page 2.

27. Ibid., both sides of page 28.

28. Ibid., the left side of page 1 and the right side of page 2.

29. In this context, we may ask whether there may be immoderate feelings among the four beginnings that are not in accordance with just principles or moderate ones among the seven feelings that to the contrary are in accordance with such principles. If there are, how can we distinguish between the four and the seven? Toegye and Gobong touched on this problem, but the thoroughgoing debate on it only began among adherents of Seongho hakpa (星湖學派, The Seongho School: Yi Ik and his disciples) in the eighteenth century.

30. Yi, "The Views on the Four-Seven and *Li-Gi* Exchanged between the Two Scholars," the right side of page 5.

31. Yi Hwang, "Dap Gi Myeong-eon" 答奇明彦 (Response to Gi Myeong-eon), in *Toegye jip*, 29:424a.

32. Originally, Toegye had thought that the seven cannot be said to be good or evil. However, after giving due weight to Gobong's argument on this matter, he revised his view and stated that the seven, though originally good, are liable to become evil.

33. Yi Hwang, "Response to Gi Myeong-eon—Revised," in *Toegye jip*, 29:413b–414a.

34. Ibid., 29:414b–415a.

35. Ibid., 29:415b–c; Zhu Xi, "Zhu Zi yu-lei," in *Zhu Zi chuan-shu* 15, Vol. 53, 1776.

36. Han Won-jin, *Juja eollon dong-i go* 朱子言論同異考 (Discrepancies in the Speeches and Writings of Zhu Zi), trans. and ann. Gwak Sin-hwan (Seoul: Somyeong Publishing Company, 2002), 107.

37. Gi, "The Views on the Four-Seven and *Li-Gi* Exchanged between the Two Scholars," the left side of page 21 and the left side of page 22.

38. Ibid., both sides of page 9, the left side of page 11, and the right side of page 12.

39. Yi, "Response to Gi Myeong-eon," 29:419c.

40. This section is a revision and supplementation of some of the contents of my thesis: Kim Hyoungchan, "Naeseong oewang-eul hyang-han du gaji gil: Toegye cheorak-eseo-ui liwa sangjereul jungsimeuro" (The Two Paths toward Becoming a Sage on the Inside and a Virtuous King on the Outside: Focused on the Concepts of *Li* and *Sangje* in Toegye's Philosophy), *Cheorak yeon-gu* 34 (2007).

41. Yi, "Response to Gi Myeong-eon," 29:423c–424a, 426d.

42. Yi Hwang used terms such as "the issuance of *li*," "the mobility of *li*," and "the arrival of *li* of its own accord" in order to explain that *li* is not like a dead thing. However, he used them in different contexts. That is, he used the issuance of *li* in the discussion of the four-seven, the mobility of *li* in the explanation of the relation of *li* and *gi*, and the arrival of *li* of its own accord in the interpretations of *gyeongmul* (格物) and *mulgyeok* (物格). In this context, Mun Seok-yun explains that the concept of "issuance" is promoted in the theory of the mind and nature, that of "mobility" is advanced in the theory of the universe, and that of "arrival" is advanced in the field of epistemology. Mun Seok-yun, "Toegye-eseo libalgwa lidong, lido-ui uimi-e dae-hayeo" (On the Meaning of Toegye's Expressions "The Issuance of *Li*," "The Mobility of *Li*," and "The Arrival of *Li*"), *Toegye hakbo* 110 (2001): 198.

43. Among the research papers that are pertinent to this debate, I have paid particular attention to the writings of Mun Seok-yun and Kim Gi-hyeon. Mun closely traced the evolution of Yi Hwang's concept of *li*, and Kim studied in great depth Yi Hwang's view on the world implied in his concept of *li*. Refer to Mun, "Toegye-eseo libalgwa lidong, lido-ui uimi-e daehayeo," and Kim Gi-hyeon, "Toegye-ui *li* cheorak-e naejae-doen segyegwanjeok hamui" (The Worldview Implied in Toegye's Philosophy of *Li*), *Toegye hakbo* 116 (2001).

44. There has been widespread debate on the dualistic nature of *li-gi*. As *li* and *gi* are neither separable nor intermingled, they cannot strictly be spoken of as two independent entities. So it may not be unequivocally said that the theory of *li-gi* can be subsumed under a dualistic rubric. However, I have referred to the "dualistic" theory of *li-gi*, as *li* and *gi* are regarded as the most primordial elements of all entities. For a more detailed discussion on this subject, refer to Kim, "Igironui irwonnonhwa yeon-gu," 1–10.

45. Yi, "Response to Gi Myeong-eon," 29:413b–415b.

46. Gi, "The Views on the Four-Seven and *Li-Gi* Exchanged between the Two Scholars," the right side of page 10.

47. Yi, "Response to Gi Myeong-eon," 29:432d.

48. Gobong's debates with Sojae and Chodang provided the momentum for a scholarly reevaluation of the relationship between *li* and *gi* in his thought and a reexamination of Toegye's view on *li-gi*. Though this evolving understanding is very important to a fuller grasp of Gobong's philosophy, I have not dealt with it here as it is beyond the remit of this book. Concerning this changing perception of Gobong's work, refer to Nam Ji-man, "Gobong Gi Dae-seung-ui seongniseol yeon-gu" (A Study on Gobong Gi Dae-seung's Theory of Human Nature and Principle [性理]) (PhD diss., Korea University, 2009), 50–67.

49. Gi Dae-seung, "The Views on the Four-Seven and *Li-Gi* Exchanged between the Two Scholars—Postscripts to the Four-Seven," in *Gobong jeonjip* II, Vol. 2, the left side of page 22 and the right side of page 25.

50. Gi Dae-seung, "The Views on the Four-Seven and *Li-Gi* Exchanged between the Two Scholars—General Remarks on the Four-Seven," in *Gobong jeonjip* II, Vol. 2, the right side of page 25 and the right side of page 27.

51. Yi, "The Views on the Four-Seven and *Li-Gi* Exchanged between the Two Scholars," the right side of page 27; "The Views on the Four-Seven and *Li-Gi* Exchanged between the Two Scholars—Toegye's Writing Presented to Gobong," in *Gobong jeonjip* II, Vol. 2, the right side of page 27 and the right side of page 28.

52. Zhu Xi, "Da Xue zhang-ju 大學章句," in *Zhu Zi chuan-shu* 6, 17.

53. Concerning the details of the controversy on *gyeongmul* and *mulgyeok* between Gobong and Toegye, refer to Nam, "Gobong Gi Dae-seung-ui seongniseol yeon-gu," 95–101.

54. "所謂致知在格物者，言欲致吾之知，在卽物而窮其理也．蓋人心之靈莫不有知，而天下之物莫不有理，惟於理有未窮，故其知有不盡也．是以大學始教，必使學者卽凡天下之物，莫不因其已知之理而益窮之，以求至乎其極．至於用力之久，而一旦豁然貫通焉，卽衆物之表裏精粗無不到，而吾心之全體大用無不明矣．此謂物格,此謂知之至也." Zhu Xi, "Da Xue zhang-ju," in *Zhu Zi chuan-shu* 6 (Shanghai: Shanghai guji chubanshe, 2002), 20. For a translation of this Chinese paragraph, refer to Wing-tsit Chan, *A Source Book of Chinese Philosophy* (Princeton, NJ: Princeton University Press, 1963), 89.

55. Zhu Xi believed that all things have their own *li* that originate from the same source and that one can recognize the universal *li* through the recognition of the *li* of an individual thing. "蓋萬物各具一理，而萬理同出一原，此所以可推而無不通也." "Da Xue huo-wen," in *Zhu Zi chuan-shu* 6, 525.

56. "Da Xue zhang-ju," in *Zhu Zi chuan-shu* 6, 17.

57. Ibid.

58. Gi Dae-seung, "Dap Toegye seonsaeng munmok" 答退溪先生問目 (Response to Master Toegye's List of Questions), in *Gobong jip*, 040:130a–b. "物格 戊申奉事，理到之言，發微不可見條下，通書註，隨其所寓，而理無不到，大學或問註，無一毫不到處，以此等言句，反覆永之，則理詣其極及極處無不到者如鄙意釋之，固無不可也."

59. Zhu Xi, "Wu-shen feng-shi" 戊申奉事 (Memorial to the King in 1188 [戊申奉事], in *Zhu Zi chuan-shu* 20, 611–12. "是以程顥常闢之曰：‘自謂窮神知化，而不足以開物成務，言爲無不周偏，而實外於倫理，窮深極微，

而不可以入堯舜之道, 天下之學, 自非淺陋固滯, 則必入於此, 是謂正路之榛蕪, 聖門之蔽塞, 闢之而後可與入道.' 嗚呼! 此眞可謂理到之言."

60. Nam Ji-man, on the basis of this quotation, defined "理到之言" as "the state-ment arriving at the principle" and argued that Gobong contributed to the establish-ment of Toegye's concept of "the arrival of *li* of its own accord." However, as he was primarily concerned with Gobong's influence on Toegye, he did not develop his discussion about the significance of Toegye's concept of the arrival of *li* of its own accord (理自到說). Nam, "Gobong Gi Dae-seung-ui seongniseol yeon-gu," 98–101. The concept "理到之言" may be translated as "the arrival of *li* at a statement" or "the arrival of a statement at *li*." I, assuming Gobong's intention in citing the concept, interpret it as "the arrival of *li* at a statement." Though it is a literal translation, I don't believe that there is scope for much variability in interpretation because anyone who is familiar with Korean can interpret it in a straightforward way. Likewise, "the arrival of *li* (理到)" was accepted as an idiomatic expression both in China at the time of Zhu Xi and in Korea at the time of Toegye and Gobong. Therefore it may be said that Toegye's ultimate concern was not to define the idiomatic and conventional expression of the concept but to discover a clue that could reveal "the role of *li*" through the concept.

61. "Tong-shu" 通書 1, in *Xing-li da-quan* 性理大全 (Seoul: Bogyeong mun-hwasa, 1994), 2: 56. "發動也, 微幽也, 言其不疾而速. 一念方萌, 而已至理而具, 所以微 而不可見也. 充光也, 周偏也, 言其不幸而至, 蓋隨其所寓, 而理無不到, 所以周而不可窮也."

62. Zhu Xi, "Da Xue huo-wen," in *Si-shu da-quan* 四書大全 I (Jinju: Suri, 2012), 76, "至善只是極好處, 十分端正恰好, 無一毫不是處, 無一毫不到處."

63. Ibid., "玉溪盧氏曰 至善, 乃太極之異名. . . . 程子所謂 '以其義理精微之極, 有不得而名'者, 故姑以至善目之."

64. Yi Hwang, "The Appended Response to Gi Myeong-eon," in *Toegye jip*, 20:466c–467b. "前此滉所以堅執誤說者, 只知守朱子理無情意, 無計度. 無造作之說, 以爲我可以窮到物理之極處, 理豈能自至於極處, 故硬把物格 之格, 無不到之到, 皆作己格己到看, . . . 然而又曰, 理必有用, 何必又說是 心之用乎, 則其用雖不外乎人心, 而其所以爲用之妙, 實是理之發見者, 隨人心 所至, 而無所不到, 無所不盡, 但恐吾之格物有未至, 不煥理不能自到也. 然則方 其言格物也, 則固是言我窮至物理之極處, 及其言物格也, 則豈不可謂物理之極處, 隨吾所窮而無不到乎. 是知無情意造作者, 此理本然之體也, 其隨寓發見 易無不到者, 此理至神之用也. 向也, 但有見於本體之無爲 而不知妙用之能顯行, 殆若認理爲死物, 其去道不亦遠甚矣乎."

65. Zhu Xi, "Da Xue huo-wen," 81. "物格者, 事物之理, 各有以詣其極而無餘之謂 也. 理之在物者, 既詣其極而無餘, 則知之在我者, 亦隨其詣而無不盡矣."

66. The understanding of the statement "*li* arrives of its own accord" not as a meta-phor but as a fact has caused misunderstanding and debate. In fact, not only scholars of Toegye's era but also modern scholars continue to argue about this perception. Mark Johnson details multiple instances in which metaphors have been applied to the discussion of moral issues and argues for the necessity of the figurative use of words even in the exercise of concrete moral judgments and the evaluation of behavior.

Refer to Mark Johnson, *Moral Imagination: Implication of Cognitive Science* (Chicago: University of Chicago Press, 1993).

67. H. I. Dreyfus and S. E. Dreyfus maintained that seasoned experts, unlike novices, do not necessarily have to undergo the process of encoding their objects of study into language in the process of making moral judgments and in their behavior. However, Andy Clark criticized their view by emphasizing the importance of communication even among experts. I think that it is necessary to distinguish cases in which language is needed for communication from cases in which it is omitted from the moral judgments and behavior of experts. Hubert I. Dreyfus and Stuart E. Dreyfus, "What Is Morality? A Phenomenological Account of the Development of Ethical Expertise," in *Universalism vs. Communitarianism*, ed. David Rasmussen (Cambridge: MIT Press, 1990); Andy Clark, "Connectionism, Moral Cognition, and Collaborative Problem Solving," in *Mind and Morals*, ed. Larry May, Marilyn Friedman, and Andy Clark (Cambridge: MIT Press, 1998).

68. Gi Dae-seung, "Seongsaeng jeon sangjang panbusataek" 先生前上狀判府事宅 (To Master Toegye), in *Gobong jeonjip*, 244a. "所辯無爲之體, 至神之用等語, 闡發幽隱, 尤極精密. 反復玩味, 若承面誨, 欽復尤深. 但細看其間, 恐有道理不自在之累, 未知如何."

69. "Cheong-hyang so," in *Gobong jeonjip*, 580, "大升答曰 無爲之體 至神之用等語, 闡發幽隱, 尤極精密. 但細看其間, 恐有不自在之累云."

70. Ibid., "後來諸儒論辨曰 高峯此言, 雖寂寥一句語, 見其自在字, 則實得或問 理詣其極之意, 此似精的, 當以是爲正云."

Chapter 4

Yulgok Asks and Toegye Answers 2

On The Doctrine of the Mean
(May–October 1570)

In 1570, the last year of his life, seventy-year-old Toegye received two let-ters from Yulgok containing lists of questions and sent him replies. Yulgok was no longer the young man who had been preparing for the civil service examination twelve years earlier; he was a thirty-five-year-old man in his seventh year as a government official in the Royal Court who was enjoying the favor of King Seonjo. Nonetheless, it seems that Yulgok wrote letters to Toegye whenever he encountered an issue he couldn't understand unaided, and Toegye answered his every question in clear terms.

In his first list of questions to Toegye in 1558, Yulgok asked about *The Great Learning*, whereas his second and third lists were mainly related to *The Doctrine of the Mean* and *Ten Diagrams on Sage Learning*. Twelve years earlier, Yulgok had asked primarily general, all-encompassing questions, whereas in 1570, he immersed himself in the details of the texts and dissected them. This led to debate on crucial questions concerning the optimal mode of engaging in self-cultivation on the path to the Way and the even more funda-mental issue of the distinction between the effort to understand and embody the Way and the Way itself. This hinged on the question of the "golden mean," or the achievement of self-discipline, which in turn led to debate on whether this was an external, behavioral phenomenon or a more intrinsic one. Finally, the two scholars debated who the path to the Way was open to and whether epistemological priority should be given to the Way itself as a noumenal reality or to human beings in their strivings to achieve it.

The correspondence between the two Confucian scholars, which seems to have taken place over the course of several months, shows how lively their debate was. As time went by, Yulgok's understanding of the topics in ques-tion clearly deepened. It is possible or even likely that there were frequent questions, answers, and exchanges of opinion between them, but although there might well have been more letters exchanged between Yulgok and Toegye, they are no longer extant.

In the case of the second exchange of letters, we have Toegye's reply to Yulgok but not Yulgok's list of questions. Therefore we have no choice but to speculate about what Yulgok's questions were. In the third exchange of letters, some of the questions in the second list of questions were revisited and discussed in more depth. I have extracted some of the important topics from their lengthy letters, which can help us understand their thoughts and perspectives. Because the topics covered in the second and third pairs of letters are linked, I have organized the questions in terms of two categories—those related to *The Doctrine of the Mean* and those concerning *Ten Diagrams on Sage Learning*—and have reviewed them according to the topics under discussion.

HOW TO READ

Toegye's second reply to Yulgok tells us that the latter posed two questions about the annotations to "Du Zhong Yong fa (讀中庸法, How to Read *The Doctrine of the Mean*)," which had been inserted at the beginning of *Zhong Yong zhang-ju* (中庸章句, *The Doctrine of the Mean in Chapters and Verses*). In this letter, what is notable is their different approaches to and perspectives on the text they were discussing, rather than the content of the letter. Yulgok pointed out and criticized logical inconsistencies he had found in the text, and Toegye advised him to examine it in its overall context. Toegye's answers were offered without qualifications, which demonstrates how candid their relationship as mentor and disciple had become. Toegye's tone in the letter was much more informal than it had been twelve years earlier, which suggests that they had built friendship and trust over the years.

Because we only have Toegye's reply, let's take a closer look at some of its passages:

【1】 The explanation of Zhen Xi-shan (the pen name of Zhen De-xiu) is slightly at odds with Zhu Xi's intention. But Zhu Xi explained how mysterious it is when one's sincere reverence (篤恭) reaches its utmost extent, which also means that this intangible, soundless, and scentless mysteriousness comes from sincere reverence. Because that is the case, Xi-shan also simply said that mysteriousness arises from sincere reverence. He didn't argue that one can gradually reach the ultimate stage by engaging in diligent practice after one has become sincerely reverential. Xi-shan's erudition is not shallow like that. You should be careful not to mislead about the author's true intention in your writing.[1]

【2】 Rao (饒氏)[2] explained[3] that *The Great Learning* is concerned with how to teach people, and specifically how to engage in learning and to cultivate oneself, and that *The Doctrine of the Mean* is concerned with the optimal method of preaching the Way (道, Dao), namely by elaborating on what the Way is. Because the intentions of the two books are not the same, their teachings are applicable to different types of activity. Rao was not wrong, but you've argued that "It is not reasonable to see learning and the Way through different prisms." You've misunderstood it. (Have you read what Zhu Xi wrote about the difference between "being capable (能)" and "what can be done (所能)" in his reply to Lü Ziyue (呂子約)?[4] You must understand that the Way, practice, learning, and righteous principle are different from one another in their deepest senses. Generally speaking, learning is "being capable," whereas the Way is "what can be done"; you shouldn't confuse them in order to form a coherent theory. Zhu Xi's letter to Lü Ziyue is in chapter 27 of volume 48 of *The Complete Works of Master Zhu* (朱子大全). But I recommend that you read other letters in chapters 25 and 26 as well in order to grasp the full meaning of what I've said.)[5]

The literal translation of Zhen Xi-shan's annotation that Yulgok pointed out in excerpt 【1】 is as follows:

Zhen Xi-shan said, "*The Doctrine of the Mean* begins with the line, 'What Heaven has conferred is called nature (天命之謂性),' and ends with the line, 'Neither sound nor smell (無聲無臭).'" These phrases sound elegant and mysterious. However, this book also admonishes us to "be prudent and cautious (戒愼)," "be fearful and anxious (恐懼)," "be watchful over yourself when you are alone (謹獨)," and "be sincerely reverential (篤恭)," all of which instruct people on the correct forms of behavior. It means that one can fully develop one's virtuous nature only after one has become prudent and cautious, fearful and anxious, and watchful over oneself when one is alone. It also implies that one can reach the ultimate, numinous stage or the stage of soundlessness and scentlessness only after one has become sincere and reverential. In other words, it does not say that one must give one's whole mind to the profound and refrain from concrete practice."[6]

It seems that Yulgok's question was, "'The stage of soundlessness and scentlessness' is equal to the ultimate stage one can reach when one cultivates oneself in a sincere and reverential manner. So isn't it wrong to say that cultivating oneself in a sincere and reverential manner is the prerequisite of reaching that stage?" It is true that Zhen Xi-shan used the phrase "only after becoming sincere and reverential (必篤恭而後)," so Yulgok's criticism was not without foundation. Toegye, however, answered that what Zhen Xi-shan meant to say was not at odds with what Zhu Xi argued, maintaining that "the utmost extent of sincere reverence" is the ultimate stage of soundlessness and scentlessness. And Toegye added, "Xi-shan's erudition is not shallow like that. You should be careful not to mislead about the author's true intention in your writing."

In excerpt 【2】, Yulgok asked a similar question to the one in excerpt 【1】. His question was whether Rao Lu (饒魯) differentiated between learning and the Way. Toegye pointed out that *The Great Learning* was concerned with informing people about how to cultivate themselves, while *The Doctrine of the Mean* was concerned with informing them of what the Way means, and that thus the intentions of the two books were not the same. He added that if Yulgok criticized Rao Lu for differentiating between learning and the Way on the basis of Rao Lu's explanation, he had "misunderstood it."

Yulgok tried to apply the same logic to the understanding and explanation of self-cultivation and its results and of learning and the Way. Toegye told him that it was wrong to differentiate between self-cultivation and its results and between learning and the Way. This would also mean that, once one understands that they are the same, one can differentiate between them in order to help readers better understand them. It is possible that Yulgok's criticism of others' texts reminded Toegye of Gobong, who had argued that one should not differentiate between the four beginnings and the seven feelings or between *li* and *gi*.

In the debate between Toegye and Gobong over the four beginnings and the seven feelings, Toegye criticized Gobong's point of view as follows:

> You must understand that two things that look the same have differences, and at the same time, their differences arise from common ground. In order to keep things in perspective, you must realize that viewing them as two different things does not prevent them from "not being independent of one another" and that viewing them as the same thing does not necessarily mean they are "interdependent on each other."[7]

All phenomena undergoing comparison are composed of common ground and differences. While paying attention to their differences, one must understand that they have common ground, whereas, in paying attention to their common ground, one must understand that they have differences. This is what Toegye intended to convey.

Gobong criticized Toegye for focusing on the differences between the four beginnings and the seven feelings, arguing that they are all human emotions. Gobong considered that the four beginnings and the seven feelings have the same structure from the viewpoint of the theory of *li-gi* or of ontology. Toegye gently refuted his argument, saying that Gobong must see their sameness as well as their differences and urging him to think about why the ancient sages had differentiated between the purely good four beginnings and the seven feelings, which tend to become evil.

Yulgok's criticism of Zhen De-xiu and Rao Lu for differentiating between self-cultivation and its results, and between learning and the Way, is consistent with Gobong's argument. Toegye believed that Yulgok was focusing solely on their sameness or identity and that he did not understand that Zhen De-xiu and Rao Lu were explaining the differences present within sameness. It seems understandable that, when Yulgok had a debate with Ugye (the pen name of Seong Hon) about the four beginnings and the seven feelings two years after Toegye passed away, he adopted a similar position as Gobong. It may be that his perspective on the four beginnings and the seven feelings was already determined as early as the 1570s, when he exchanged letters with Toegye. Yulgok was one of the observers of the eight-year-long debate between Toegye and Gobong on the four beginnings and the seven feelings.

It is common for intellectuals to seek to explain the world through the rubric of a single logical system that is compatible with their perspective or level of understanding. This tendency represents their intellectual desire to explain the world in a simple and logical way. However, the mysterious natural order does not always proceed logically and coherently; sometimes nature seems to deviate from its normal path. On the other hand, if one examines the issue more closely, one realizes that it deviates in an internally consistent way. Problems arise when one devises one's own logical system within one's intellectual parameters or comfort zone and then tries to apply it to the logic of the universe and of nature. Such a closed theoretical system cannot explain the breadth and depth of the mechanisms of the universe and, eventually, excludes this complexity. A species of intellectual violence occurs when intellectuals argue that it is wrong to discuss things that are excluded by their own logical systems.

The phrase "You must understand that two things that look the same have differences, and at the same time, their differences arise from common ground" in all likelihood means that one must escape the frame of reference one has developed and open one's mind and eyes to the world outside this frame. Whatever perspective or theoretical system one chooses to apply for the sake of coherent explanation, one must bear in mind that there is a broader, more variegated world than one's theory encompasses, a world outside of one's frame of reference or theoretical system. There certainly is a gap between language that describes facts and the facts themselves. Choosing a particular perspective is a useful way to explain and understand certain facts. However, the perspective one has chosen is not the absolute truth, and one should not judge whether others' opinions are right or wrong based solely and rigidly on one's choice of perspective. In this light, Toegye attempted to explain to Gobong and Yulgok that other people's modes of explanation can be understood differently in varied contexts.

METHODS OF ENGAGEMENT IN SELF-CULTIVATION

Ideally, self-cultivation is the practice one engages in when one's mind is tranquil or stimulated. This is a never-ending activity for Confucian scholars who strive to achieve the ideal of becoming a sage. But it is necessary for the way one cultivates oneself to vary depending on whether one's mind is tranquil or not and whether one's main focus is self-cultivation in a state of tranquility or of stimulation.

Yulgok asked Toegye about the practice of self-cultivation carried out by controlling one's human mind and moral mind with a judicious and unwavering attitude. This was the core maxim that King Shun (舜) in ancient China proposed to his successor King Yu (禹) when he passed the crown to him, and it was considered by Confucian scholars to be central to self-cultivation and by Zhu Xi to be the key to the dissemination of Confucian ideals.

This idea originated from the imperative, four Chinese characters in length, that King Yao (堯) bequeathed to his successor King Shun (舜):

Sincerely strive for the golden mean (允執厥中).[8]

King Shun (舜) elaborated the phrase in sixteen Chinese characters when he gave advice to his successor, King Yu (禹):

The human mind is always treacherous and the moral mind is always subtle. Thus, be judicious and steadfast, and sincerely strive for the golden mean (人心惟危, 道心惟微, 惟精惟一, 允執厥中).[9]

King Shun thought that this admonition was the key to world peace. Confucian scholars who admired King Yao, King Shun, and King Yu regarded it as a fundamental principle of learning and cultivation. Even Jeong Yak-yong (pen name: Dasan, 1762–1836), who argued that this passage was retrospectively fabricated by others, nevertheless acknowledged its value as a resounding message that contains the crux of Confucian teachings.[10]

The human mind is always treacherous because of selfish human desire, so one must cultivate one's mind by refining it and being wary of acting in a way that is contrary to what is right. The moral mind is never antithetical to what is right, but it is very subtle, so one must pursue one's moral mind steadfastly. The issue of the human mind and the moral mind was discussed by Yulgok and Ugye when they debated the four beginnings and the seven feelings, and during this interaction, Yulgok clarified his position on this issue. However, it is obvious that, in his letter to Toegye, he had not yet developed his own position. And it is assumed that Toegye influenced Yulgok's perspective on the human mind and the moral mind.

Toegye's engagement with Yulgok with regard to this issue is evident in the following response:

Regarding the annotation of Wu-zhai Cheng-shi (勿齋程氏)[11] to "Zhong Yong zhang-ju xu (中庸章句序, Preface to *The Doctrine of the Mean in Chapters and Verses*)," you wrote that his explanation was not reasonable. So I would like to ask you, what is learning or cultivation when your mind is tranquil? When King Shun talked about the human mind and the moral mind, he was referring to them in the context of a stimulated mind (已發處). Therefore the admonition to "be judicious and steadfast, and sincerely strive for the golden mean (惟精惟一, 允執厥中)" is not a call for you to cultivate yourself when your mind is tranquil. You should focus on the original words and put them into practice and should not add unnecessary words to the original words and confuse self-cultivation in a state of stimulation with self-cultivation in a tranquil state. Such a mistake occurs when you apply too many additional meanings to the original meaning and eventually distort and confuse the original intention of the words. This is the worst reading habit, and Zhu Xi's disciples were especially cautioned against it. As you pointed out in your letter, Mencius said what Confucius had not said, and Master Cheng (Cheng Yi) and Master Zhu (Zhu Xi) said what Mencius had not. You are trying to integrate everything they said into a single argument. And this is not right.[12]

As we can see, Toegye replied in a stern tone. He chided Yulgok for having "the worst reading habit" and admonished him not to engage in it again.

Here is the passage from Wu-zhai's annotation that Yulgok had pointed out:

Wu-zhai said, "(When one's mind) responds to external things and is stimulated, one's mind can be at last manifested as the human mind or as the moral mind, and in this context, the phrase 'be judicious and steadfast, and sincerely strive for the golden mean' is concerned with learning or cultivation in a state of stimulation."[13]

Yulgok problematized Wu-zhai's explanation that one must cultivate the human mind and the moral mind when one's mind is stimulated by external things. He believed that one must cultivate them regardless of one's state of mind and criticized Wu-zhai for limiting their cultivation to periods when the mind is stimulated.

In his reply to Yulgok, Toegye agreed with Wu-zhai's explanation, arguing that the human mind and the moral mind that King Shun had discussed were linked to the stimulated mind. And he chided Yulgok for adding unnecessary interpretations to the original meaning and of distorting it, calling such behavior "the worst reading habit."

However, when we look at Toegye's position on the human mind and the moral mind during his debate with Gobong and at the position Yulgok took on them in later years, it seems that Toegye and Yulgok reversed their positions. Toegye argued that, like the four beginnings and the seven feelings, the moral mind can be inextricably linked to *li* and the human mind to *gi*. According to him, what made the human mind and the moral mind different from each other was the fact that the former was linked to the material boundaries of *gi*, while the latter was linked to the purely good morality of *li*. Toegye, on the other hand, focused on the fundamental reason for the differences between the four beginnings and the seven feelings and between the moral mind and the human mind. He highlighted the importance of self-cultivation in a tranquil state of mind or when the mind has yet to be spurred into active thought (未發時) rather than when the mind has been stimulated by external things (已發時).[14] Yulgok attempted to apply the sixteen-character Chinese phrase about the human mind and the moral mind to the discussion of the stimulated and the tranquil mind. And Toegye, in his reply, corrected Yulgok, explaining that both the human mind and the moral mind are concerned with the stimulated mind.

In later years, Yulgok argued that it is difficult to control the direction of one's mind consciously when it has yet to be stimulated or to take any particular direction and that once the original moral nature at the core of one's mind evolves into moral emotions, one must make conscious efforts to control the direction of one's mind. Yulgok emphasized that the moment when one's mind is stimulated, one must aim to turn the human mind into the moral mind through self-cultivation and self-discipline.

Yulgok's position became clear two years after Toegye passed away, when Yulgok and Ugye argued over the four beginnings and the seven feelings as well as over the human mind and the moral mind. When Yulgok sent the letter discussed earlier to Toegye, he didn't have any particular position on the issue of the human mind and the moral mind and on how to discipline oneself in order to control them. Given later changes in Yulgok's theory on the human mind and the moral mind, it seems that he accepted Toegye's opinion that the two are linked to the stimulated mind, as well as Toegye's advice that he should stay true to the original meaning of texts in order to avoid "the worst reading habit." By doing so, Yulgok renewed his understanding of the human mind and the moral mind, paid attention to the task of self-cultivation in a stimulated state of mind, and eventually made his position clear: he argued that the human mind can become the moral mind and vice versa (人心道心相爲終始說).[15]

ON PERCEPTION

Yulgok's next question was about the perception (知覺) of the mind. In the "Preface to *The Doctrine of the Mean in Chapters and Verses*," Ge-an (格菴趙氏)[16] added an annotation to the phrase "There is only one unencumbered and spiritual perception (虛靈知覺)," which was written by Zhu Xi, and Yulgok raised an issue about it, as follows:

In your letter, you were also wrong about what Ge-an Zhao-shi (格菴趙氏) wrote regarding "unencumbered and spiritual perception." Although every living thing has perception, the biased and stubborn perception of birds and beasts is never the same as the most spiritual perception of human beings. Moreover, the perception explained by Ge-an is based on the Confucian sages' method of mental cultivation (心法), as he writes: "The human mind is always treacherous and the moral mind is always subtle. Thus, be judicious and steadfast, and sincerely strive for the golden mean (人心惟危, 道心惟微, 惟精惟一, 允執厥中)." The word "perception" he described is preceded by "unencumbered and spiritual" to indicate how profound and mysterious the essence (體) and the function (用) of the human mind are. Those who read can understand facts and truths correctly only by focused mental perception and by appreciating and realizing the essential issues, and ultimately by thinking rigorously. You should not taint the original meaning of human perception by referring to the perception of birds and beasts, and by having doubts about things that should be believed. Ordinary people's perception is different from sages' perception in that ordinary people are influenced by their disposition and blinded by their selfishness, and they lose their ability to perceive accurately. How could you base your opinion on the perception of birds and beasts and have doubts about the human mind's (inherent) ability to appreciate and realize truth? 【In your letter, you said, "It may be wrong to interpret perception like this. Not only ordinary people but also birds and beasts have perception. So, how could it be right to say that they all know 'the normative principle (所當然, what ought to be so)' and realize 'the natural principle or cause (所以然, the reason for which it is so)'?"】[17]

Ge-an interpreted "perception (知覺)" as follows:

To "know (知)" is to appreciate "the normative principle" and to "sense (覺)" is to realize "the natural principle or cause."[18]

In response to that interpretation, Yulgok asked Toegye whether it is possible to understand "the normative principle" and "the natural principle or cause" through perception, which is possessed not only by humans but also by beasts. "The normative principle" refers to obligatory or moral norms, whereas "the natural principle or cause" means inescapable forces or existential rules. The core impulses of Neo-Confucianism are to grasp the fact that existential rules (the reason that existence is as it is) and moral norms (what ought to be so) are based on a shared principle, to understand that it is inevitable that we conform to moral norms and existential rules, and to put moral norms into practice. In this regard, understanding "the normative principle" and "the natural principle or cause" is not possible without a great deal of learning and self-discipline. Yulgok's question centered on whether it was possible to judge the ability to understand "the normative principle" and "the natural principle or cause" based on "perception," a faculty that does not differentiate human beings from beasts.

Toegye answered that "perception" in this context was "human beings' most spiritual perception" rather than the "biased and stubborn perception of beasts," and he pointed out that, even though many ordinary people have lost part of their ability to perceive accurately, spiritual perception is inherent to every human being. And he chided Yulgok for ignoring the original intent of the author and for interpreting the text out of context.

As Yulgok understood, "perception" also means the cognitive function of humans and other animals. However, in Neo-Confucianism, it further entails the understanding of how nature and society operate[19] because, as mentioned earlier, existential rules and moral norms are based on a shared principle. For example, one's duty of serving one's parents devotedly is as natural as the physical law that any object with mass falls from its previous position according to gravitational pull. Such an idea indicates that moral norms are considered inescapable in the same way that existential rules are and that moral norms control us in the same way that physical laws always hold.

Years later, when Yulgok established his own theory of the human mind and the moral mind, the concept of "perception" served as an important element of his thought. One of the critical reasons why Yulgok took a different position to Toegye on the human mind and the moral mind was that he had a different conception of what "perception" entailed. Yulgok believed that "perception" was what made the human mind different from the moral mind and was a faculty that only humans possessed. At the time when Yulgok sent this letter to Toegye, he was probably not firm in his position on "perception." Presumably, Toegye's reply made him reconsider its meaning and role in terms of the human mind and the moral mind.

Toegye gave Yulgok advice to enable him to understand Ge-an's text proper, and Yulgok took his advice and delved deeper into the concept of perception and, eventually, established his own theory. Toegye discussed the human mind, the moral mind, and perception only briefly in relation to the four beginnings and the seven feelings, whereas Yulgok developed these concepts based on Toegye's teachings. Therefore it is fair to say that in this respect Yulgok surpassed his master Toegye.

ON THE CULTIVATION OF THE MIND

The Way (道, Dao) is invisible. Human nature, which is said to have originated from the Way, is impalpable. Neo-Confucianism presupposes that humans have an original moral nature, which is fundamentally equal to the Way of nature. One of the reasons why Mencius is considered an orthodox Confucian scholar and Xun Zi is not is that Mencius claimed that people contain within them the purely good original moral nature, which accords with the Way. However, even though this is the case, we experience a variety of emotions every day—emotions such as happiness, sadness, anger, fear, anticipation, and anxiety. Neo-Confucianism emphasizes that people should acquire a systematic understanding of how these emotions arise from their original moral nature and should learn how to control their personal selfishness and nurture good human nature, which accords with universal order.

Sindok / xin-du (慎獨, watching oneself carefully when alone), a stricture that is discussed in *The Doctrine of the Mean*, is one method of self-cultivation and self-discipline that can lead to such a virtuous life. This phrase emphasizes the importance of focusing more on self-cultivation and self-discipline when one is alone because this is when one becomes prone to indolence and debauchery. Zhu Xi went even further in his interpretation of the phrase, arguing that one should "be cautious when you know [something] alone."[20] What is more important than displaying virtuous emotions and performing good deeds is ensuring that one's good deeds are sincere. In other words, one should not hide one's true intentions and pretend to do good deeds.

It seems that Yulgok asked Toegye about the section in chapter 1 of *The Doctrine of the Mean* in which "watching oneself carefully when alone" is discussed. Toegye answered as follows:

Regarding the phrase "The visible and the revealed all partake of the Way," written by Rao Lu (饒魯), you asked this question: "Both what is wrong and what is right are in secluded and dark places or in small and subtle things. Is it right to say that 'they all partake of the Way'?" Given that Zhu Xi and other sages argued that everything was composed of good and evil dimensions, Rao Lu's opinion is problematic. Zi-si (子思) and Zhu Xi argued that the Way is everywhere and that even though the Way is very subtle, one cannot prevent it from manifesting itself. In this regard, the imperative of "watching oneself carefully when alone" was proposed simply as a method of ensuring the Way's integrity. It is unrelated to the idea that the visible and the revealed all partake of the Way.[21]

Let's first take a look at the related passage in *The Doctrine of the Mean.*

The Way (Dao) may not be forgotten for an instant. If it could be, it would not be the Way. On this account, the superior man does not wait until he sees worrying things in order to be cautious, nor until he hears threatening things in order to be apprehensive.

There is nothing more visible than what is secret, and nothing more manifest than what is minute. Therefore the superior man is watchful over himself when he is alone.[22]

The Way is the basic operational principle of the universe, nature, and society. Therefore everyone is influenced by it. The Way is not only the order of nature but also of moral norms. Although it is not a personal God who assigns reward and punishment, its accurate and stern order evokes respect and fear. No matter how hard one tries to avoid the Way, it is still there. No matter how skillfully one hides one's true self, the "eyes and ears" of the Way will always make note of who one is.

Regarding the passage from *The Doctrine of the Mean* excerpted earlier, Rao Lu wrote that "the visible and the revealed all partake of the Way,"[23] and Yulgok questioned this interpretation. Rao Lu probably meant that the Way reveals itself no matter how assiduously one tries to conceal it. But Yulgok made the objection that dark places and subtle things have both good sides and bad aspects and that it is wrong to say that all of them constitute the Way. Toegye agreed with Yulgok's view. What this passage conveyed was that one should watch oneself when one is alone and be careful not to act contrary to the dictates of the Way, and Toegye thought Yulgok's view did not run counter to his emphasis on self-cultivation and self-discipline. Their discussion about the passage does not end there, as we can see here:

In your letter, you referred to Rao Lu's argument that *The Great Learning* did not mention "being watchful and fearful (戒慎恐懼)." You made the same mistake here as you did when you argued that the phrase "be judicious and steadfast, and sincerely strive for the golden mean" did not include the admonition to cultivate oneself when one's mind is tranquil. *The Great Learning* did not discuss "being watchful and fearful." Zhu Xi interpreted the meaning of "to rectify" (正) in *The Great Learning* based simply on the word "to examine" (察) in an annotation to the chapter on *jeongsim / zheng-xin* (正心, the rectification of the mind).[24] And then he extracted the words "*jon / cun* (存, to retain)" and "*gyeong / jing* (敬, to be reverentially mindful)" from an annotation to the phrase "visible but cannot be seen (視不見)" and mentioned in a sub-annotation that a problem arises when one fails to sustain one's mind.[25] Zhu Xi suggested the solution for this problem as explained above, even though he didn't directly discuss "being watchful and fearful." Yun-feng Hu-shi (雲峯胡氏)[26] also means the same thing in saying, "Think first, act later (前念後事)." No one has argued that "being watchful and fearful" is discussed in the chapter on the rectification of the mind. In your letter, however, you argued that this chapter is about "being watchful and fearful," which is not correct. 〖In your letter, you asked me, "How can it be possible to clarify luminous virtue (明德) without making efforts to be watchful and fearful?" You are right to recognize the difficulty. This is why Zhu Xi said, "*The Elementary Learning* (小學) explains in detail how people used to cultivate their nature, and *The Great Learning* (大學) made *gyeongmul chiji* (格物致知, the extension of knowledge through the investigation of things) the priority," and he supplemented the self-cultivation discussed in *The Elementary Learning* with the phrase "*gyeong* (敬, reverent mindfulness)." This is how to cultivate oneself. Although *The Great Learning* does not directly mention the phrase "being watchful and fearful," it suggests the need to "always reflect on oneself (顧諟)"[27] and to "always be reverent (敬止)."[28] These two phrases imply "being watchful and fearful." And although "being stable (定)" and "being tranquil (靜)" are the result of "knowing where to stop (知止)," you should understand that they are also related to cultivating oneself by attending to one's studies when one's mind is tranquil. One should not argue that something was said even though it was not said.][29]

Yulgok raised another question about Rao Lu's comment on this passage in *The Doctrine of the Mean*. Rao Lu wrote that "*The Great Learning* discussed 'watching oneself carefully when alone' but not 'being watchful and fearful,'"[30] but Yulgok wondered how it was possible to clarify luminous virtue without being watchful and fearful. He argued that the chapter on the rectification of the mind in *The Great Learning* is about "being watchful and fearful." Toegye replied that Rao Lu said that what was not addressed in *The Great Learning* was not in the book and that Yulgok should not falsely argue it was already addressed in *The Great Learning*.

But Toegye acknowledged that the argument of *The Great Learning* was not unrelated to the issue of "being watchful and fearful," and to illustrate this point he drew on examples in the writings of Zhu Xi and Yun-feng. Toegye paid attention to the words and phrases "retaining (存)," "reverent mindfulness (敬)," and "a problem arises when one fails to sustain one's mind." As Zhu Xi said, "*The Elementary Learning* explains in detail how people used to cultivate their nature, and *The Great Learning* made *gyeongmul chiji* the priority." Nevertheless, this does not obviate the need for one to be "watchful and fearful" and to cultivate oneself when one's mind is tranquil.

In comparison to Yulgok, in fact, it was Toegye who placed more emphasis on the need to cultivate oneself before one's mind is stimulated by external things or phenomena or to do so when one's mind is tranquil. Yulgok argued that such self-cultivation must be, and is, mentioned in *The Great Learning*, but Toegye refuted him, saying that such method of self-cultivation was implied in the words of *The Great Learning* according to explanation of scholars like Zhu Xi and Yun-feng. Ultimately, Yulgok's debate with Toegye as to the difference and relationship between self-cultivation when one's mind is tranquil and when one's mind is stimulated, the different conscious and intentional levels of self-discipline, such as "being watchful and fearful," and how each level operates served as the foundation for his theory of self-discipline. In later years, Yulgok put greater emphasis on conscious self-cultivation and self-discipline in a stimulated rather than in a tranquil state of mind. But it seems that, at the moment when he sent this letter to Toegye, Yulgok had not fully determined his position on this matter.

ON THE DIFFERENCE BETWEEN A
SAGE AND A WISE MAN

In his letter to Toegye twelve years earlier, Yulgok had asked him whether it was possible for anyone to become as wise as Yan Hui (顏回) if they made great efforts. In an annotation to the first chapter of *The Great Learning*, Zhu Xi wrote that "the phrase that 'Only with peace of mind do we produce the capacity to think (安而後能慮)' applied only to Yan Zi (Yan Hui)." And Yulgok asked Toegye if it was impossible to have that capacity unless you were as wise as Yan Zi, who was one of the disciples of Confucius. Toegye's answer was that "generally speaking, even those whose level of wisdom is unexceptional can make efforts to reach that goal. But, in reality, it is unattainable unless you are as sagacious as the great wise men (大賢)."

Yulgok put a similar question to Toegye twelve years later. Again, he inquired about the passage that says it is hard even for Yan Zi (顏子) and Zeng Zi (曾子) to become as wise as Confucius. Toegye answered as follows:

> In the section of *Questions and Answers on The Doctrine of the Mean* (中庸或問) that addresses the first chapter of *The Doctrine of the Mean*, Chen-shi (陳氏)[31] said, "Although only sages (聖人) and men-gods (神人) can achieve *junghwa / zhong he* (中和, balance and harmony) and the state where 'Heaven and Earth are in their proper positions, and all things are nourished and flourish (位育),' those who set their hearts on learning also are able to achieve or to approach this state through learning if they make great efforts."[32] You commented on this passage in your letter. I believe that once one achieves "balance and harmony," one can certainly achieve the state in which "Heaven and Earth are in their proper positions, and all things are nourished and flourish." However, the possibility of approaching this state refers to the learning and cultivation of wise men. Although "one can reach the level of a sage if one makes great achievements,"[33] when you take into account the ability to make extraordinary changes and to accomplish profound and mysterious things, Confucius's ability "to make people turn to him by bringing peace to them and to prompt them to work in harmony by motivating them"[34] was not easily attainable by Yan Zi or Zeng Zi.[35]

This passage is related to an annotation to the statement "When balance and harmony is actualized, Heaven and Earth are in their proper positions, and all things are nourished and flourish (致中和, 天地位焉, 萬物育焉)" in the first chapter of *The Doctrine of the Mean*. According to Zhu Xi, "balance and harmony" refers to the capacity to fully manifest one's original moral nature in the form of moral feelings and to activate the original moral nature throughout the world. The original moral nature is consistent with the principles and norms of the universe and of nature, so if one is able to fully realize "balance and harmony," Heaven and Earth, which work in accordance with the principles and norms of the universe and of nature, will be in their proper positions and all things will be nourished. If one can realize one's moral nature and impact directly on the workings of Heaven and Earth and the nourishing of all things, it is supportable to say that one will have achieved the spiritual level of a sage. But this is the level of Confucius, a level that was not readily attainable by Yan Zi or Zeng Zi. Such an explanation distinguishes the spiritual level of Confucius from that of Yan Zi and Zeng Zi. Confucius was a sage, whereas Yan Zi and Zeng Zi were wise men. Yulgok, who firmly believed that anyone could become a sage, seemed unsatisfied by Toegye's answer.

Confucius is the most revered sage in Confucianism. He once said, "In my seventieth year, my heart knew what was right for me, and I never went to extremes."[36] This is the ultimate level of perfection that humans can possibly reach, and they should strive to do so. This is the level at which Heaven and the human are united as one (天人合一). However, Confucius was not born with a great ability to achieve that level. He was born to a poor family and made great efforts to elevate himself spiritually and intellectually throughout his life. When he turned seventy, he finally achieved that level. Confucius was proud of being a person "who was not born with knowledge, but, with a deep affinity for the past, I have been eager to seek out its wisdom,"[37] and he expressed this pride by saying "I learned here and reached up there."[38]

The idea that there are no born sages and that anyone can become one if they make tremendous efforts as Confucius did is very important in Confucianism. In Confucius's era, people were treated according to their social status. However, Confucius did not care about the status of his disciples, and his attitude was reflected in the Confucian focus on the prerequisites of becoming a sage.

Of course, Confucianism has other criteria for determining those who have the potential to become sages. Confucius said, "There are the wise of the highest class, and the stupid of the lowest class, who cannot be changed."[39] According to him, there are those who are born with knowledge and those who gain knowledge through learning, but there are also those who are faced with challenges and do not learn wisdom.[40] This means that it is impossible for those who have faced challenges and have not learned wisdom as a result to become sages. However, in essence, it is a tenet of Confucianism that if one gains theoretical knowledge or if one produces great achievements by putting into practice one's knowledge, the outcome is the same, no matter

how one obtains knowledge.[41] Yulgok's question was based on this idea, and
Toegye acknowledged the fact that "one can reach the level of a sage if one
makes great achievements."

However, Confucius was the last person in Chinese history who became a
sage on the strength of his own efforts. The lineage of sages who based their
thinking on adherence to Confucian ideals, which started with ancient Chinese kings such as Yao, Shun, Yu, Tang, Wen, We, and the Duke of Zhou,
finally ended with Confucius. They had been considered by many to be paragons in terms of their capacity to check or moderate the power of the political
authorities and had been respected by later kings as exemplary figures. As a
result, people began to see them as representing ideals that were far removed
from practical reality.[42] Toegye acknowledged that, in general, anyone could
become a sage if they dedicated themselves to this quest, but at the same
time he believed that sages (including Yao, Shun, and Confucius), wise men
(such as Yan Zi and Zeng Zi), and later Confucian scholars (like Toegye
himself) could not be considered in the same light. Given that Confucianism
emphasized the need to respect and emulate the sages and required Confucian scholars and kings to make ceaseless efforts to become sages, Toegye's
perspective was defensible.

The point here is that Yulgok, who twelve years earlier had asked Toegye
whether it was impossible for ordinary people to become sages like Yan Zi,
was in his second letter asking him whether it was impossible for Yan Zi and
Zeng Zi to become as wise as Confucius. Toeyge's answer was that it was
technically impossible, but Yulgok was not satisfied with this. So in his third
letter to Toegye, he asked a similar question again:

【Question】 In the section of *Questions and Answers on The Doctrine of the
Mean* that addresses the first chapter of *The Doctrine of the Mean*, Chen-shi
said, "One who becomes wise through learning is nearly able to reach the state
where Heaven and Earth are in their proper positions, and all things are nourished and flourish." But I was not fully convinced by his argument and thought
that whether one was born wise or learned wisdom, once one produced great
achievements, the outcome would be the same. In your reply, you wrote, "Confucius's ability to 'make people turn to him by bringing peace to them and to
prompt them to work in harmony by motivating them' was not easily attainable
by Yan Zi or Zeng Zi." You are absolutely right about that. However, I think
those who are born with knowledge (生而知之) and those who gain knowledge
as a result of learning (學而知之), despite their differences in attributes, display
no differences once they reach the state of becoming great through self-transfor-
mation (大而化之).[43] Even though Yan Zi "became wise through learning," he
could not quite attain the status of a sage. If he had lived a few years longer and
had the chance to transform himself, he would have become as wise as Confucius, who was able to "make people turn to him by bringing peace to them and

to prompt them to work in harmony by motivating them." If what Chen-shi said was right, those who become wise as a result of learning would never be able to reach the state where Heaven and Earth are in their proper positions and all things are nourished. If that is the case, scholars would never be able to become sages no matter how mightily they strove. You also said in your letter that this state is "not easily attainable," which is true. But it would be wrong to say that this state is "never attainable." This is the reason why I am not fully convinced by Chen-shi's argument.[44]

It seems that Yulgok half-conceded the point. He acknowledged that, as Toegye said, becoming as wise as Confucius was "not easily attainable." But he asked Toegye whether it was right to say that this outcome was "never attainable." In his third letter to Yulgok, possibly believing that this question had already been answered, Toegye passed over this query and moved on to the next one. But the answer Yulgok wanted to hear from Toegye, by repeatedly asking similar questions in three letters, was that "anyone can become a sage." Yulgok believed that establishing the goal of "becoming a sage" through learning is the starting point of learning and cultivation. This conception is also included in *The Secret to Dispelling Ignorance* (擊蒙要訣), a textbook for young beginners, and *The Essentials of Sage Learning* (聖學輯要), a textbook for kings, both of which were written by Yulgok.

Confucius said that people "by their nature are similar, but through their habits they are very distinct."[45] But Toegye believed that, even though people are similar in nature, they are different in the degree to which they can achieve their purposes. Meanwhile, Yulgok argued that anyone can become a sage like Confucius if they make tremendous efforts. According to Yulgok, as sages who realize balance and harmony can facilitate Heaven and Earth in finding their proper positions and hence make all things nourished, ordinary people can realize an ideal society through their own efforts.

DIFFERENT PERSPECTIVES: ASSIMILATION OR DIFFERENTIATION

Yulgok asked Toegye about the relationship between "balance and harmony (中和)" and "the mean (中庸)" addressed in *The Doctrine of the Mean*. He did not agree with the way Rao Lu (饒魯) distinguished between them. But Toegye criticized Yulgok for having the unfortunate tendency of too easily associating disparate things with each other or forcibly coalescing them instead of distinguishing between them (喜合惡離之病). *The Doctrine of the Mean* is concerned with "balance and harmony" and "the mean," and Toegye and Yulgok were in agreement about what the meanings and implications of these two terms were. However, the two scholars saw the relationship between them from different perspectives, which reflected their fundamental philosophical divergence. Yulgok was still not convinced by Toegye's answer. Their argument on this matter continued in their third exchange of letters, as seen in the following excerpt from Toegye's reply to Yulgok's second letter:

> In your letter about Rao Lu's explanation of the second chapter (of *The Doctrine of the Mean*)[46], you said "'balance and harmony' and 'the mean' cannot be differentiated in terms of the inside and the outside." In essence, they are not different. But if we discuss how each of these phrases is used in context, they are certainly different from one another. For example, You Zuo (游酢)[47] said that the term "balance and harmony" is used in the context of human nature and emotions, which is the inside, and that the term "the mean" is employed in discussion of virtuous conduct (德行), which is the outside. When we explain the two terms in the context of "human nature and emotions" and "virtues and behavior," it is impossible to say that "balance and harmony" is concerned with the outside. 【Toegye's supplementary explanation: Virtue (德), which is the result of practicing the Way, is concerned with both the inside and the outside. However, behavior (行) amounts to elements of one's daily activities, which are no doubt related to the outside.】
>
> Rao Lu supplemented You Zuo's explanation, and I have not yet seen error in Rao Lu's account. If we assume that you are right, then we can't avoid discerning your unfortunate tendency of unnecessarily associating things with each other and your antipathy toward distinguishing between them. As a result, it becomes difficult to gain a correct understanding of what Zi-si (子思) wanted to say by using different terms depending on context. 【Toegye's supplementary explanation: The term "the mean" does not apply to the first chapter and the term "balance and harmony" does not apply to the second and subsequent chapters.】[48]

In short, Yulgok raised an issue about Rao Lu's explanation, which was based on what You Zuo had said, that "balance and harmony" was related to the inside or "human nature and emotions" and that "the mean" was related to the outside or "virtuous conduct." And Toegye supported You Zuo's position.

Here is the explanation of "balance and harmony" and "the mean" described in the first and second chapters of *The Doctrine of the Mean*:

> The state before the feelings of pleasure, anger, sorrow, and joy (喜怒哀樂) are aroused is called "balance or equilibrium (中)." The state in which these feelings are aroused and each and all attain due measure and degree is called "harmony (和)." Balance or equilibrium is the great foundation of the world, and harmony its universal way. When balance/equilibrium and harmony are

realized to the highest degree, Heaven and Earth will attain their proper order and all things will be nourished and flourish.

Confucius says that a virtuous man actualizes the mean, while a mediocre man acts contrary to its dictates. [Zhu Xi's annotation: "The mean" is a term meaning neither on one side nor the other and neither to overshoot nor to fall short. In other words, it is Heaven's will, which must be obeyed, and is both precise and mysterious to the highest degree. Only a virtuous man is able to put it into practice; a mediocre man acts contrary to it.] A virtuous man actualizes the mean because he always embodies it; a mediocre man's nonactualization is due to his heedlessness.[49]

"Balance and harmony" designates the state of being at one with what is right as a result of the manifestation of moral feelings. Moral feelings arise not from personal feelings but from the original moral nature, which is consistent with the principles of the universe and nature. In other words, when the state of "balance and harmony" is realized, Heaven and Earth are in their proper positions and all things are nourished. The manifestation of moral feelings is ultimately indistinguishable from feeling, thinking, and acting in accordance with the principles of the universe and nature or of "uniting Heaven and the human." If one lives a life of feeling, thinking, and acting in accordance with the principles of the universe and nature, one can become a proactive participant of the workings of the universe and nature. *The Doctrine of the Mean* includes the phrase "the feelings of pleasure, anger, sorrow, and joy" because, at the time when this book was written, there was no conceptual distinction between human nature and emotions. However, Rao Lu, who had learned the fundamental tenets of Neo-Confucianism, recognized that the phrase encompasses both the original moral nature and moral feelings, and he used the term "human nature and emotions" in his explanation.

In addition, "the mean" designates the putting into practice of "balance and harmony." Those who actualize "the mean" are virtuous men, and those who act contrary to it are mediocre men. Zhu Xi explained that "the mean" was "a term meaning neither on one side nor the other, and neither to overshoot nor to fall short. In other words, it is Heaven's will, which must be obeyed, and is both precise and mysterious to the highest degree." Therefore, in some contexts, "the mean" includes the meaning of "balance and harmony."

Logically speaking, there is little difference between "the mean" and "balance and harmony." But *The Doctrine of the Mean* explained that "balance or equilibrium" was a state "before the feelings of pleasure, anger, sorrow, and joy are aroused" and that "harmony" was a state "when these feelings are aroused and each and all attain due measure and degree." It also explained "the mean" using the concepts of a virtuous and a mediocre man. In this context, it is plausible to differentiate between "human nature and emotions" and

"virtuous conduct" or between the inside and the outside. But Yulgok repeatedly raised concerns about the activity of differentiating between the terms
and Toegye seemed increasingly irritated at his questions. He chided Yulgok
for having an unfortunate tendency of unnecessarily associating things with
each other and of failing to distinguish between them, and he tried to bring
this argument to a close, explaining that the first chapter of *The Doctrine of
the Mean* didn't discuss "the mean" and that subsequent chapters didn't mention "balance and harmony."

However, Yulgok didn't cease taking issue with Toegye's perspective in
his third letter to him.

【**Question**】 Even though I have learned from you about the reasons why Rao
Lu considered "balance and harmony" to be the inside and "the mean" to be
the outside, my doubts persist. Rao Lu's theory that, in general, "human nature
and emotions" are related to "balance and harmony" and "virtuous conduct" is
related to "the mean"[50] is correct and reasonable. However, the phrase "balance
and harmony existing in perfection (致中和)" means that "human nature and
emotions" include "virtuous conduct," and the fact that the concept of "'balance'
in 'the mean' is actually the same as 'balance and harmony'"[51] means that "virtuous conduct" is the same as "human nature and emotions." This explanation
runs counter to Rao Lu's complicated theory that differentiated "balance and
harmony existing in perfection" and "practicing the mean" as learning and cultivation on the inside and learning and cultivation on the outside, respectively.
"The great root (大本)" and "the universal way (達道)"[52] are "human nature and
emotions," whereas "establishing the great root" and "practicing the universal
way" are "virtuous conduct." Rao Lu would be right if "establishing the great
root" is learning and cultivation on the inside and "practicing the universal way"
is learning and cultivation on the outside. But if we assume that "balance and
harmony existing in perfection" is learning and cultivation on the inside, then
both "establishing the great root" and "practicing the universal way" must constitute learning and cultivation on the inside. They should be the only methods
of learning and cultivation designed for "practicing the mean." If we pursue
"the mean" outside of "the great root" and "the universal way," there will arise
a problem worse than piling one bed on another. Zi-si (子思) clearly said that
"when 'balance and harmony' is actualized, Heaven and Earth are in their proper
positions, and all things are nourished." How is it possible to allow Heaven and
Earth to attain their proper order and all things to be nourished without learning
and cultivation on the outside? Thus, I still believe that Rao's theory is wrong.
So, once again, I would like to ask your opinion on this subject.[53]

Yulgok extended the issue of the relationship between "balance and harmony"
and "the mean" to the link between the concepts of "balance and harmony existing in perfection" and of "practicing the mean." According to him, although it
may be reasonable to consider "balance and harmony" as "human nature and

emotions" and "the mean" as "virtuous conduct," the problem in Rao Lu's theory was that he considered "balance and harmony existing in perfection" as "human nature and emotions" and "practicing the mean" as "virtuous conduct." "Balance and harmony existing in perfection" means realizing "the mean" to the highest degree, and thus includes practicing "balance and harmony." Yulgok asked Toegye to give him his teaching on this subject once again.

Toegye replied again, in a different tone this time, as follows:

> You have reminded me of Rao Lu's theory, which considered "balance and harmony" as the inside and "the mean" as the outside. It seems to me that you are overly harsh on him. Rao Lu never said that "this is learning and cultivation on the inside; that is learning and cultivation on the outside." He simply explained that "this is a way to cultivate both the inside and the outside."[54] This means that "practicing the mean" is a way to "encourage balance and harmony exist in perfection"; that "encouraging balance and harmony exist in perfection" is a way to "practice the mean"; and that finally the two are thus mutually beneficial.
>
> If we differentiate between learning and cultivation on the inside and on the outside and engage in only one of the two, it is clear that they are not mutually beneficial. In your letter, you wrote that "'balance and harmony existing in perfection' means that 'human nature and emotions' include 'virtuous conduct,' and the fact that the concept of 'balance' in 'the mean' is actually the same as 'balance and harmony' means that 'virtuous conduct' is the same as 'human nature and emotions.'" You used the expressions "include" and "is the same as" here. Doesn't that mean that they are mutually beneficial? In my view, your theory is not so different from Rao Lu's, but you are being especially hard on Rao Lu. Wouldn't you agree?[55]

Toegye pointed out that Yulgok's argument was very similar to Rao Lu's. According to Yulgok, Rao Lu already understood that "balance and harmony" and "the mean," "balance and harmony existing in perfection" and "practicing the mean," the inside and the outside, and "human nature and emotions" and "virtuous conduct" mutually include each other. In fact, although Rao Lu differentiated between the terms in each pair, he added that "the two ('balance and harmony existing in perfection' and 'practicing the mean') are ways to complementarily cultivate the inside and the outside (二者內外交相養之道也)."

Obviously, Toegye and Yulgok had different perspectives on Rao Lu's theory. It seems that Yulgok, who had been consistently critical of Rao Lu, believed that he differentiated between "balance and harmony" and "the mean" in terms of the inside and the outside, and in terms of "human nature and emotions" and "virtuous conduct," because Rao Lu did not understand the mutually inclusive relationship between the two as well as he did. However, Toegye emphasized that Rao Lu fully understood their relationship and he simply differentiated between them for the sake of convenience and that Yulgok should not belittle Rao Lu's work. Yulgok based his criticism on the logical implications of the sequence of Rao Lu's text, whereas Toegye tried to understand the broader context of Rao Lu's theory. This difference in their critical stances is consistent with how they defined the relationship between the four beginnings and the seven feelings.

THE WAY AND HUMAN BEINGS

Confucius said: "The reason why the Way is not practiced is clear to me: it is because men of wisdom tend to overshoot it, while those of lesser intelligence fail to reach the bar. The reason why the Way is not fully understood is also clear to me: it is because men of worth tend to overshoot it, while those of imperfect character fail to reach the bar."[56]

Yulgok asked Toegye about this passage, contained in the fourth chapter of *The Doctrine of the Mean*. Rao Lu said that "the practice referred to in the phrase 'is not practiced' in this passage does not mean that the agent is human."[57] But Yulgok believed that both practicing and fully understanding the Way can be engaged in only by humans. And Toegye acknowledged that, basically, it is humans who can practice and fully understand the Way, but he said that it is also possible to interpret the passage as implying that the Way is the agent. Here is an excerpt from Toegye's reply:

With regard to chapter 4 of *The Doctrine of the Mean*, Rao Lu wrote, "Practice does not mean that the agent is human . . . ," and you wrote in your letter that "practicing and fully understanding the Way can be engaged in only by humans." Indeed, when humans don't practice the Way, the Way can't be practiced, and when humans don't fully understand the Way, the Way can't be fully understood. However, Rao Lu's phrase "the Way is not practiced" doesn't necessarily mean that humans don't practice the Way. And "the Way is not fully understood" doesn't necessarily mean that humans don't fully understand the Way. Therefore Rao Lu was not wrong about this issue.[58]

There are many points of contention between Toegye's thought and Yulgok's, and their perspectives on the Way and human beings display the most striking differences. Simply put, Toegye focused on the role of the Way, whereas Yulgok focused on the role of humans. Yet there is one aspect that is especially noteworthy when comparing Toegye's view with that of Yulgok, namely that both of their strands of thought are grounded in Neo-Confucianism (in particular, the teachings of Zhu Xi). At the time, Neo-Confucianism was considered one of the most progressive philosophies in the Chinese cultural sphere. Based on Neo-Confucianism, Toegye and Yulgok explored ways to enhance humanity and improve society. And what we know of their philosophies constitutes the achievements they produced through these efforts. Toegye and Yulgok had different philosophies, practical proposals, and political views based on the reality they faced, the issues that most concerned them, and their personal proclivities. However, they shared common ground that transcended these differences.

Although Neo-Confucianism was a critical part of their common ground, it was simply a tool for them to further their thinking. It is natural that they used the most advanced theoretical and empirical tools available at the time in order to unearth the most effective solutions for the issues that concerned them. Wonhyo (元曉), Jinul (知訥), Jeong Yak-yong (丁若鏞), and other respected Korean philosophers did the same thing, using the most promising methods to diagnose current problems and to devise contemporary philosophical alternatives, and these alternatives became important elements of Korean philosophical history. Toegye and Yulgok's efforts and achievements were widely acknowledged at the time in Joseon and had a significant influence on Korea for a long period of time.

They essentially agreed on the premise of Neo-Confucianism that there exist principles and norms that govern the universe and nature and that the ideal life is one that is in accord with these principles and norms. And they devoted their lives to theoretically exploring ways of realizing a society and state in which people could live the ideal life and to putting Neo-Confucian principles and norms into practice in the political world. The question raised by Yulgok in his letter to Toegye was concerned with how to interpret and explain humanity's role in putting into practice the principles and norms that govern the universe and nature, which together constitute the Way.

At first glance, they had different understandings of the same phenomena or facts. These differences depended on whether they focused more on "being capable (能)" or on "what can be done (所能)."[59] If one focuses on "being capable," the extent to which the Way is practiced or fully understood is dependent on the degree to which humans attempt to do so. In other words, whether or not the Way is practiced and fully understood depends on what humans do. This was the position taken by Yulgok. As Confucius said, "It is people who can broaden the Way, not the Way that broadens people."[60]

However, even if humans make efforts to do so, ultimately, according to the alternative interpretation, it is the Way that should be practiced and fully understood. And humans do not determine whether this occurs or not. This method of interpretation and Rao Lu's annotations, which were criticized by Yulgok, are based on the concept of "what can be done," defined by Zhu Xi.

> Being practiced does not mean that people practice the Way but that the Way itself penetrates Heaven and Earth; being fully understood does not mean that people fully understand the Way but that the Way itself illuminates Heaven and Earth.[61]

Adherents of Yulgok's philosophy may pose the question of whether it is not humans that effectively practice and fully understand the Way. However, focusing on the Way, which is being practiced and fully understood, can have a greater impact than focusing on people, who practice and fully understand the Way.

During his debate on the four beginnings and the seven feelings, Toegye said that *li* (理) was what made the four beginnings different from the seven feelings. The four beginnings are purely good because *li* is purely good. When you see a little child crawling toward a well, you naturally feel you want to protect the child. This is an instinctive feeling unwittingly derived from the pure goodness of moral feelings, and *gi* or human will plays a secondary, or even negligible, role. The pure goodness of moral feelings overwhelms *gi* or human will. By focusing on the fundamental power of good feelings and understanding the metaphysical driving force of this power, Toegye recognized the necessity of living a moral life and advocated the need to build a society and state in which people could live morally. He emphasized that "the Way" and *li* are not simply principles and norms that can be actualized by means of the physical role of *gi* but collectively the primary agents that permeate Heaven and Earth.

Yulgok, on the contrary, interpreted the structures and circulations of the universe, those of nature, and those of society as working in cooperation between *li* and *gi*, which are neither inseparable nor intermingled with each other. He also believed that *li* is inherently good and complete and that human agency in this context cannot engage in the functioning of *li* itself. For Toegye, this view entailed the risk of regarding *li* as a dead thing. For his part, Yulgok believed that Toegye's view risked undermining the absolute goodness and completeness of *li*. Yulgok looked for ways to allow *li* to fully realize its goodness and completeness by purifying changeable *gi*, and he focused on the human will that can transform *gi*. The differences in Toegye and Yulgok's perspectives on the role of humans and that of the Way were already clear at the time when they exchanged their letters. And their differences became even more obvious when they discussed solutions to political problems in terms of their role as members of the intelligentsia and as bureaucrats within the political system.

NOTES

1. Yi Hwang, "Dap Yi Sukheon munmok" 答李叔獻問目 (Response to Yi Sukheon), in *Toegye jip*, 29:375d–376a.
2. Rao shi (饒氏) is Rao Lu (饒魯, ? –?), a student of Zhu Xi's son-in-law and leading disciple, Huang Gan (黃幹). His pen name was Shuang Feng (雙峯).

3. Annotations to "Du Zhong Yong fa (How to Read *The Doctrine of the Mean*)," in *Zhong Yong* (The Doctrine of the Mean). "雙峰饒氏曰, 學是說學, 中庸是說道理, 會得大學透徹, 則學不差, 理會得中庸透徹, 則道不差."

4. Lü Ziyue (呂子約) is Lü Zujian (呂祖儉, ? –1196), a civil servant of the Southern Song Dynasty.

5. Yi Hwang, "Response to Yi Sukheon," in *Toegye jip*, 29:376a–b.

6. Annotations to "Du Zhong Yong fa," in *Zhong Yong*. "西山眞氏曰, 中庸, 始言天命之性, 終言無聲無臭, 宜若高妙矣. 然, 曰戒愼, 曰恐懼, 曰謹獨, 曰篤恭, 則皆示人以用力之方. 蓋必戒懼謹獨而後, 能全天性之善, 必篤恭而後, 能造無聲無臭之境, 未嘗使人馳心窈冥而不踐其實也."

7. Yi Hwang, "Toegye dap Gobong sadan chiljeong bun ligi byeon" 退溪答高峯四端七情分理氣辯 (Response to Gobong's Questions Regarding the Four Beginnings and the Seven Feelings), in *Gobong jeonjip*, Vol. 1, the right side of page 5 in part 1.

8. "Counsels of the Great Yu (大禹謨)," in *Shu Jing* (書經, *The Book of Documents*).

9. Ibid.

10. Jeong Yak-yong, "Maessi seo pyeong" 梅氏書平 (An Evaluation of Mei Ze's *Shu Jing*), in Jeongbon Yeoyudang jeonseo 定本 與猶堂全書 (The Standard Edition of the Collected Works of *Yeoyudang*) 13 (Seoul: Dasan Cultural Foundation, 2012), 353–55.

11. Wu-zhai Cheng-shi (勿齋程氏) is Cheng Ruo-yong (程若庸, ? –?), a scholar of the Song Dynasty.

12. Yi Hwang, "Response to Yi Sukheon," in *Toegye jip*, 29:376b–c.

13. "Zhong Yong zhang-ju xu" 中庸章句序 (Preface to *The Doctrine of the Mean in Chapters and Verses*)," in *Zhong Yong*. "勿齋程氏曰, 人生而靜, 氣未用事, 未有人與道之分, 但謂之心而已, 感物而動, 始有人心道心之分焉, 精一執中, 皆是動時工夫."

14. For more details on how Toegye emphasized cultivating oneself "when one's mind is yet to be stimulated," see Kim Hyoungchan, "The Theory and Practice of Sage Politics: The Political Philosophies and Neo-Confucian Bases of Yi Hwang and Yi I," *Acta Koreana* 17, no. 1 (2014): 262–70.

15. Details of Yulgok's discourse on the human mind and the moral mind are discussed in chapter 7.

16. Ge-an Zhao-shi (格菴趙氏) is Zhao Shun-sun (趙順孫, 1215–1277), a civil servant of the Song Dynasty.

17. Yi Hwang, "Response to Yi Sukheon," in *Toegye jip*, 29:376c–d.

18. "Zhong Yong zhang-ju xu," in *Zhong Yong*. "格庵趙氏曰, 知是識其所當然, 覺是悟其所以然."

19. According to Lee Gi-yong, perception includes "sensuous cognition in terms of feeling, rational or moral cognition, and awareness of the will to act upon what is recognized." See Lee Gi-yong, "Yulgok Yi I-ui Insim dosim ron yeon-gu" (A Study on the Theory of Human Mind and Moral Mind in the Philosophy of Yulgok Yi I) (PhD diss., Yonsei University, 1995).

20. Zhu Xi, Chapter 1, in *Zhong Yong zhanng-ju ji-zhu* 中庸章句集注 (Collected Commentaries on *The Doctrine of the Mean in Chapters and Verses*).

21. Yi Hwang, "Response to Yi Sukheon," in *Toegye jip*, 29:376d.

22. Chapter 1, in *Zhong Yong*. "道也者, 不可須臾離也, 可離非道也. 是故君子戒慎乎其所不睹, 恐懼乎其所不聞. 莫見乎隱, 莫顯乎微, 故君子慎其獨也."

23. Zhu Xi, Chapter 1, in *Zhong Yong zhanng-ju ji-zhu*. "雙峯饒氏曰 . . . 見與顯, 皆是此道."

24. Zhu Xi, Chapter 7, in *Da Xue zhang-ju ji-zhu* 大學章句集註 (Collected Commentaries on *The Great Learning in Chapters and Verses*).

25. Ibid.

26. Yun-feng Hu-shi (雲峯胡氏) is Hu Bingwen (胡炳文, 1250–1333?), a scholar of the Yuan Dynasty.

27. "Zhuan 1" 傳1章, in *Da Xue* 大學 (The Great Learning). "大甲曰 顧諟天之明命."

28. "Zhuan 3" 傳3章, in *Da Xue*. "詩云 穆穆文王, 於緝熙敬止."

29. Yi Hwang, "Response to Yi Sukheon," in *Toegye jip*, 29:377a–b.

30. Zhu Xi, Chapter 1, in *Zhong Yong zhang-ju ji-zhu*. "雙峯饒氏曰 . . . . 大學只言慎獨, 不言戒懼."

31. Chen-shi (陳氏) is Chen Li (陳櫟, 1252–1334), a scholar of the Yuan Dynasty.

32. Annotation to "或問喜怒哀樂之未發謂之中 . . . ," in *Zhong Yong huo-wen* 中庸或問 (Questions and Answers on The Doctrine of the Mean). "新安陳氏曰 由位育推其本於致中和, 故曰萬化之本原. 自致中和極其功於位育, 故曰一心之妙用. 究極之, 惟大聖人能與於此, 乃聖神之能事, 降聖人一等而論之, 由教而入者, 果能盡致中和之工夫, 則其學問之極功, 亦可庶幾乎此也."

33. Chapter 20, in *Zhong Yong zhang-ju*. "或生而知之, 或學而知之, 或困而知之, 及其知之一也. 或安而行之, 或利而行之, 或勉强而行之, 及其成功一也."

34. Confucius, "Book 19," in *The Analects*. "夫子之得邦家者, 所謂立之斯立, 道之斯行, 綏之斯來, 動之斯和. 其生也榮, 其死也哀, 如之何其可及也."

35. Yi Hwang, "Response to Yi Sukheon," in *Toegye jip*, 029:377c–d.

36. Confucius, "Book 2," in *The Analects*. "七十而從心所欲不踰矩."

37. Ibid., "Book 7." "子曰 我非生而知之者, 好古, 敏以求之者也."

38. Ibid., "Book 14." "下學而上達."

39. Ibid., "Book 17." "子曰 唯上知與下愚不移."

40. Ibid., "Book 16." "孔子曰 生而知之者, 上也; 學而知之者, 次也; 困而學之, 又其次也; 困而不學, 民斯爲下矣."

41. Chapter 20, in *Zhong Yong zhang-ju*. "或生而知之, 或學而知之, 或困而知之, 及其知之一也. 或安而行之, 或利而行之, 或勉强而行之, 及其成功一也."

42. For more details on how Confucius was idolized or idealized, see Mark Edward Lewis, *Writing and Authority in Early China* (Albany: State University of New York Press, 1999), 218–40.

43. Mencius, "Jin-xin II" 盡心下, in *Mencius*. "可欲之謂善, 有諸己之謂信, 充實之謂美, 充實而有光輝之謂大, 大而化之之謂聖, 聖而不可知之之謂神."

44. Yi I, "Sang Toegye seonsaeng munmok" 上退溪先生問目 (Inquiries Presented to Master Toegye), in *Yulgok jeonseo*, 44:182a–b. This is the first question in Yulgok's third list of questions to Toegye and is related to questions in his second list.

45. Confucius, "Book 17," in *The Analects*. "子曰 性相近也, 習相遠也."

46. Chapter 2, in *Zhong Yong zhang-ju ji-zhu*. "雙峯饒氏曰 . . . 中和以性情言, 人心本然純粹之德也; 中庸以事理言, 天下當然之則, 不可過, 亦不可不及者也. 二者雖同此中理, 而所指各異. 故致中和者, 則欲其戒懼愼獨, 以涵養乎性情, 踐中庸者, 則欲其擇善固執, 以求合乎事理. 二者內外交相養之道也."

47. You Zhu (游酢, 1053–1123) was a civil servant of the Song Dynasty and is considered one of the four disciples of Cheng Ming-dao (程明道).

48. Yi Hwang, "Response to Yi Sukheon," in *Toegye jip*, 29:377d–378a.

49. Chapters 1 and 2, in *Zhong Yong zhang-ju ji-zhu*. "喜怒哀樂之未發, 謂之中, 發而皆中節, 謂之和. 中也者, 天下之大本也, 和也者, 天下之達道也. 致中和, 天地位焉, 萬物育焉. 仲尼曰 君子中庸, 小人反中庸. [朱子注: 中庸者, 不偏不倚, 無過不及, 而平常之理, 乃天命所當然, 精微之極致也. 惟君子爲能體之, 小人反是.] 君子之中庸也, 君子而時中, 小人之中庸也, 小人而無忌憚也."

50. Annotation to Chapter 2, in *Zhong Yong zhang-ju ji-zhu*.

51. Ibid.

52. Chapter 1, in *Zhong Yong zhang-ju*. "喜怒哀樂之未發, 謂之中, 發而皆中節, 謂之和. 中也者, 天下之大本也, 和也者, 天下之達道也."

53. Yi I, "Inquiries Presented to Master Toegye," in *Yulgok jeonseo*, 44:182b–c.

54. Chapter 2, in *Zhong Yong zhang-ju ji-zhu*. "雙峯饒氏曰 . . . 中和以性情言, 人心本然純粹之德也; 中庸以事理言, 天下當然之則, 不可過, 亦不可不及者也. 二者雖同此中理, 而所指各異. 故致中和者, 則欲其戒懼愼獨, 以涵養乎性情, 踐中庸者, 則欲其擇善固執, 以求合乎事理. 二者內外交相養之道也."

55. Yi Hwang, "Response to Yi Sukheon," in *Toegye jip*, 29:379c–d.

56. Chapter 4, in *Zhong Yong*. "子曰 道之不行也, 我知之矣. 知者過之, 愚者不及也. 道之不明也, 我知之矣. 賢者過之, 不肖者不及也."

57. Chapter 4, in *Zhong Yong zhang-ju ji-zhu*. "雙峯饒氏曰 . . . 行不是說人去行道, 是說道自流行於天下, 明不是說人自知此道, 是說道自著明於天下."

58. Yi Hwang, "Response to Yi Sukheon," in *Toegye jip*, 29:378a.

59. In his reply to Yulgok's second list of questions, Toegye recommended that Yulgok read chapters 25 through 27 of volume 48 of *Zhi Zi da-quan* (朱子大全, *The Complete Collection of Master Zhu Xi*) for more details on "being capable" and "what can be done." Yi Hwang, "Response to Yi Sukheon," in *Toegye jip*, 29:376a–b.

60. Confucius, "Book 15," in *The Analects*. "子曰 人能弘道. 非道弘人."

61. Chapter 4, in *Zhong Yong zhang-ju ji-zhu*. "雙峯饒氏曰 . . . 行不是說人去行道, 是說道自流行於天下, 明不是說人自知此道, 是說道自著明於天下."

Chapter 5

Yulgok Asks and Toegye Answers 3

On Ten Diagrams on Sage Learning *(May–October 1570)*

The list of questions in Yulgok's third letter to Toegye is composed of queries about *The Doctrine of the Mean* and about *Ten Diagrams on Sage Learning*. The questions about *The Doctrine of the Mean* were addressed in the previous chapter because they are supplementary to questions in Yulgok's second letter to Toegye. His questions about *Ten Diagrams on Sage Learning* are related to three of the ten diagrams in the volumes "The Diagram of the Western Inscription (西銘圖)," which was concerned with the hierarchy of being, leading to a debate on the status of sages; "The Diagram of the Study of the Heart-Mind (心學圖)," which was concerned with self-cultivation; and "The Diagram of the Explanation of Humanity (仁說圖)." The issue of the ordering of *Ten Diagrams on Sage Learning* as a whole was also taken up in terms of its schematization according to the order of nature and the moral life. Yulgok paid special attention to "The Diagram of the Study of the Heart-Mind," and Toegye's explanations to and rebuttals of Yulgok are very detailed.

Ten Diagrams on Sage Learning was written by Toegye in 1568 for submission to King Seonjo. At the time, the king was seventeen years old, and sixty-eight-year-old Toegye collated the knowledge of Neo-Confucianism he had gained during his lifetime into ten diagrams, which were accompanied by his commentary to help the young monarch become a sage king. Because the book contains the essence of the respected Neo-Confucian scholar's studies of his later years, it would have been seen as almost beyond criticism and reproach. However, Yulgok raised a few questions about this text. Partly as a result, after Toegye presented his *Ten Diagrams on Sage Learning* to King Seonjo, he revised the book several times based on feedback from Gobong, Yulgok, and other scholars.[1]

Some of Yulgok's criticisms were accepted and others were rejected by Toegye. Yulgok's argument was centered on his views on Cheng Fu-xin (程復心, 1257–1340),[2] whose thinking influenced Toegye's academic work on the study of the heart-mind. On the other hand, Yulgok did not accept Cheng Fu-xin's theories and strongly criticized them. Obviously, Toegye and Yulgok had very different ideas about the study of the mind.

THE "WESTERN INSCRIPTION"

Yulgok's first question related to *Ten Diagrams on Sage Learning* pertained to the "Western Inscription," one of the major works of Zhang Zai (張載, 1020–1077), a scholar of the Northern Song Dynasty who played an important role in establishing Neo-Confucianism. The message of the "Western Inscription" is as follows: Heaven is the father, Earth is the mother, the people who live between Heaven and Earth are one's siblings, and all living things are one's companions. In the context of his conception of the world's structure, Zhang Zai explained the levels of status and the roles of kings, ministers, sages, and wise men. Based on his philosophy of *gi* (氣), he explained convincingly the relationship between all living things and humans coexisting on Earth. For that reason, the "Western Inscription" was considered important among Confucian scholars.

Therefore it would be natural to include it in any textbook on sage learning (聖學), which was based on Confucianism. Cheng Fu-xin drew "The Diagram of the Western Inscription (西銘圖)" based on Zhang Zai's text, and in writing the second chapter of *Ten Diagrams on Sage Learning* Toegye incorporated the "Western Inscription" and "The Diagram of the Western Inscription" and integrated his commentary with them. Subsequently, Yulgok posed a question about Cheng Fu-xin's "The Diagram of the Western Inscription," as follows:

> *Ten Diagrams on Sage Learning* is clear and appropriate in its purpose and meaning, so young scholars should be careful when criticizing it. However, a question came to mind when I was reading this book. I couldn't help but ask you this question, with all due modesty. It is about the passage in the "Western Inscription" commencing with the phrase "King Yu hated sweet wine (惡旨酒)" and proceeding to "Bo Qi (伯奇)" who obeyed his parents with courage, a passage that compares people serving their parents to people serving Heaven. It simply describes Bo Qi's need to "take care of his parents (顧養)" and to "nurture people who are dutiful to their parents (錫類)." But it doesn't imply that the people who performed these actions fulfilled their duties to the highest degree. The passage simply selects one of the actions that each person had performed in his life. However, "The Diagram of the Western Inscription" merely

says that "sages and wise men fulfilled their duties (聖賢各盡道)." According to this expression, King Shun, King Yu, and Zeng Zi truly fulfilled their duties, but it is very questionable whether figures like Ying Kao Shu (穎考叔) and Shen Sheng (申生) also did so.[3]

Here is the section in the "Western Inscription" that Yulgok took issue with:

King Yu hated sweet wine because he wanted to take care of his parents; talented people were nurtured so that more people would be dutiful to their parents as Ying Kao Shu had; King Shun never ceased attempting to please his parents despite many hardships and this is one of his achievements; Shen Sheng didn't run away and instead waited to be cooked to death in a cauldron, and this shows his perseverance; Zeng Shen (曾參) kept his body, which his parents had bestowed on him, intact; and Bo Qi obeyed his parents with courage.[4]

Yulgok's criticism was, as he himself explained, aimed at examples that were used to "compare people serving their parents to people serving Heaven." Zhang Zai discussed some people who could be considered exemplary. But Yulgok believed that it was wrong for Cheng Fu-xin to place all of them in the same category as sages and wise men, who "fulfilled their duties." King Shun, King Yu, and Zeng Zi were widely considered sages, but Ying Kao Shu, Shen Sheng, and Bo Qi were not considered as great as sages. Although it is true that Ying Kao Shu and Shen Sheng, who lived in the Spring and Autumn period of ancient China, and Bo Qi who appeared in *Shi Jing* (詩經, *The Book of Odes*) had behaved in such a way as to show their filial piety, they were not sages. Therefore, according to Yulgok, it is wrong to say that they "fulfilled their duties."

Toegye answered as follows:

Zhang Zai did not mean that Ying Kao Shu and Shen Sheng fulfilled all of their duties. They were merely mentioned as examples of those who performed actions that served Heaven. In this sense, it is right to acknowledge that they fulfilled their duty to serve Heaven. But you are clouding the issue by comparing their characters with those of sages, such as King Shun and King Yu, in order to argue that they didn't fulfill their duties. This would confuse people who serve Heaven, and as a result they wouldn't be able to fulfill their duties to serve Heaven when they face challenges, as these exemplary people did. That is why Lin-yin (林隱, the pen name of Cheng Fu-xin) merely said that they "fulfilled their duties." In your letter, you wrote that Zhang Zai "simply selects one of the actions that each person had performed in his life." Then I assume that you may understand what he really meant to say. In the same vein, you should consider what Lin-yin tried to explain in his "The Diagram of the Western Inscription."

【Toegye's added remark: Was it really necessary to criticize Lin-yin for confusing the characters of sages with those of people who were not as great as sages?】[5]

Toegye thought that Yulgok's criticism was excessive. He pointed out that Zhang Zai took one action of each of these people as examples, as Yulgok had also pointed out, and that Cheng Fu-xin used these examples in "The Diagram of the Western Inscription" to show that they all fulfilled their duties in these particular cases. Cheng Fu-xin was the second most frequently cited scholar in Toegye's *Ten Diagrams on Sage Learning*, after Zhu Xi. Cheng Fu-xin designed not only "The Diagram of the Western Inscription" but also the First Diagram (上圖) in "The Diagram of the Saying 'The Heart-Mind Combines and Governs Nature and the Feelings' (心統性情圖)" and "The Diagram of the Study of the Heart-Mind (心學圖)," and he wrote "The Explanation of the Diagram of the Saying 'The Heart-Mind Combines and Governs Nature and the Feelings' (心統性情圖說)" and "The Explanation of the Diagram of the Study of the Heart-Mind (心學圖說)." Toegye's tone in his letter to Yulgok had a hint of reproach, suggesting that it was impossible that Cheng Fu-xin had not understood what Yulgok understood. Toegye thought highly of Cheng Fu-xin, but Yulgok had severe reservations about his work. Yulgok repeatedly raised issues about "The Diagram of the Study of the Heart-Mind," which was based on Cheng Fu-xin's diagram and theory. Eventually, he suggested that Toegye delete the diagram and theory in question from *Ten Diagrams on Sage Learning*.

"THE DIAGRAM OF THE STUDY
OF THE HEART-MIND"

Among the chapters of *Ten Diagrams on Sage Learning*, "The Diagram of the Study of the Heart-Mind" caused the greatest controversy between Toegye and Yulgok. Toegye strongly refuted Yulgok's argument, and later he added his refutation to *Ten Diagrams on Sage Learning* in order to clarify his position. The two scholars were at odds with each other over Cheng Fu-xin and the study of the heart-mind.

Yulgok raised the following issues:

I am very dubious about "The Diagram of the Study of the Heart-Mind," drawn by Lin-yin Cheng-shi (林隱程氏). First of all, the mind of a great man is the same as the mind of a sage, and is in the same category as an immovable mind (不動心) and a mind with which one can follow what one's heart desires without transgressing what is right (從心).[6] Therefore how can the mind of a great man be placed in a superior position to the moral mind? Even those without wisdom retain their original mind, but you can't have the mind of a great man unless you cultivate your virtues to the highest degree and keep your original mind intact. How is it possible to have the mind of a great man without culti-vating yourself? Moreover, it is not reasonable to divide self-cultivation into the two parts of resisting human desires and of upholding Heaven's principles. Furthermore, the sequence of the preserved mind (心在) and the thinking mind (心思) seems to be incorrect.

"The Diagram of the Study of the Heart-Mind" displays the acts of "watching oneself carefully when alone (愼獨)," "overcoming one's desire and rededicat-ing oneself to propriety (克復)," preserving the mind (心在)," followed by the act of "seeking for the mind that was lost (求放心)." After thinking about this over and over again, I still think that the sequence or order of these priorities is incorrect. You explained that Yan Zi (顔子) sought for the mind that he had lost,[7] which is not appropriate either. In general, there are two types of word used by sages and wise men: those that are precise (精) and those that are vague or ill-defined (粗). You should not seek something ill-defined in something precise, and vice versa. Mencius's theory of seeking for the mind that was lost[8] was intended for scholars in general, and thus is ill-defined; Confucius's theory of overcoming one's desires and rededicating oneself to propriety (克己復禮)[9] was intended solely for Yan Zi, and thus is precise. It would be possible to apply a precise theory to something ill-defined, and to apply an ill-defined theory to something precise, but this is neither just nor fair.

In addition, if "watching oneself carefully when alone" is close to "resisting human desires," acts of introspection should all be included under the rubric of "resisting human desires"; if "being watchful and fearful" is close to "uphold-ing Heaven's principles," acts of self-cultivation (涵養) should all be included in "upholding Heaven's principles." But in "The Diagram of the Study of the Heart-Mind," "fully realizing the mind (盡心)" is included in the process of self-cultivation, even though it is part of knowing (知), whereas "rectifying the mind (正心)" is included in the category of introspection, even though it is part of doing (行). This is highly questionable. I believe these terms used in "The Diagram of the Study of the Heart-Mind" are merely meaningless reiteration, and it is not necessary to refer to them.[10]

Yulgok's criticism of "The Diagram of the Study of the Heart-Mind" and "The Explanation of the Diagram of the Study of the Heart-Mind" was very harsh. He pointed out that neither the structure and sequence of the diagram nor the classification of the methods of self-cultivation were correct. His criti-cism was focused on the unsystematic arrangement of the words placed around "heart-mind (心)" and "reverent mindfulness (敬)" in Cheng Fu-xin's "The Diagram of the Study of the Heart-Mind." He also disagreed with Cheng Fu-xin's classification of "watching oneself carefully when alone" as a component of "resisting human desires" and of "being watchful and fearful"

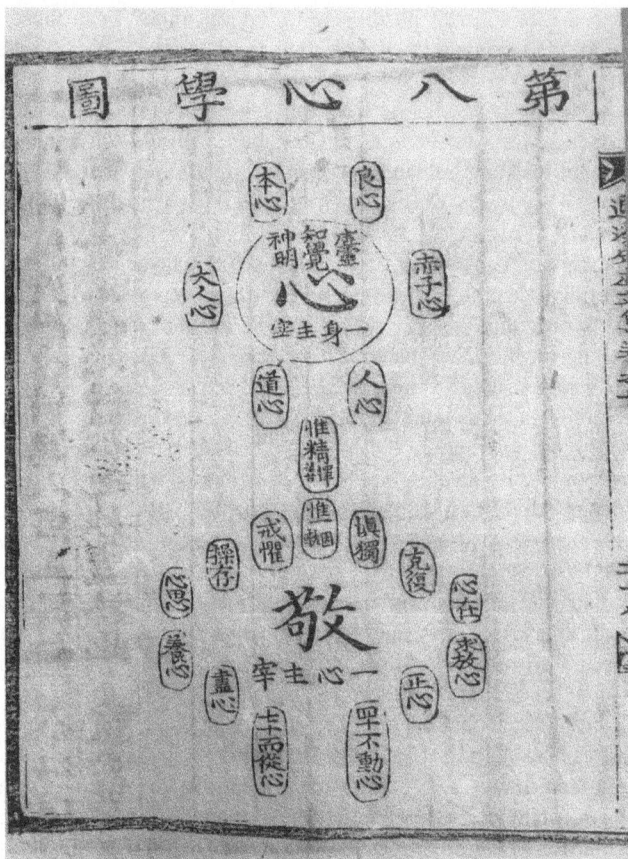

Image 5.1   Cheng Fu-xin's "The Diagram of the Study of the Heart-Mind" in *Ten Diagrams on Sage Learning*. *Source*: "Simhak do 心學圖" (Vol.7, p. 28) in *Toegye seonsaeng munjip* 退溪先生文集. Author: Yi Hwang 李滉. Publisher: Dosan seowon 陶山書院, Korea Date of publication: 1697. Used here with permission from Korea University Library.

as being an aspect of "upholding Heaven's principles." There is very little respect for Cheng Fu-xin's philosophy in Yulgok's letter. He even suggested that Toegye exclude "The Diagram of the Study of the Heart-Mind" from *Ten Diagrams on Sage Learning*.

However, Toegye disagreed and wrote a full-length reply. Yulgok's letter was not brief, but Toegye's response was even longer, to the point where it is difficult to extract some salient passages from it. It seems that Toegye was offended by Yulgok's suggestion that he omit "The Diagram of the Study of the Heart-Mind" from his book. As is evident from *Ten Diagrams on Sage Learning*, he thought highly of Cheng Fu-xin, and Yulgok knew that.

But Yulgok was not sparing in his criticism of the explanation of Cheng Fu-xin. Because Toegye's letter is long, I will summarize it instead of extracting a few passages from it.

In summary, Toegye acknowledged that there was some truth to Yulgok's criticism that there were errors in the sequencing and logical construction of "The Diagram of the Study of the Heart-Mind." But he also pointed out that Cheng Fu-xin had not classified and sequenced the methods of self-cultivation in the manner Yulgok described, and thus he couldn't fully accept Yulgok's criticism. Toegye's reply was focused on defending Cheng Fu-xin and on criticizing Yulgok's mode of interpreting the writings of the ancient sages.

In his letter, Toegye wrote, "When I was young, I read *Xin Jing* (心經, *The Classic of the Heart-Mind*), which I had borrowed from someone. And this diagram ('The Diagram of the Study of the Heart-Mind') was one of my favorites in the book."[11] "The Diagram of the Study of the Heart-Mind," along with annotations by Cheng Fu-xin, appears in the first part of *Xin Jing fu-zhu* (心經附註, *Supplementary Annotations to the Classic of the Heart-Mind*), a Confucian textbook combining the writings of ancient sages compiled by Zhen De-xiu, one of the leading figures in the Zhu Xi School, and supplementary annotations written by Cheng Min-zheng (程敏政). The study of the heart-mind was at the core of Toegye's philosophy, and the scholars of the Toegye School even equated his philosophy with the study of the heart-mind. Indeed, some modern scholars also consider Toegye's *oeuvre* as primarily focused on the study of the heart-mind rather than of *li*.[12] Toegye's study of the heart-mind was essentially concerned with the cultivation of the mind and its safeguarding from temptation. From his perspective, it is important to understand the structures and workings of the human mind, human nature, and human emotions. But such theoretical and analytical understanding is simply groundwork for the practice of self-cultivation and for leading the mind in the right direction.

Toegye himself also had some doubts about the structure of "The Diagram of the Study of the Heart-Mind," but he wrote in his letter to Yulgok that he had realized the precise and detailed meaning of Cheng Fu-xin's diagrams and commentary, which he had borrowed from someone about ten years earlier. He wrote, "The categorization of the six kinds of human mind into two groups is a very insightful path to take in terms of its logic and context. Although Cheng Fu-xin didn't discuss the virtues and necessary sequence of methods of self-cultivation, his understanding is not shallow."[13]

In addition, Toegye criticized Yulgok, saying that Yulgok understood Cheng Fu-xin's "The Diagram of the Study of the Heart-Mind" in the same way as "someone . . . telling a fool a dream he had," and he showed his disappointment, saying, "I did not believe that this diagram would be so hard to appreciate for scholars like you, who have wisdom and insight." Toegye assumed that Yulgok was overzealous in his criticism of Cheng Fu-xin, and wrote that "it wouldn't be easy to surpass Cheng Fu-xin by making an impromptu argument."[14]

Toegye later included Yulgok's criticism and his counterargument in *Ten Diagrams on Sage Learning* and concluded the chapter on "The Diagram of the Study of the Heart-Mind" as follows:

> Cheng Fu-xin's courtesy name was Zi-jian (子見). He was born in Xin-an (新安). He sequestered himself from the world, didn't take up any public office, and followed the path of righteousness. He studied the classics until his later years and acquired wisdom from them. In the end, he wrote *Si-shu zhang-tu* (四書章圖, *The Diagrams of the Chapters of the Four Books*), comprised of three volumes. During the reign of King Ren-zong (仁宗) of the Yuan Dynasty (1311–1320), he was recommended for public office and the king offered him a position, but he didn't take up the offer. Then, he was appointed to a provincial professorship (鄉郡博士), but again he resigned and retired to his hometown. Is it not impossible that such an erudite man drew a diagram carelessly without knowledge of the subject in question?[15]

Toegye thought that Cheng Fu-xin had no ambition to succeed in the practical world and that he strove to concentrate on learning for the cultivation of his own self (爲己之學) and that "The Diagram of the Study of the Heart-Mind" created by such a man of noble character should not be disparaged.

It could be that Yulgok had never agreed with Toegye's study of the heart-mind during more than a decade of interactions with him, or alternatively that Yulgok had always been unhappy with Toegye's fascination with Cheng Fu-xin's study of the heart-mind, and that Toegye's *Ten Diagrams on Sage Learning* provided Yulgok with the opportunity to show his disapproval of Cheng Fu-xin's theory. Clearly, there was a chasm between Toegye and Yulgok when it came to Cheng Fu-xin's "The Diagram of the Study of the Heart-Mind" and the study of the heart-mind itself. Their different standpoints became clear in Yulgok's theory of the four beginnings and the seven feelings, and of the human mind and the moral mind, which he put forward after Toegye passed away. Yulgok either didn't understand or opposed Toegye's stance on the study of the heart-mind, and that was one of the reasons why he took a different theoretical path than Toegye.

THE STRUCTURE AND SEQUENCE OF
TEN DIAGRAMS ON SAGE LEARNING

The argument between Toegye and Yulgok over "The Diagram of the Study of the Heart-Mind" was so heated that it became almost personal; they were unflinching in their criticisms because they were very close, but there were some criticisms in their letters that could have aggrieved the other person. However, ultimately this potential pitfall did not transpire, and in his reply Toegye gladly accepted Yulgok's suggestions.

Yulgok had suggested that Toegye alter the order of "The Diagram of the Explanation of Humanity (仁說圖)" and "The Diagram of the Study of the Heart-Mind" in *Ten Diagrams on Sage Learning*.

【Yulgok's question】 I think "Chapter 8: The Diagram of the Explanation of Humanity" should be placed before "The Diagram of the Study of the Heart-Mind." What is your feeling on that?[16]

【Toegye's answer】 I very much agree with and am impressed by your idea. I realized the need to change their order when I returned from Hanyang (present-day Seoul) last year, and your letter made me more confident in that idea. So I immediately acted on it. There may be more corrections to be made, and I'll do so as soon as I become aware of them, as it will not cause me anxiety no matter how many times I need to make corrections. However, it is very difficult for me to inform the king every time I make corrections after I presented *Ten Diagrams on Sage Learning* to His Highness. The fact that my lack of academic knowledge exposes me to faults and mistakes makes me increasingly fearful of doing so. I'm planning to write a letter to His Highness and to wait for a corresponding penalty for the errors I made. But I haven't found time for this yet, because I have to decide first whether or not to resign from public service. Kim Seong-il (金誠一, 1538–1593) and Kim Chwi-ryeo (金就礪, 1526–?) have other revised versions, so you can borrow them from them if you would like to.[17]

It is understandable why Toegye readily accepted Yulgok's suggestion to change the sequence of "The Diagram of the Explanation of Humanity" and "The Diagram of the Study of the Heart-Mind" in light of the overall structure of *Ten Diagrams on Sage Learning*. Toegye divided the text into two parts, consisting of chapters 1 through 5 and chapters 6 through 10. According to Toegye, the first part is "based on the Way of Heaven (天道) and its virtue is to allow people to illuminate morality and concentrate on performing virtuous deeds"[18] and the second part is "based on the heart-mind and human nature (心性) and its point is to enable people to strive to cultivate themselves every day and practice showing respect for others."[19] To put it in another way, the first part is focused on the practice of morality based on the understanding of the order of nature, whereas the second part concentrates on the optimal ways of living a moral life based on the understanding of the heart-mind and human nature.

When Toegye described the ontological basis of Neo-Confucianism in the first diagram, "The Diagram of the Supreme Polarity (太極圖)," and in the second diagram, "The Diagram of the Western Inscription," he explained it from the perspective of the theory of the *li*-principal (主理) within the frame-work of *liilbunsu / li-yi-fen-shu* (理一分殊, *li* is one but its manifestations are many), which is based on the doctrines of Zhu Xi. The two diagrams are followed by "The Diagram of the Elementary Learning (小學圖)," "The Diagram of the Great Learning (大學圖)," and "The Diagram of the Rules of the White Deer Hollow Academy (白鹿洞規圖)"—diagrams that illustrate that the purpose of the ontological theory, which prioritizes *li* (principle), is to enable the practice of morality and ethics. "The Diagram of the Elementary Learning" and "The Diagram of the Great Learning," in particular, empha-sized "reverent mindfulness (敬)" as an attitude and method of practical learning and cultivation, in order to clarify that "sage learning" is a practice-oriented form of learning.

The sixth, seventh, and eighth diagrams illustrate that a human's original moral nature is derived from nature, and thus emotions, which arise from the original moral nature, should follow the order of nature. They also sug-gest that "watching oneself carefully when alone" and "being watchful and fearful" are some of the ways to control the interactions between the original moral nature and the emotions, and that such practices can lead to "reverent mindfulness," a concept Toegye had been constantly stressing. The ninth and tenth diagrams demonstrate how to deal with the original moral nature and emotions of everyday life. They put particular emphasis on not only understanding and following the order of the nature and of the human being, but also maintaining reverence for metaphysical entities symbolized as *li* (理, principle), the Way (道, Dao), and *Sangje / Shang-di* (上帝, the Lord on High), demonstrating that Toegye's philosophy was profound not only in terms of its theoretical but also its ideological aspects.[20]

The original sequence between the sixth diagram and the tenth diagram was "The Diagram of the Saying 'The Heart-Mind Combines and Governs Nature and the Feelings,'" "The Diagram of the Study of the Heart-Mind," "The Diagram of the Explanation of Humanity," "The Diagram of the Admonition for Mindfulness Studio (敬齋箴圖)," and "The Diagram of the Admonition on Rising Early and Retiring Late (夙興夜寐箴圖)." Yulgok suggested that Toegye change the order of "The Diagram of the Explana-tion of Humanity" and "The Diagram of the Study of the Heart-Mind," and Toegye accepted his suggestion. *Ten Diagrams on Sage Learning* in *Toegye jip* is the version that incorporated Yulgok's suggestions. "The Diagram of the Saying 'The Heart-Mind Combines and Governs Nature and Feelings'" demonstrates the process and principle of how emotions arise from the origi-nal moral nature, and thus it was necessary to place it at the beginning of the second part—chapters 6 through 10—which is based on "the heart-mind and human nature." "The Diagram of the Explanation of Humanity" shows that "humanity (仁)," a concept that is representative of the original moral nature

in Confucianism, is based on the form of the order of nature called "life (生),"
in order to make the case that a moral life is the most natural one to live.
"The Diagram of the Study of the Heart-Mind" illustrates that the mind governs the body and that the working of the mind should be governed by "reverent mindfulness," thereby showing how sage learning can be practiced to
perfection. And the following two diagrams—"The Diagram of the Admonition for Mindfulness Studio" and "The Diagram of the Admonition on Rising
Early and Retiring Late"—explain how to practice morality in everyday life.
Therefore "The Diagram of the Study of the Heart-Mind," which describes
how to study sage learning, had to be placed between "The Diagram of the
Saying 'The Heart-Mind Combines and Governs Nature and Feelings" and
"The Diagram of the Explanation of Humanity," which illustrate the principles of the heart-mind and human nature, and "The Diagram of the Admonition for Mindfulness Studio" and "The Diagram of the Admonition on Rising
Early and Retiring Late," which illustrate practical ways of living fruitfully.
Yulgok understood the structure of *Ten Diagrams on Sage Learning* at once
and suggested that Toegye change the order of the two diagrams without
hesitation, and Toegye immediately accepted Yulgok's suggestion. Despite
significant differences in their positions, Toegye and Yulgok maintained a
productive relationship, criticizing what needed scrutiny while acknowledging what was productive.

NOTES

1. For more details of revisions to *Ten Diagrams on Sage Learning*, see Mun
Seok-yun, "Toegye-ui *Seonghak sipdo* sujeong-e gwanhan yeon-gu" (A Study on
Toegye's Revision of *Ten Diagrams on Sage Learning*), *Toegye hakbo* 130 (2011).
2. A scholar of the Yuan Dynasty.
3. Yi I, "Sang Toegye seonsaeng munmok" 上退溪先生問目 (Inquiries Presented to Master Toegye), in *Yulgok jeonseo*, 44:182d.
4. Yi Hwang, "*Seonghak sipdo*: Je-2-Seomyeong do" 聖學十圖: 第二西圖
(*Ten Diagrams on Sage Learning*: Chapter 2: The Diagram of the Western Inscription), in *Toegye jip*, 29:202c. "惡旨酒, 崇伯子之顧養; 育英才, 穎封人之錫類,
不弛勞而底豫, 舜其功也; 無所逃而待烹, 申生其恭也. 體其受而歸全者, 參乎;
勇於從而順令者, 伯奇也."
5. Yi Hwang, "Response to Yi Sukheon," in *Toegye jip*, 29:379d–380a. The sentence in square brackets is in *Toegye jip* but not in *Yulgok jeonseo*.
6. Confucius, "Book 2," in *The Analects*. "七十而從心所欲, 不踰矩."
7. Yi Hwang, "*Seonghak sipdo*: Je-8-Simhak do" 聖學十圖: 第八心學圖 (*Ten
Diagrams on Sage Learning*: Chapter 8: The Diagram of the Study of the Heart-
Mind), in *Toegye jip*, 29:210c.
8. Mencius, "Gao Zi I" 告子 上, in *Mencius*.

9. Confucius, "Book 12," in *The Analects.*

10. Yi I, "Inquiries Presented to Master Toegye," in *Yulgok jeonseo,* 44:183a–c.

11. Yi Hwang, "Response to Yi Sukheon," in *Toegye jip,* 29:380d. Toegye wrote that he borrowed *The Classic of the Heart-Mind* from someone. However, it is assumed that "The Diagram of the Study of the Heart-Mind" was added when Cheng Min-zheng was compiling *Supplementary Annotations to the Classic of the Heart-Mind.* Therefore what Toegye borrowed was *Supplementary Annotations to the Classic of the Heart-Mind,* not *The Classic of the Heart-Mind* itself.

12. This standpoint is also found in the following papers: An Byeong-ju, "Toegye-ui hangmun-gwan: Simgyeong huroneul jungsimeuro" (Toegye's View of Learning: Focusing on "Postscripts to the Classic of the Heart-Mind"), *Toegyehak yeon-gu* 1 (1987); Sin Gwi-hyeon, "Toegye Yi Hwang-ui 'Simgyeong buju' yeon-guwa geu-ui siimhak-ui teukjing" (Toegye's Study on *Supplementary Annotations to the Classic of the Mind-and-Heart* and the Characteristics of His Study of the Mind), *Minjok munhwa nonchong* 8 (1987); Kim Jong-seok, "Ma-eum-ui cheorak: Toegye simhak-ui gujo bunseok" (The Philosophy of the Mind: A Structural Analysis of Toegye's Study of the Mind), *Minjok munhwa nonchong* 15 (1994); and Hong Won-sik, "Toegye-hak, geu jonjae-reul munneunda" (What Are Toegye Studies?), *Oneurui dong-yang sasang* 4 (2001). Hong Won-sik attempted to reintegrate Toegye's study of *li* into his study of the heart-mind, and Kim Jong-seok made consistent efforts to reinterpret the theory of the four beginnings and the seven feelings from the perspective of the study of the heart-mind. However, given that Toegye's study of the heart-mind is greatly dependent on his study of *li,* further research is needed to elaborate the theoretical structure of Toegye's study of the heart-mind to the level of his study of *li.* For more details on this issue, see Kim Hyoungchan, "Toegye's Philosophy as Practical Ethics: A System of the Learning, Cultivation, and Practice of Being Human," *Korea Journal* 47, no. 3 (2007).

13. Yi Hwang, "Response to Yi Sukheon," in *Toegye jip,* 29:380d.

14. Ibid., 29:380d.

15. Yi Hwang, "*Ten Diagrams on Sage Learning*: Chapter 8: The Diagram of the Study of the Heart-Mind," in *Toegye jip,* 29:210c–d.

16. Yi I, "Inquiries Presented to Master Toegye," in *Yulgok jeonseo,* 44:184a.

17. Yi Hwang, "Response to Yi Sukheon," in *Toegye jip,* 29:382d–383a.

18. Yi Hwang, "*Seonghak sipdo*: Je-5-Baengnokdonggyu do" 聖學十圖: 第五白鹿洞規圖 (*Ten Diagrams on Sage Learning*: Chapter 5: The Diagram of the Rules of the White Deer Hollow Academy," in *Toegye jip,* 29:205c.

19. Yi Hwang, "*Seonghak sipdo*: Je-10-Sukeungyamaejam do" 聖學十圖: 第十夙興夜寐箴圖 (*Ten Diagrams on Sage Learning*: Chapter 10: The Diagram of the Admonition on Rising Early and Retiring Late," in *Toegye jip,* 29:213a–b.

20. For more details on the structure and meaning of *Ten Diagrams on Sage Learning,* see Kim Hyoungchan, "*Seonghak sipdo* hajae" (A Bibliographical Introduction to *Ten Diagrams on Sage Learning*), in *Yeokjuwa haeseol Seonghak sipdo* (*Ten Diagrams on Sage Learning*: Translation Notes and Interpretations), ed. The Research Institute of Korean Studies at Korea University (Seoul: Yemoon seowon, 2009), 22–26.

Chapter 6

The Four Beginnings and Seven Feelings; the Human Mind and the Moral Mind

The Debate between Yulgok and Ugye

In 1572, two years after the death of Toegye, Yulgok had a scholarly debate with his lifelong friend and political comrade Seong Hon (成渾, 1535–1598; pen name: Ugye). The debate began when Ugye, who had agreed with Toegye's theory of the four beginnings and the seven feelings, asked Yulgok's opinion on Toegye's theory. Through this debate, Yulgok critically reviewed Toegye's theory and systematically presented his own. He seems to have already established his position to some extent while following the prior debate between Toegye and Gobong.

Ugye essentially agreed with Toegye's stance but asked Yulgok's opinion in a considered way. Yulgok provided a clear, textbook-like response by defining the concepts involved and explaining the structure of Neo-Confucian theory. This was in sharp contrast to Ugye's response, which was simply, "I can't explain it in words."[1] The perfectly logical letters that Yulgok wrote, which were composed of clear and concise points, are examples of why he was called "gudo jangwon gong (九度壯元公, one who has won first place in the state examination nine times)."[2] Rarely could others summarize the relationship between metaphysical and polysemous Neo-Confucian concepts as lucidly as he did. Although Toegye's influence on him was still strong, Yulgok had a different opinion that he was so confident in that he could not downplay it any longer.

THE HUMAN MIND AND THE MORAL MIND

The reason why Ugye asked Yulgok's opinion while agreeing with Toegye's theory on the four beginnings and the seven feelings was because he thought that the four and the seven could be distinguished in the same way as the human mind and the moral mind. He believed that the essence of the mind revealed through phenomena can be divided into the human mind and the moral mind. The human mind refers to the part of the mind that seeks to satisfy physiological needs or to achieve self-gratification, whereas the moral mind refers to the part that pursues moral principles or public morality. While the four beginnings and seven feelings are simply moral emotions, the human mind and the moral mind are concepts that encompass both moral emotions and the domain of the mind that judges and amends these moral emotions. Ugye believed that the method of separating the ideal (four beginnings) and the common moral emotions (seven feelings) was basically the same as that of distinguishing the human mind from the moral mind.

> To explain the moral mind and the human mind, the sages have described the separate revelations of *li* and *gi*. So the argument of Toegye itself can't be wrong, can it?[3]

According to Ugye, because the old sages distinguished between the moral mind and the human mind by defining the former as the revelation of *li* and the latter as the revelation of *gi*, Toegye's theory that divides the four beginnings and the seven feelings in the same way could not be wrong.[4] The criteria for distinguishing between dividing both the moral/human mind and the four beginnings/seven feelings were the moral principles of Confucianism and Neo-Confucianism. Whether these two distinctions are identical can be determined from the perspective of the theory of *li-gi*. When *li* is completely revealed without the interruption of *gi*, it becomes the moral mind/four beginnings, whereas when the moral goodness of *li* is revealed accompanied by distortions due to the interruption of *gi*, it becomes the human mind/seven feelings. Based on Zhu Xi's theory, which claims that the moral mind and the human mind are separable because the cause of the former is "innate nature (性命)" and that of the latter is "material disposition (or physical matter, 形氣),", which are effectively *li* and *gi*, Ugye believed that such a distinction could also be applied to the four beginnings and the seven feelings.

However, Yulgok argued that the human mind and the moral mind were originally one mind and that thus they have the same origin. The mind is originally a single entity but is divided into the human mind and the moral mind immediately after perception arises in response to external perturbations. While Ugye considered the moral mind and the human mind to be as distinctive as *li* and *gi*, Yulgok rebutted Ugye's perspective by focusing on the fact that both the human mind and the moral mind originated from one mind. Throughout six letters he sent to Yulgok, Ugye consistently justified Toegye's theory on the four beginnings and the seven feelings in terms of the distinction between the human mind and the moral mind. However, Yulgok contended that they were not actually separate. He argued that the relationship between the four beginnings and the seven feelings is closer to that between "innate pure nature (*bonyeon jiseong / ben-ran-zhi-xing* 本然之性)" and "physical nature (*gijil jiseong / qi-zhi-zhi-xing* 氣質之性)" rather than to that between the human mind and the moral mind. Although Ugye and Yulgok could not find middle ground, Yulgok's theory was systematically presented through this debate, and the discussions about *li*, *gi*, and "the heart-mind and nature" developed continually in Joseon after their debate. This controversy was caused by Zhu Xi's statement about the human mind and the moral mind, which is as follows: "One (the human mind) arises from the selfish disposition of physical matter while the other (the moral mind) originates in the justness of innate nature (或生於形氣之私, 或原於性命之正.)." In the "Preface to *The Doctrine of the Mean in Chapters and Verses*," Zhu Xi wrote that Zi-si (子思) compiled *The Doctrine of the Mean* in order to propagate the learning of the Way (道學) and explained the great tradition based on the adherence to Confucian ideals by quoting *The Book of Documents*. The core content of the tradition was the proposition that one should "sincerely strive for the golden mean (允執厥中)," which was an admonition offered by King Yao to King Shun. This was extended to the proposition that "the human mind is always treacherous and the moral mind is always subtle. Thus, be judicious and steadfast, and sincerely strive for the golden mean (人心惟危 道心惟微 惟精惟一 允執厥中)," which was a dictum conveyed by King Shun to King Yu. Zhu Xi interpreted the human mind and the moral mind as follows:

> Although there is only one disinterested and numinous perception (虛靈知覺) of the mind, the human mind and the moral mind are considered to be different. This is because one of these arises from the selfish disposition of physical matter while the other originates in the justness of innate nature, and thus they perceive things differently.[5]

Here Ugye focused on the phrase. "one of these arises from the selfish disposition of physical matter while the other originates in the justness of innate nature." The demonstration of the marvelous perceptual abilities of the mind proves that it is not two but one. Nevertheless, King Shun spoke as if there are two minds because one of them arises from the selfish disposition of physical matter while the other originates in the justness of innate nature. As long as it was based on this statement of Zhu Xi, Toegye's theory cannot be considered to be wayward because it divided the mind into the human mind and the moral mind according to Zhu Xi's intentions and applied a *li-gi* theory-based distinction to the four beginnings and the seven feelings. According to Toegye, if the ideal moral mind and the ordinary person's mind are distinguished based on *li* and *gi*, this standard can also be applied to the division between ideal moral feelings and ordinary moral feelings. However, in Zhu Xi's "Preface to *The Doctrine of the Mean in Chapters and Verses*," this statement is immediately succeeded by the following:

> They perceive things differently. Thus, one of them (the human mind) is in a precarious and unstable state and the other (the moral mind) is subtle and recognized only with great difficulty. . . . (Therefore) if one engages in this field of study with continuous effort and lets the moral mind govern one, and allows the human mind to follow its lead, the precarious component (the human mind) becomes stable and the subtle one (the moral mind) becomes manifest. Thus, whatever one does, including moving, standing still, speaking, or working, nothing will fall short or be overextended.[6]

Yulgok based his argument on these propositions, which stipulate that the human mind and the moral mind are not divided from the beginning prior to their instantiation but are instead distinguished after the perception of the mind begins to operate in response to external disturbance. In the process of this emotional revelation, one should control oneself in such a way that the human mind will adhere to the strictures of the moral mind. According to Yulgok, Zhu Xi's proposition that "one of these arises from the selfish disposition of physical matter while the other originates in the justness of innate nature (或生於形氣之私, 或原於性命之正)" does not mean that the human mind and the moral mind have different origins, but simply explains the reason for the division between them when the two were revealed after the act of perception initially took place.

> The statement that one of these arises from the selfish disposition of physical matter while the other originates in the justness of innate nature was made after observing the awakening (of the mind). Through investigation, it was found that the revelation of principles and righteousness (理義) originated from the innate pure mind. Thus, this is called the moral mind. Conversely, the revelation of desire for food and sex was found to originate in "matter and shapes (血氣成形)," which consists of physiological drives and disposition. Thus, this is called the human mind. Therefore Zhu Xi's above statement is different from Toegye's theory of *hobal / hu-fa* (互發, the mutual issuance of *li* and *gi*), which claims that one of them is the revelation of *li* whereas the other is the revelation of *gi* and that thus they have different origins.[7]

According to Yulgok, although we can distinguish the human mind from the moral mind, they were not originally divided as Toegye or Ugye insisted but were instead divided from the moment when the act of perception arose. On the manifestation of the mind, people divided the mind into the moral mind and the human mind depending simply on the purpose and cause of their perception. If their perception was in the service of promoting and embodying moral principles and was caused by the justness of innate nature, it was called the moral mind; if their perception was in the service of the desire for food or sex and was caused by the selfish disposition of physical matter, it was called the human mind.

However, dividing the cause of the manifestation of the mind into innate nature and material disposition, after realizing that a part of the mind was manifested for a moral purpose and the other came about as a result of the desire for food or sex, can be seen as dividing them in their very origin. Ugye pointed this out and argued that the moral mind and the human mind originated from *li* and *gi*, respectively, and that the relationship between them can also be seen as commensurate with the distinction between the four beginnings and the seven feelings,[8] but this theory was not accepted by Yulgok. He contended that both the human mind and the moral mind stem from a single innate nature but that a part of this nature can be considered to be the human mind if *gi* interferes, while the other part is considered to be the moral mind if *gi* does not intrude.[9]

Yulgok emphasized that the four beginnings and the seven feelings can neither be divided nor converted into one another, unlike the human mind and the moral mind. Instead he explained the four beginnings and the seven feelings using the concepts of innate pure nature (本然之性) and physical nature (氣質之性).

INNATE PURE NATURE AND PHYSICAL NATURE

When we understand the reason for the division between the human mind and the moral mind in relation to material disposition and innate nature, the difference between the two can be explained in terms of *gi* and *li*. Not only Toegye and Ugye but also Yulgok agreed with this. However, Yulgok still stressed that the human mind and the moral mind are originally one mind. According to him, a single mind partakes of innate nature and expresses emotions. Unlike Toegye or Ugye, he believed that the human mind and the moral mind are divided at the moment when the individual mind perceives external objects, that is, when the mind reacts to external disturbance or perturbation. This argument was based on the theory of *li-gi*, which asserts that *li* and *gi* are originally inseparable (理氣不相離). According to this theory, the moral mind and the human mind are composed of the inseparable *li* and *gi*, and thus the moral mind and the human mind essentially have the same origin. However, the difference between the two arises when *gi* obstructs the complete issuance of *li*. Based on this theory, Yulgok proposed the theory that by altering *gi*, the human mind can be converted into the moral mind, and vice versa (人心道心相爲終始說); in other words, if the human mind is the beginning of the process, then the moral mind could be the end, and vice versa.

Yulgok thought that unlike the contrast between the human mind and the moral mind, in the case of the four beginnings and the seven feelings, the former is included in the latter. Among the seven feelings, those in which the pure goodness of *li* emerges completely without being interrupted by *gi* are the four beginnings. In order to describe this relationship between the four beginnings and the seven feelings, Yulgok drew on the explanation of the relationship not between the human mind and the moral mind but between innate pure nature and physical nature. According to him, the relationship between the moral mind and the human mind is similar to that between the *li*-principal (主理) and the *gi*-principal (主氣), while in the case of innate pure nature and physical nature, the former is included in the latter. The theory of *li-gi* maintains that the *li* of physical nature is called innate pure nature, while physical nature encompasses *gi*.

The concepts of innate pure nature and physical nature constitute a more advanced perspective on human nature than Mencius's view that it is inherently good and Xun Zi's view that human nature is inherently evil. While Mencius's stance focuses on the moral characteristics of human beings and Xun Zi's stresses their evil traits, the duality of innate pure nature and physical nature more convincingly explains the intermingling of goodness and evil latent in human beings. It describes the complexity of innate nature as the combination of the virtuous axiological characteristic of *li* and of the various material characteristics of *gi* by applying the Neo-Confucian theory of *li-gi* to the concept of innate nature.

According to Neo-Confucianism, human nature is identical to *li*, conceptualized in the proposition that "innate human nature is *li* (性卽理)," but it is distinguished from the *li* conceptualized as "*li* is included in *gi* (氣中之理)." Yulgok claimed that the concept of physical nature refers to *li*, which is encompassed by *gi*, while innate pure nature (the nature conferred by Heaven and Earth [天地之性] or the nature conferred by Heaven [天命之性])[10] refers solely to *li* and not to *gi*.[11] Therefore physical nature is the combination of *gi* and *li*, whereas innate pure nature is only *li*. While Toegye distinguished innate pure nature from physical nature as the *li*-principal and the *gi*-principal depending on their intent (所就而言之 or 所指), Yulgok's explanation more clearly showed how the structure of innate pure nature and physical nature had a close affinity with the conception of the theory of *li-gi*.

The distinction made between innate pure nature (the nature conferred by Heaven and Earth) and physical nature by contrasting the two concepts originated in the work of Zhang Zai (張載, 1020~1077) in the Northern

Song Dynasty. He pointed out that the nature of each entity was not separately derived but stemmed from the sole origin of all things,[12] and he stated,
"Since physical nature is created after the formation of individual matter (*gi*),
the nature conferred by Heaven and Earth can be preserved by restoring its
origin."[13] Zhang Zai contrasted physical nature and the nature conferred by
Heaven and Earth because he wanted human beings to overcome obstacles
created by *gi*, which constitutes the universe, and live by the Mandate of
Heaven (天命) or the laws of nature. He believed that only by fulfilling their
own nature conferred by Heaven and Earth could human beings completely
embody the nature of all things conferred by Heaven and Earth and could
further attain a life consistent with the Mandate of Heaven.[14]

Zhu Xi focused on the division between the nature conferred by Heaven
and Earth and the physical nature that was conceptualized by Zhang Zai and
linked this to the theory of the cultivation of the mind (修養論), which was
based on changes in the material disposition (or physical matter) of the
individual. He stated that because the nature conferred by Heaven and Earth
is the state of the highest, purest goodness in existence before the manifestation of human nature, and that physical nature is the state in which the
whole substance of the Supreme Polarity permeates the physical matter of
the individual mind, it is necessary to overcome one's corrupt matter (*gi*) so
that the realization of the nature conferred by Heaven and Earth, which is the
Supreme Polarity, is not obstructed.[15] As such, the distinction between the
nature conferred by Heaven and Earth and physical nature was originally proposed to enable one's physical matter or material disposition to be adjusted
so that the original characteristics of innate nature could be fully realized in
accordance with the Mandate of Heaven.

Focusing on past sages' original intention of conceptually distinguishing
between innate pure nature (the nature conferred by Heaven and Earth) and
physical nature, Toegye distinguished them according to their meanings,
with innate pure nature designating *li* as an origin of human nature, and
physical nature designating the nature formed after *li* and *gi* were combined.
Toegye argued that Zi-si's conception of the nature conferred by Heaven
(天命之性), Mencius's innate good nature (性善之性), Confucius's theory
regarding the completion of human nature in accordance with nature's goodness (繼善成性說), and Zhou Dun-yi's theory of the Indeterminate and the
Supreme Polarity (無極太極說) all refer to the origin of *li* (原頭本然處).
He also claimed that the intention of the sages in discussing innate nature was
to teach the pure goodness utterly free of evil (純善無惡) of *li*. Conversely,
the concept of physical nature was reluctantly introduced to explain phenomenal entities by Cheng Yi and Zhang Zai.[16] Taking into account the fact that
the sages pursued the full realization of the nature conferred by Heaven and
Earth and that physical nature was simply an instrumental reality established

for the realization of this nature, it is important to clearly distinguish between the two in terms of their differing purposes. Thus, regarding Gobong's claim "While the nature conferred by Heaven and Earth is solely *li*, physical nature is a combination of *li* and *gi*," Toegye disagreed, arguing that, under the principle of the inseparable relationship between *li* and *gi*, the nature conferred by Heaven and Earth also comprises not only *li* but also *gi*.[17] This argument drew attention to the original intention to distinguish between the nature conferred by Heaven and Earth and physical nature, as it is indicated in the discussion that the explanation focusing on the formal structure of the theory of *li-gi* is not the only way to understand the human mind. Furthermore, Toegye asserted that such a relationship between the nature conferred by Heaven and Earth and physical nature can be applied to the four beginnings and the seven feelings. With the same logic of dividing the human mind into the moral mind and the human mind, Toegye considered innate nature (the nature conferred by Heaven and Earth), the moral mind, and the four beginnings as partaking of the *li*-principal, and physical nature, the human mind, and the seven feelings as being constituted of the *gi*-principal.

However, just as Gobong had, Yulgok believed that only the *li* in physical nature constitutes innate pure nature (the nature conferred by Heaven and Earth), and he saw the relationship between innate pure nature and physical nature as commensurate with the relationship between the four beginnings and the seven feelings. According to him, the four beginnings simply refer to virtuous elements among the seven feelings. Yulgok's explanation that innate pure nature and the four beginnings refer only to *li*, while physical nature and the seven feelings encompass *gi*, is helpful in clearly separating the roles of *li* and *gi* in the human mind, where *li* is encompassed by *gi*. By contrast, Toegye and Ugye made a distinction between the issuances of *li* and *gi*, which is the distinction between the *li*-principal and the *gi*-principal, and applied this dynamic between the moral mind and the human mind to the relationship between the four beginnings and the seven feelings. This clearly shows the core issue that brought about the axiological difference between the two sides.

In paying attention to the fact that *li* and *gi* are in an inseparable relationship, Yulgok explained that innate pure nature or the four beginnings refer only to *li* in the state in which *li* and *gi* are combined, that is, the state of physical nature or the realm of the seven feelings. He said that innate pure nature or the four beginnings is not an independent form of *li* but is instead the *li* in physical nature or the seven feelings, which is a combination of *li* and *gi*. Yulgok criticized Toegye and Ugye for distinguishing between the issuances of *li* and *gi* or the *li*-principal and the *gi*-principal because this division means that *li* and *gi* are separable and that one precedes the other. In the belief that the explanation of the relationship between *li* and *gi* plays a key role in disproving Toegye's theory of the mutual issuance of *li* and *gi*, Yulgok proposed a new form of explanation called *litong-giguk* (理通氣局, *li* pervades and *gi* delimits).

LI PERVADES AND *GI* DELIMITS

Yulgok's argument can be divided into an "explanation solely of *li*" and an "explanation that includes *gi*." While adhering to the principle of an inseparable relationship between *li* and *gi*, this enabled the conceptual division of innate pure nature and physical nature or of the four beginnings and the seven feelings. However, on Ugye's agreement with Toegye's theory of the mutual issuance of *li* and *gi*, Yulgok sought a way to more clearly demonstrate the principle of an inseparable relationship between *li* and *gi*. By defining *li* and *gi* in different ways, first by explaining only *li* and second by offering an explanation that included *gi*, he showed that the principle of an inseparable relationship between them still holds, even when only *li* is explained, as follows:

> Cheng Yi said, "Since human beings are born with *gi*, there are both goodness and evil in *li* (人生氣稟, 理有善惡)." These eight Chinese letters greatly enlighten people. The *li* described here does not refer to the original *li* (理之本然) but to the *li* that courses through things while riding on *gi* (乘氣流行之理). The original *li* is truly virtuous, but the concept of *li* becomes various when riding on *gi*. Because human beings are born with *gi* and have both goodness and evil, *li* also has goodness and evil.[18]

Based on Cheng Yi's proposition that "both goodness and evil exist in *li*," Yulgok divided *li* into the original *li* and the *li* that courses through things while riding on *gi* by applying the concepts of innate pure nature and physical nature to *li*. That is, because *li* and *gi* are inseparable, *li* becomes the original *li* when only *li* is described, while it becomes the *li* riding on *gi* (乘氣之理) when *li* and *gi* are described together. Yulgok used this method of explanation of *li* (describing only *li* or *li* and *gi* together) in order to show that, although all things include the virtuous *li*, in actuality both *li* and *gi* exist and are inseparable. However, he found a way to reveal that *li* and *gi* are inseparable even in the case of the original *li*, in other words that *li* cannot exist without *gi*. This means that even the original *li* does not exist in isolation but is combined with the original *gi* (本然之氣). He explained that the original *li* is combined with the original *gi* and that the *li* riding on *gi* is with reference to the *gi* that changes (所變之氣). In this way, Yulgok refuted Toegye and Ugye by pointing out that not only innate pure nature/physical nature and the four beginnings/the seven feelings but also the human mind/the moral mind cannot avoid the principle of there being an inseparable relationship between *li* and *gi*.

> Although the moral mind stems from innate nature, *gi* is manifested instead of *li*. Thus, it cannot be called the issuance of *li*. Both the human mind and the moral mind are the manifestations of *gi*. If *gi* follows the original *li*, *gi* is also the original *gi*. Therefore the *li* riding on the original *gi* becomes the moral mind. If *gi* corrupts the original *li*, the original *gi* is also corrupted. Therefore the *li* riding on the corrupt *gi* becomes the human mind, which is sometimes excessive and sometimes insufficient.[19]

As seen earlier, Yulgok emphasized the principle of an inseparable relationship between *li* and *gi* once again by explaining that the original *li* is combined with the original *gi* and that the *li* riding on *gi* is combined with the *gi* that changes. Then he criticized Toegye's theory of *hobal* (mutual issuance). Yulgok wrote:

> The two letters *hobal* (互發) of Toegye's may not have been caused by a mistake in expression but by a mistake in understanding the nuanced logic of an inseparable relationship between *li* and *gi*.[20]

There was another reason for Yulgok to stress the inseparable relationship between *li* and *gi* to this extent. Although he was called an advocate of the theory of the *gi*-principal, in terms of which his thinking was contrary to Toegye's, he maintained his focus on the fact that *li* and *gi* play different roles, and in particular that *li* always plays the dominant role in the relationship with *gi*. He believed that *li* is a virtuous, categorical principle and always presides over *gi*, and thus its dominant role should not be overlooked, not only in the case of innate pure nature/the four beginnings but also in the case of physical nature/the seven feelings. In other words, even in the case of physical nature/ the seven feelings, in which the attributes of *li* are not fully manifested due to the influence of *gi*, as well as in the case of innate pure nature/the four beginnings, the fact that *li* always accompanies *gi* as sovereign over the latter must not be forgotten. For this reason, Yulgok used the term "*li*-principal" in the case of innate pure nature/the four beginnings, while he never used the term "*gi*-principal" in the case of physical nature/the seven feelings.

In order to explain this relationship between *li* and *gi* based on the principle of an inseparable relationship between them, Yulgok suggested the proposition *litong-giguk* (理通氣局), which can be interpreted as *li* pervades and *gi* delimits.

> Because *li* and *gi* are inseparable, they can be regarded as a single thing. However, they are different from each other in that *li* does not have a shape while *gi* does, and *li* does not function while *gi* does. Without a form or a function

(無形無爲), *li* is sovereign over that which has a form and a mode of functioning (有形有爲), whereas *gi*, which has a form and a mode of functioning, becomes a tool of that which has no form or mode of functioning. While *li* does not have a form, *gi* does. While *li* is omnipresent over any entity without any restriction, *gi* is limited to a specific time and space. While *li* does not have any function, *gi* does. Therefore *gi* is manifested and *li* rides on it (氣發理乘).[21]

This theory of *litong-giguk* was newly proposed by Yulgok to explain the relationship between *li* and *gi*, which had been conceptualized in Neo-Confucianism in the form of the proposition *liilbunsu / li-yi-fen-shu* (理一分殊, *li* is one but its manifestations are many) or the proposition *lidong-giyi / li-tong-qi-yi* (理同氣異, *li* concurs but *gi* differs). Cheng Yi and Zhu Xi's *liilbunsu* explained the fundamental identity and the phenomenal diversity of all things in the universe by focusing on *li*, and their *lidong-giyi* explained the functional difference between *li* and *gi*, which are neither separate nor intermingled (理氣不相離·不相雜). However, based on the principles of an inseparable relationship between *li* and *gi* and the unmixable nature of *li* and *gi*, Yulgok explained the formlessness and nonfunctionality of *li* and the form and functioning of *gi*, including the fundamental identity and phenomenal diversity of *li* and *gi*.

According to Yulgok, *gi* is originally calm, consistent, clear, and somewhat empty (湛一淸虛). However, due to its inherent, contradictory characteristics of *yin* and *yang*, *gi* continuously and arbitrarily moves up and down (升降飛揚) and becomes inconsistent (參差不齊), causing all kinds of generation, change, and movement. While coursing through all things, *gi* sometimes loses its original nature and sometimes does not. If *gi* loses its original nature, complete, clear, calm, constant, and somewhat empty *gi* (湛一淸虛之氣) becomes skewed and opaque *gi*, akin to waste or ashes (糟粕煨燼之氣). This is what "*gi* is circumscribed (氣局)" means. This attribute is in contrast to the fact that *li* always maintains its subtle nature in all things. *Li* retains its original subtle characteristics regardless of the condition of the accompanying *gi*, whether complete or skewed, clear or opaque, or pure or impure. This is what "*li* pervades (理通)" means.[22] *Li* always determines the various functions of *gi* from a dominant position based on its inherent nature. This method of coexistence in a relationship of *litong-giguk* was expressed in the proposition "*gi* is manifested, but *li* is riding on it (氣發而理乘之)." This relationship also applies to the dualisms of innate pure nature/physical nature, the four beginnings/the seven feelings, and the moral mind/the human mind.

What enables the diverse and ever-changing phenomena in the universe to maintain identity and consistency is not the identity/consistency of *gi* but the universality of *li*, and what enables *li* to display diversity in the phenomenal world is the circumscription of *gi*.[23] As a result, the grounds of both identity and diversity are the universality of *li* and the specificity of *gi*, respectively. However, although constant order is maintained in every case through the sovereignty of *li*, the clear, opaque, pure, or impure nature of *gi* may interfere with the complete realization of *li*. Therefore the attempt at self-cultivation and self-regulation must focus completely on controlling *gi* and on recuperating its original nature. However, because *li* is originally good (理本善), no supplement is needed. All that is required of *li* is that it should reveal its original nature through the recovery of the original nature of *gi*.[24] From this perspective, *li*, which maintains its original subtle characteristics, coexists with *gi* in every case, and only in this way can *li* reveal its original nature through self-cultivation. For this reason, Yulgok criticized Toegye for regarding the seven feelings and physical nature as constitutive of the *gi*-principal and as the manifestations of *gi* (氣發) and stressed that *li* always coexists with and has sovereignty over *gi*.

Yulgok, who emphasized the inseparable relationship between *li* and *gi*, interpreted *liilbunsu* (理一分殊) as denoting "essence and function (體用)." He said that *li* as a root principle of all entities is the "essence (體)" of *li*, while *li* as manifested in the multifarious phenomena is the "function (用)" of *li*. According to Yulgok, various phenomena are caused by the unevenness of *gi* because *li* always courses through all things while riding on *gi*.[25] As mentioned earlier, this means that the original *li* combines with the original *gi* and the *li* riding on *gi* combines with the *gi* that changes. Thus, from this perspective, Luo Qin-shun (羅欽順, pen name: Zheng-an 整庵, 1465–1547) was criticized for seeing *li* and *gi* as one, and Toegye was criticized for proposing that one precedes the other. Yulgok said that they somewhat misunderstood Cheng Hao's dictum "the vessel is also the Way; the Way is also the vessel (器亦道, 道亦器)" and Zhu Xi's argument "*li* and *gi* are definitively two things (理氣決是二物)."[26] However, Yulgok judged that Toegye had made a greater mistake than Luo Qin-shun, who was criticized for treating *li* and *gi* as one. According to Yulgok, although Luo misunderstood Zhu Xi by doubting that the latter had formed a conceptual distinction between *li* and *gi*, he did in fact understand the fundamental principle of the inseparable relationship between *li* and *gi*. However, Toegye was obsessed with the mutual issuance of *li* and *gi* and thus overlooked the essential principle of the inseparable relationship between them.[27] Thus, Yulgok attempted to maintain the balance between the inseparable relationship between *li* and *gi* and the simultaneous impossibility of their intermingling. In this way, he rejected Toegye's division of *li* and *gi* in terms of their sequence and Luo Qin-shun's treatment of *li* and *gi* as one.

For this reason, Yulgok proposed that *li* superintends and rides on *gi* and that *li* and *gi* are neither one nor two (一而二, 二而一, they are one but also can be two; and they are two but also can be one).[28] This shows that *li* and *gi* are inseparable and unmixable and thus that it is impossible to identify the sequence of *li* and *gi*.[29] Yulgok called this a delicate relationship between *li* and *gi* (理氣之妙).

He adhered to the principles of the inseparable relationship between *li* and *gi* and the unmixability of the two, avoiding the explanations of the *li*-principal, the *gi*-principal, the manifestation of *li*, and the manifestation of *gi*. The basic logic of his thinking was that all things and functions in the phenomenal world are composed of the combination of *li* and *gi*, but the purely good *li* always exists in its aloofness. Yulgok wanted to argue for *li* as a purely good entity while also adhering to both the inseparability and the unmixability of *li* and *gi* in actuality.

As seen earlier, Yulgok's theory of *li-gi*, which focused on *litong-giguk*, attained quite a high level of compatibility with the Neo-Confucian theory of *li-gi*, which attempted to explain the creativity, transformative capacity, and mobility of nature (the view of nature) and the process of realizing moral ideals (the view of the human and of society) within a single framework based on the principles of the inseparability and unmixability of *li* and *gi*.[30]

THE HUMAN WILL: THE MIND EXPRESSED

The theory of *litong-giguk* (理通氣局) is useful in explaining the reason why phenomena in actuality are good or evil within the *li-gi* framework, but it is helpless when faced with the task of transforming an evil world into a good one. In other words, Yulgok's theory of *li-gi* is quite fruitful in explaining the fact that as *li*, which constitutes universal principles and norms, evolves into various phenomena in accordance with the diversity of *gi*, which is matter or energy, various types of good and evil emerge in the world. However, there is no dynamic or driving force that can lead such a world in the direction of good in this conceptualization of *li-gi*. Confucianism or Neo-Confucianism, which seeks to promote the ideal of "sage on the inside, virtuous king on the outside (內聖外王)," is not a theoretical system that is designed to "explain" phenomena but a form of learning that aims to "create" an ideal, moral society. Thus, a method of extending the realm or scope of goodness (virtue) and of suppressing evil or transforming evil into good is necessary. If Yulgok's theory of *li-gi* merely explains phenomena, it will lose its utility as a Confucian or Neo-Confucian theory. Therefore Yulgok paid attention to the human will, which can transmute evil into virtue.

This focus was based on his view of nature and human beings as a single organic body and of the central human role in all things. Yulgok thought that human beings have a special connection with the universe and nature through the dynamic of *li-gi*. Of course, because his theory of *li-gi* was based on Neo-Confucianism, which saw both the universe and nature as being composed of the combination of *li* and *gi*, it was applicable to animals and plants as well as human beings. However, he felt that human beings are in a different position from other entities in the universe and nature. This argument was based on the traditional theory of *samjae / san-cai* (三才, trinity/three substances) in Confucianism, which claims that, along with Heaven and Earth, human beings are one of the three subjects that oversee the operation of the universe. Yulgok focused on the fact that unlike other entities that arise with fixed, opaque characteristics, human beings are born with various material dispositions and have the capacity to undergo transformation, rendering them clear and pure, through the will and effort of the individual. He believed that phenomena in nature and in human society can be logically explained by *li* and *gi*, which are in a relationship of inseparability yet unmixability, and argued that in light of this it is the responsibility of human beings to change an evil or amoral reality.

Through the theory of *litong-giguk*, Yulgok tried to explain *li* as the necessary ideal to be realized and as the only universal principle, which is not only the origin of the universe but can also exist anywhere in the phenomenal world. Based on the fact that the human mind seems to be empty yet has mystical insight and possesses multifarious senses, he also thought that human beings can change impure and opaque *gi* into pure and clear *gi*, and that the will to achieve and the capacity for such learning and cultivation can only be found in human beings.[31] Taking into account the fact that Heaven and Earth are composed solely of pure and clear matter (*gi*), while other animals and plants are generated with impure and opaque matter, which are unchangeable, human beings, born with diverse forms of matter, are the only beings who can alter their own makeup.

In that sense, Yulgok believed that human judgment and behaviors have a great impact on the universe and nature. His "Cheondo chaek (天道策, A Proposal on the Way of Heaven)" provides a good explanation of the relationship between nature and human beings. This text was submitted as an answer when he won first place in a state examination when he was twenty-three years old in 1558, which was the year when he first met Toegye. Because this was written as an answer in an examination, it must have been tailored to the specific predilections of the examiner. Nevertheless, it contains the quite clear and logical stance of Yulgok on the relationship between Heaven/Earth and human beings in the framework of *li-gi*. Many of his existing *chaengmun / ce-wen* (策文, answers to state examination questions) other than "Cheondo chaek" also describe how Neo-Confucianism can explain and amend the world in various respects. The fact that the question books for high-ranking official exams consisted of such themes or issues shows that explaining virtue/vice and merits/demerits and eventually amending or improving the world on the basis of theoretical considerations was the universal concern of the intellectuals and bureaucrats of the time. Yulgok had obtained high scores for his exemplary answers to such questions, which contain his point of view and philosophical position.

According to Yulgok, among the many constituents of nature, human beings correspond to the "mind" of the world and have a significant impact on the entirety of nature. When a country is well governed by a sage king, the functioning of Heaven and Earth is also harmonious, but when a country is in a chaotic state, some harmful natural events also occur.[32] In that sense, the role of human beings is not limited to human society but affects the whole of nature.[33]

However, as mentioned earlier, in Yulgok's *li-gi* system, there is no motive force to lead the phenomenal world in which good and evil coexist in a positive direction. According to Yulgok, *gi* arbitrarily moves up and down and becomes clear/opaque or pure/impure due to its inherent nature, but *li* is the cause of this instability. This clearly distinguishes the roles of *gi* and *li*, which are neither separable nor mixable. It was also said that *li* and *gi*, which play such different roles, are always partnered in the state of *litong-giguk*. However, the existence of evil is not fully attributable to the inherent nature of *gi* because the cause of this nature is *li*. Although *gi* may interfere with *li* due to its uneven nature, the superintendence of *li* is omnipresent. Without the sovereignty of *li*, *gi* would have never been independently involved in such fundamental phenomena.[34] So does this mean that purely good *li* makes *gi* opaque or impure? If we focus only on understanding and explaining that the diversity of *gi* creates diversity in the world of phenomena from the perspective of ontology, this may not be problematic. However, Yulgok could not overlook the fact that the diversity of *gi* is directly connected with the issue of good/evil in terms of axiology. The reason why not only good but also evil exist in reality, despite the functioning of purely good *li* as a cause or a governor of *gi*, required explanation. Furthermore, it was necessary to stress the goal of Neo-Confucianism, which attempted to build a morally ideal society by transforming evil into good.

Therefore Yulgok focused on "human will/consciousness (*ui / yi* 意)." According to him, as a key function of the mind, the human will plays a role in observing and examining with precision the manifestation of one's original nature through emotions when they transpire.[35] Thus, the human will has the functions of intentional awareness and judgment.

However, the role of the will is subject to the manifestation of the heart-mind because the will's functioning commences on the revelation of the emotions.[36] This conception is different from Toegye's thinking in that he tried to distinguish the four beginnings from the seven feelings and the moral mind from the human mind, even before the manifestation of the mind. While Toegye discriminated between good and evil emotions from the point of their origin and focused on preserving, cultivating, and examining the origin of good emotions through self-cultivation even before the manifestation of the mind, Yulgok's self-cultivation is focused on the issues that arise after the revelation of emotions.

Toegye emphasized *gyeong* (敬), the attitude of being reverently mindful toward innate nature (nature = *li*) that exists even before the revelation of moral emotions, because he thought that innate nature itself is a perfect ethical principle or norm, with a tendency to realize pure goodness. Therefore, through propositions related to *li*, such as "*li* issues (理發)," "*li* moves (理動)," and "*li* arrives of its own accord (理自到)," Toegye stressed these characteristics of *li* and the reverence for the origin of *li*, the Mandate of Heaven. His philosophy also focused on the full realization of *li* through learning and cultivation. However, the will that Yulgok stressed was not morally good will in itself. Because the will as a kind of rigorous thinking begins with the revelation of an emotion, he said, "If thinking follows *li*, good emotions are immediately revealed without any possible corruption by evil thoughts. However, if thinking loses righteousness, an evil mind arises."[37] According to Yulgok, good emotion is not the automatically revealed potentiality of innate nature (nature = *li*). In order to achieve the full manifestation of good emotions, when innate nature is revealed in the form of emotions in response to external objects, the will must lead the emotions in a good direction by having them follow *li*. Yulgok emphasized *seong-ui* / *cheng-yi* (誠意, sincerity of will = making the will truthful) as a method of study or self-cultivation because enlisting the human in the task of truly obeying the rule of *li* was the key to moral judgment and behavior.

Of course, because *gyeong-oe* / *jing-wei* (敬畏, reverent mindfulness and the feeling of awe) and *seong-ui* are the basic attitudes of learning in Neo-Confucianism, both Toegye and Yulgok emphasized them. However, when comparing these two scholars in terms of their methods of study and self-cultivation, Toegye emphasized *gyeong-oe*, while Yulgok stressed *seong-ui*. Their tendencies were so strong that it is common to contrast the learning of Toegye and Yulgok based on their respective emphases on *gyeong* (敬) and *seong* / *cheng* (誠). The point of this comparison is that this difference between the two arose from whether they emphasized *li* (moral spontaneity stemming from a law of nature) or *ui* / *yi* (意, moral judgment and will).

A SUMMARY OF THE DEBATE

Ugye and Yulgok conducted a debate through a correspondence consisting of twelve letters, but they were not able to bridge their differences.

The failure to reach a consensus despite their long-running correspondence over several months shows how difficult it was to convince or persuade the other party through discussion. Through a comparative analysis of the moral mind and the human mind and the four beginnings and the seven feelings, Ugye believed the four beginnings and the seven feelings partook of the *li*-principal and the *gi*-principal, or the manifestations of *li* and *gi*, respectively, and he supported Toegye's theory of the four beginnings and the seven feelings. As for Yulgok, as a result of his applying the framework of innate pure nature and physical nature to the four beginnings and the seven feelings, he criticized Toegye's theory. In other words, Yulgok regarded the four beginnings and the seven feelings from a different perspective and explained the former by describing only *li* and the latter by describing the modality of *li* that is accompanied by *gi*.

Of course, it cannot be said that Ugye's thinking is precisely compatible with Toegye's theory. Although Ugye agreed with Toegye's stance of considering the moral mind and the four beginnings as constitutive of the *li*-principal and the human mind and the seven feelings as constitutive of the *li*-principal, he simply meant that they can be divided into the *li*-principal and the *gi*-principal depending on what they are semantically referring to. Ugye in fact adopted the same position as Gobong in that he formed this division solely in terms of "what they refer to (所指)" and "what they further imply (所就而言)." Just as Gobong understood the perspective of the "origin (所從來)" ontologically, Ugye also thought that this *li*-principal/*gi*-principal distinction could not be applied to the four-seven and to the human mind/moral mind in terms of their origin. In this sense, Ugye understood Toegye's "manifestation of *li*" as the manifestation of *gi* following *li* (氣之順理而發), just as Gobong did.[38] However, as seen earlier, Toegye made it clear to Gobong that such an understanding was a misconception of the manifestation of *li*.

Through this debate, Yulgok achieved significant philosophical progress by proposing his own ideas, such as the theory of *litong-giguk* (理通氣局) and the theory that the human mind can be transformed into the moral mind and vice versa (人心道心相爲終始說). When the debate concluded, Yulgok had established his mature scholarly position, which was comparable to Toegye's theory of *li*, *gi*, the heart-mind, and nature (理氣心性說). Since then, scholarly comparison between Toegye and Yulgok has been carried out based on this theory of *li*, *gi*, the heart-mind, and nature. As representative members of the intelligentsia in the Joseon Dynasty of the sixteenth century, their philosophical differences led to the adoption of different political stances on their parts. Their acts of political engagement best represent their political positions, but the evaluation of their stances must be made by historians. In this book, their philosophy and political thought, which brought about their political actions, is examined through their writings on politics.

UNDERSTANDING AND EVALUATION
OF THE FOUR-SEVEN DEBATE[39]

The dispute concerning the four beginnings and the seven feelings was one of the most important intellectual disputes in Joseon Confucianism. It was also an exchange of ideas that had a decisive effect on the development of the philosophy of that era. It was necessary for all Joseon intellectuals at a minimum to adopt positions and to express their opinions on this dispute, regardless of the originality or lack thereof of their own thinking. However, when discussing the issues of the original moral nature and moral emotions in terms of the concepts of *li* and *gi*, it is quite difficult to clearly explain the relationship between these abstract concepts and their roles. Confucian scholars of the time sought effective methods of explanation to overcome such difficulties by comparing the concepts and usages of *li*, *gi*, the heart-mind, innate nature, and feeling, and modern scholars have also tried to solve this problem using such explanations.

Daeseol (對說, the proposition that *li* and *gi* are independent of each other) and *inseol* (因說, the proposition that *li* and *gi* can be interlocking), suggested by Gobong to Toegye; *jeon* (專, specific usage) and *chong* (總, general usage), proposed by the Seongho School (星湖學派) and elaborated by Jeong Yak-yong (pen name: Dasan); and *hoenggan* (橫看, the horizontal viewpoint) and *sugan* (竪看, the vertical viewpoint), promoted by Yi Sang-jeong (pen name: Daesan), Yi Jin-sang (pen name: Hanju), and Jeong Jae-gyu (pen name: Nobaekheon), were the explanatory frameworks proposed by scholars in the Joseon Dynasty. Modern scholars have also used those frameworks to explain the theory of *li*, *gi*, the heart-mind, and nature in Joseon Confucianism.

Discussions centered around the Seongho School, spanning from the thinking of Yi Ik (李瀷, 1681–1763; pen name: Seongho), who considered himself a successor to Toegye, to that of Jeong Yak-yong, which was mainly focused on dividing the usages of *li* and *gi* into specific and general categories through the analysis of relevant concepts. Based on such discussions by respected Seongho scholars, including Seongho, Shin Hu-dam (慎後聃; pen name: Habin), and Yi Byeong-hyu (李秉休; pen name: Jeongsan), Dasan compared the thinking of Toegye and Yulgok in terms of the theory of the four beginnings and the seven feelings. He discerned the reason for the different positions of the two scholars in the contrasting uses they made of the conceptual implications of *li* and *gi*. While Toegye employed *li* and *gi* as specific concepts applicable to the special domain of the mind, Yulgok used them as general concepts applicable to the entirety of nature. Dasan divided them into *jeon* (specific usage) and *chong* (general usage). He evaluated Toegye's stance as more appropriate for the use of *li* and *gi* as specific concepts applicable to the domain of the mind in order to explain the four beginnings and the seven feelings because the discussion of the four and the seven is concerned with the human mind.[40]

Toegye's *li* and *gi* as specific or limited concepts can be called the "*li* and *gi* of the mind," while Yulgok's *li* and *gi* as general concepts can be called the "*li* and *gi* of nature." Toegye believed that the crucial difference between the four beginnings and the seven feelings derives from the fact that the four beginnings are purely good, whereas the seven feelings can with great facility become evil, and he reintegrated the issue of the four-seven into the issue of good and evil in the mind. He also distinguished the four beginnings, which originated from pure, good, and complete *li*, from the seven feelings, which originated from clear/pure or opaque/impure *gi* from the axiological perspective, which espouses the concept of the "*li* and *gi* of the mind." Conversely, Yulgok forthrightly adhered to the basic usage of *li* and *gi* suggested by the theory of *li-gi*, which proposed that *gi* is manifested but that *li* causes this manifestation. He explained the four beginnings and the seven feelings by focusing on their ontological structure through the use of the concept of the "*li* and *gi* of nature."

The evaluation of Bae Jong-ho to the effect that "Toegye saw *li-gi* in terms of its anthropological value whereas Yulgok firstly understood nature on the basis of *li-gi*, and then explained human existence through this understanding"[41] was arrived at based on the conception of the specific/general usage of *li-gi* proposed by scholars from Seongho to Dasan, and especially Dasan's dualism of "the *li-gi* of the mind"/"the *li-gi* of nature." Due to the ambiguity of the concept of *li-gi* and the multilayered theoretical structure of Neo-Confucianism in which *li-gi* is combined with the theory of the heart-mind and nature and is furthermore linked with the theory of learning and cultivation, the explanatory method that contrasts the usages of the concepts of *li-gi* in accordance with disparate examples or viewpoints is also useful to today's scholars. In addition to Dasan's method, the *daeseol/inseol* (對說/因說) and *hoenggan/sugan* (橫看/竪看) methods are also commonly mobilized.[42]

Daeseol/inseol is a dualism proposed by Gobong in his argument with Toegye on the four beginnings and the seven feelings. Gobong explained the meaning of *daeseol* and *inseol* as follows:

Daeseol refers to the left and the right, which are counterparts, while *inseol* refers to up and down, which entails connection.[43]

Gobong claimed that the explanation of Zhu Xi, "The four beginnings are the manifestation of *li* and the seven feelings are the manifestation of *gi*," which was quoted by Toegye to support his theory of the mutual issuance of *li* and *gi* (理氣互發說), is not *daeseol* but *inseol*.[44] That is, Gobong, who argued for the centrality of *inseol*, asserted that even Zhu Xi's explanation was given from the perspective of *inseol*. This, of course, differed from Toegye's thought, but Toegye did not raise any objection to such a *daeseol/inseol* dualistic explanatory method per se.[45]

In terms of the application of the method of *daeseol/inseol*, Toegye's viewpoint on the four beginnings and the seven feelings entailed the propositions "*li* issues and *gi* follows it (理發而氣隨之)" and "*gi* issues and *li* rides on it (氣發而理乘之)," which correspond to *daeseol*, and Gobong's view of both the four beginnings and the seven feelings in terms of the proposition that "*gi* issues and *li* rides on it (氣發而理乘之)" corresponds to *inseol*. This interpretation clearly shows the characteristics of the theory of the four-seven of each of the two scholars, Toegye and Gobong. Yi Sang-eun focused on this explanation and concretely summarized the controversies on the four-seven between Toegye and Gobong by employing the *daeseol/inseol* dualistic structure.[46]

Hoenggan and *sugan* refer to "seeing horizontally" and "seeing vertically," respectively, which was a commonly employed contrast in the Joseon Dynasty. Because it was typically used for reading account books or lists of items even before its application to the theory of *li*, *gi*, the heart-mind, and nature, countless usages can be found in the literature of Joseon. This simple method of contrast, which was very familiar to the people of the time, was naturally used when explaining the theory of *li*, *gi*, the heart-mind, and nature and when contrasting the theories of the four-seven of Toegye and Yulgok. Many scholars, including Yi Sang-jeong (李象靖, 1710–1781; pen name: Daesan), Yi Jin-sang (李震相, 1818–1886; pen name: Hanju), and Jeong Jae-gyu (鄭載圭, 1843–1911; pen name: Nobaekheon) used such a method. Nobaekheon described *hoenggan/sugan* as follows:

> From a horizontal viewpoint (橫看), the logic of all creation does not exist alone but has a counterpart, while from a vertical viewpoint (竪看), the logic of all creation does not originally have any counterpart.[47]

This conception was described by Nobaekheon as the relationship between *li* and *gi*, but its wider usefulness is easily confirmed when applying these two viewpoints to the theory of the four-seven of Toegye and Yulgok. Toegye's theory of the mutual issuance of *li* and *gi* contrasted the four beginnings and the seven feelings as pure goodness and the great potential to become evil (易流於惡), which originated from *li* and *gi*, respectively. The horizontal perspective of *hoenggan* clearly demonstrates the fact that Toegye's theory of the four beginnings and the seven feelings contrasts the four and the seven by defining them as "the issuance of *li* (理發[而氣隨之])" and "the issuance of *gi* (氣發[而理乘之])," respectively. In comparison, Yulgok's theory stipulating that "only *gi* issues and *li* rides on it (氣發理乘一途說)" displays the same structure of the four and the seven by asserting that *gi* is manifested in both the four beginnings and the seven feelings but that the cause of this manifestation is *li*. The vertical axis of *sugan* clearly demonstrates Yulgok's position that the four beginnings and the seven feelings have the same structure as *li-gi*, and this method of explanation is still employed today.[48]

The advantage of the dualisms of *daeseol/inseol* and *hoenggan/sugan* is that they schematize the major issues involved in the controversies on the four-seven, enabling greater comprehension of them by presenting the *li-gi* theory-based structure of the four beginnings and the seven feelings in a spatial arrangement. First, *daeseol* and *hoenggan* describe well the characteristics of Toegye's theory of the mutual issuance of *li* and *gi* (理氣互發說), which emphasizes that the distinction between the four beginnings and the seven feelings stems from *li* and *gi*. *Inseol* and *sugan* clearly illustrate the structure of Yulgok's theory, which entails that "only *gi* issues and *li* rides on it (氣發理乘一途說)" and which implies that both the four beginnings and the seven feelings are manifested through the functioning of *gi* superintended by *li*. *Daeseol* and *hoenggan* also demonstrate Toegye's viewpoint that the four beginnings and the seven feelings are contrasting concepts, and *inseol* and *sugan* illustrate Yulgok's position that the seven feelings encompass the four beginnings.

However, Confucianism or Neo-Confucianism, which pursue the embodiment of the Confucian ideal of "sage on the inside, virtuous king on the outside (內聖外王)," consider learning and cultivation (內聖) to be a tool for the realization of thought or the ideal (外王). Because Neo-Confucianism is a body of learning aimed at the realization of a morally ideal society, facts that preclude the consideration of the moral value of recognition, judgment, and behavior are not its concern. That is, academic investigation and discussion in terms of the analysis of facts that are independent of moral cognition, judgment, and behavior are meaningless in Confucianism or Neo-Confucianism.

After Confucius and Mencius presented Confucian thought and philosophy, their followers in the Northern Song Dynasty systematized the theory of *li-gi* in order to theoretically support and justify their teachings. However, whether its theoretical structure was explained from the perspective of the theory of *li-gi* or schematized from the viewpoint of *hoenggan/sugan*, it was simply an explanatory framework aimed at contrasting the four beginnings and the seven feelings or a means of explaining the Neo-Confucian theory of *li*, *gi*, the heart-mind, and nature to novices. In addition, it is true that such methods were useful in early modern studies in explaining in terms of modern language and logic the theory of *li*, *gi*, the heart-mind, and nature or the theory of four beginnings and the seven feelings, in which scholars had lost interest.

These schemata arranged and explained the two sides in terms of an oppo-sitional structure, but it is important that, originally, the key to Neo-Confucian debates on issues such as the theory of the four beginnings and the seven feel-ings was not to identify whose position was correct or incorrect. In particular, controversies on the four beginnings and the seven feelings were not focused on an examination of the authenticity of the *li-gi* theory-based structure of the four and the seven. While Gobong pointed out that Toegye's theory of the mutual issuance of *li* and *gi* may encourage people to understand *li* and *gi* dif-ferently, Toegye argued that, although there may be different opinions arising from varying viewpoints, his explanation was more useful for the purpose of education and edification in terms of the original goal of Neo-Confucianism. Ultimately, this was essentially not a dispute over who was more correct but a discussion that aimed to identify which perspective was more effective in furthering the understanding and practice of Neo-Confucian values or its worldview.

Therefore the focus of the understanding and evaluation of the theory of *li*, *gi*, the heart-mind, and nature should not be on the comparison and analysis of *li-gi* theory-based structures but on which perspective plays a more effec-tive role in achieving the purpose of Neo-Confucianism and is more appropri-ate for contemporary circumstances.

Joseon Confucian scholars, including Toegye, Gobong, Ugye, and Yulgok, did not initiate disputes in order to reveal the ontological structures of *li*, *gi*, the heart-mind, and nature. They debated in order to discern the path to the realization of a moral life through the amendment or perfecting of moral emotions. They recognized that each other's concepts of *li* and *gi* had both a general usage (in terms of nature) and a specific or dedicated usage (in terms of the mind), and they adopted viewpoints that could accommodate the dif-ference in sameness (同中有異) and the sameness in difference (異中有同), depending on where their focus was.[49] In other words, scholars who partici-pated in the debates on the four beginnings and the seven feelings discussed which method was more effective in understanding moral emotions and in realizing or achieving a moral life, either through a focus on distinguishing the moral emotions of human beings based on the axiological standard of good and evil (同中有異) or a focus on the fact that all moral emotions have the same foundation as each other in terms of the structure of the theory of *li-gi* (異中有同). In addition, it was more important for them to transform the contemporary world in which facts and values were inseparable into a virtu-ous world than to avoid the difficulties of understanding caused by ambigu-ous language or conceptual usage.

Toegye stressed the distinctiveness of the four beginnings and the seven feelings by focusing on the distinction between good and evil, whereas Gobong and Yulgok stressed the fact that the four and the seven have the same *li-gi* theory-based structure by focusing on the relationship between *li* and *gi* and their roles. Nevertheless, Toegye partially accepted Gobong's comment that he should not cause in others the misunderstanding that *li* and *gi* were separate, and he made it clear that the four beginnings and the seven feelings were based on the ontological foundations of the theory of *li-gi*, which consist of the inseparability of *li* and *gi* (理氣不相離) and their simultaneous independence (理氣不相雜). While also emphasizing that the four beginnings and the seven feelings have the same structure in terms of the theory of *li-gi*, Gobong and Yulgok emphasized that the realization of purely good moral emotions can be ensured only by clarifying the relationship between *li* and *gi* and their roles. The key point of this argument is not that they explained the four beginnings and the seven feelings in terms of different *li-gi* theory-based structures, but that, despite their different arguments, they together led the way in the conceptualization of the ontological structures of *li* and *gi* and in the axiological adjustment of moral emotions. This strand of thought succeeded the original preoccupations of Neo-Confucianism, which had been centered on the attempt to strengthen the legitimacy of moral standards to the level of ontological necessity by providing an ontological foundation for these moral standards.

What people today can gain from the theory of *li*, *gi*, the heart-mind, and nature and the theory of the four beginnings and seven feelings in Neo-Confucianism may be the initiation and the experience of discussions that attempt to raise the level of normative justification of a moral life to the level of the law of nature by seeking the basis of human and social morality in the fundamental homogeneity of phenomena and in the essential identity of natural principles. In addition, the method of realizing a morally ideal society, pursued through such discussions, also requires sober assessment, which can help lead modern society in a desirable direction. In other words, in order to establish a debate that can contribute to the creation of a better society, we should pay attention to multifaceted issues, namely the advantages and disadvantages of integrating Confucianism with an ontological foundation; the implications of its resulting theories, including the theory of *li*, *gi*, the heart-mind, and nature and the theory of the four beginnings and the seven feelings; the experience of developing a society and operating a legal system based on those theories; the development of theories based on this experience; and the principles and experience of social cohesion obtained through the reproduction mechanisms advanced by such theories and practices.

Toegye and Yulgok attempted to put into practice what they had learned from their discussions about the theory of *li*, *gi*, the heart-mind, and nature. As they were practical intellectuals often engaged in public duties, this book focuses on the strands of political philosophy that provided a foundation for their political activities.

NOTES

1. Seong Hon, "Yeo Yulgok non igi Je-2-seo" 與栗谷論理氣 第二書 (Discussing *Li* and *Gi* with Yulgok—Letter No. 2), in *Ugye jip* 牛溪集 in *Han-guk munjip chonggan*, 43:91b.

2. Yulgok was called "gudo jangwon gong" because he won first place in nine state examinations. It is presumed that he actually did so than nine times because "gudo (九度, nine times)" also means "the greatest number of times" or "very many times."

3. Seong Hon, "Yeo Yulgok non igi Je-1-seo" 與栗谷論理氣 第一書 (Discussing *Li* and *Gi* with Yulgok—Letter No. 1), in *Ugye jip*, 43:089a.

4. Seong Hon, "Discussing *Li* and *Gi* with Yulgok—Letter No. 1," in *Ugye jip*, 43:89a; "Byeolji" 別紙 (Enclosure), in *Ugye jip*, 43:089b; "Je-2-seo" 第二書 (Letter No. 2), in *Ugye jip*, 43:90d.

5. Zhu Xi, "Zhong Yong zhang-ju xu" 中庸章句序, in *Si-shu zhang-ju ji-zhu* 四書章句集注 (Collected Commentaries on the Four Books in Chapters and Verses) (Beijing: Zhong-hua Shu-ji, 1983), 14. "心之虛靈知覺, 一而已矣, 而以爲有人心道心之異者, 則以其或生於形氣之私, 或原於性命之正, 而所以爲知覺者不同."

6. Ibid., 14. "而所以爲知覺者不同. 是以或危殆而不安, 或微妙而難見耳.... 從事於斯, 無少間斷, 必使道心, 常爲一身之主, 而人心每聽命焉, 則危者安, 微者著, 而動靜云爲, 自無過不及之差矣."

7. Yi I, "Dap Seong Howon" 答成浩原 (Response to Seong Howon), in *Yulgok jeonseo*, 044:200b–c.

8. Seong Hon, "Discussing *Li* and *Gi* with Yulgok—Letter No. 2," in *Ugye jip*, 43:91a–b.

9. Yi I, "Response to Seong Howon" (Yulgok's Letter No. 2), in *Yulgok jeonseo*, 44:199d–200b.

10. When contrasted with physical nature, innate pure nature, the nature conferred by Heaven and Earth, and the nature conferred by Heaven are effectively indistinguishable.

11. Yi I, "Response to Seong Howon," in *Yulgok jeonseo*, 44:209a–b.

12. Zhang Zai, "Cheng-ming" 誠明 (Sincerity and Enlightenment), in *Zheng-meng* 正蒙 (Rectifying Ignorance) of *Zhang Zi quan-shu* 張子全書 (The Complete Works of Zhang Zai) (Taipei: Taiwan Zhong-hua Shu-ju, 1996), 2:17b. "性者萬物之一源, 非有我之得私也."

13. Ibid., 18b. "形而後有氣質之性, 善反之則天地之性存焉."

14. Ibid., 18b. "盡其性能盡人物之性, 至於命者亦能至人物之命, 莫不性諸道, 命諸天. . . . 性於人無不善, 繫其善反不善反而已, 過天地之化, 不善反者也. 命於人無不正, 繫其順與不順而已, 行險以僥倖, 不順命者也."

15. Zhu Xi, "*Zheng-meng* Cheng-ming zhu" 正蒙–誠明 注, in *Zhang Zi quan-shu*, 2:19a–b.

16. Yi Hwang, "Dap Gi myeong-eon" 答奇明彥 (Response to Gi Myeong-eon), in *Toegye jip*, 29:413c–d.

17. Ibid., 029:418b–c.

18. Yi I, "Response to Seong Howon," in *Yulgok jeonseo*, 44:196c.

19. Ibid., 44:212a.

20. Ibid., 44:212c.

21. Ibid., 44:210d–211a.

22. Ibid., 44:211a–b.

23. Ibid., 44:218a.

24. Ibid., 44:211c.

25. Yi I, "Dap An Eung-hyu" 答安應休 (Response to An Eung-hyu), in *Yulgok jeonseo*, 44:250b–c.

26. Yi I, "Response to Seong Howon," in *Yulgok jeonseo*, 44:202a–b.

27. Ibid., 44:204c–205a.

28. Ibid., 44:199a.

29. Ibid., 44:199b.

30. This explanation of *litong-giguk* is based on Kim Hyoungchan's "Igironui irwonnonhwa yeon-gu" (A Study on the Monistic Tendency of the Theory of *Li-Gi*) (PhD diss., Korea University, 1996), 60–64.

31. Yi I, "Response to Seong Howon," in *Yulgok jeonseo*, 44:199c–d.

32. Toegye also agreed with the concept of mutual communication between Heaven-Earth and human beings, but he was quite critical of Yulgok's position that human behaviors are directly influenced by Heaven and Earth. Yi Hwang, "Mujin yukjo so" 戊辰六條疏, in *Toegye jip*, 29:192b–194d.

33. Yi I, "Cheondo chaek," in *Yulgok jeonseo*, 44:309c–312d.

34. Yi I, "Response to Seong Howon," in *Yulgok jeonseo*, 44:199b.

35. Ibid., 44:194d–195a.

36. Ibid., 44:251d–252a.

37. Yi I, "Eorok sang" 語錄 上 (Analects I), in *Yulgok jeonjip*, 45:232b.

38. Seong Hon, "Je-4-seo" 第四書 (Letter No. 4), in *Ugye jip*, 43:096c.

39. In this section, "Understanding and Evaluation of the Four-Seven Debate," I have summarized and rearranged, in accordance with this book's context, some contents of my article. Kim Hyoungchan, "The Li-Ki Structure of the Four Beginnings and the Seven Emotions and the Intent of the Four-Seven Debate," *Acta Koreana* 18, no. 2 (2015).

40. Jeong Yak-yong, "Ibal gibal byeon" 理發氣發辨 (The Critical Argument about the Issue of *Li* and the Issue of *Gi*), in *Yeoyudang jeonseo* 與猶堂全書 (The Complete Works of Jeong Yak-yong), Vol. 1 and 2 in *Han-guk munjip chonggan*, 281:258a–c. For Dasan's detailed opinions described in the "Issuance of *Li* and *Gi*," refer to Kim Hyongchan's "Ma-eum-ui igiwa jayeon-ui igi" (The *Li-Gi* of the Mind and the *Li-Gi* of Nature), *Han-gukhak nonjip* 40 (2010).

41. Bae Jong-ho, *Han-guk yuhaksa* (A History of Korean Confucianism) (Seoul: Yonsei University Press, 1974), 81.

42. In addition, there is the alternative explanatory method of *hollyun* (渾淪) / *bungae* (分開), which was employed by Yu Myeong-jong. This method was used by Toegye when he explained the relationship between *li* and *gi*. Yu Myeong-jong applied it to the explanation of the four beginnings and the seven feelings and called Toegye's theory *bungae* (分開) and Gobong's theory *hollyun* (渾淪). This method was quite similar to those of *daeseol/inseol* and *hoenggan/sugan* in terms of the

relevant issues dealt with and the characteristics of the explanatory framework, but Yu Myeong-jong in fact generated confusion by linking *hollyun* to *hoenggan* and *bungae* to *sugan*. He saw that Toegye's theory that the four beginnings and the seven feelings constitute the mutual issuance of *li* and *gi* (四端七情理氣互發) corresponds to *sugan* in that there is a precedence between *li* and *gi*, while also seeing Gobong's view that the seven feelings include the four beginnings (七包四) as *hoenggan* because there is no precedence between *li* and *gi* (理氣無先後). This book argues that Nobaekheon's explanation as described shortly is more valid when applied to *hoenggan/sugan*, and thus Yu Myeong-jong's theory is not separately discussed. Yu Myeong-jong, *Seongnihak-gwa Yangmyeonghak* (Philosophies of Zhu Zi and Yamgming) (Seoul: Yonsei University Press, 1994), 134–54; *Han-guk yuhak yeon-gu* (A Study of Korean Confucianism) (Seoul: Yimun Publishing Company, 1988), 142–46; Yi Hwang, "Dap Gi Myeong-eon 答奇明彦 (Response to Gi Myeong-eon), Non sadan chiljeong Je-2-seo huron 論四端七情第二書-後論 (Second Letter Discussing the Four Beginnings and the Seven Feelings), in *Toegye jip*, 29:424c–d.

43. Gi Dae-seung, "Gobong dap Toegye jaeron sadan chiljeong seo" 高峯答退溪再論四端七情書 (Gobong's Response to Toegye After Reviewing the Four Beginnings and the Seven Feelings), in *Gobong jeonjip* (Seoul: Daedong munhwa yeon-guwon at Sungkyunkwan University, 1979), 276.

44. Ibid.

45. Yi Hwang, "Response to Gi Myeong-eon," in *Toegye jip*, 29:432c–d.

46. Yi Sang-eun, "Sachil nonbyeon-gwa Daeseol/Inseol-ui uiui" (The Significance of the Four-Seven Debate and *Daeseol/Inseol*), in *Toegye-ui saeng-aewa hangmun* (Toegye's Life and Learning) (Seoul: Yemun seowon, 1999), 87–244.

47. Jeong Jae-gyu, "'Oepil' bipane daehan jaebipan" 猥筆辨辨 (A Reappraisal of the Criticism of Presuming Writing), in *Nobaekheon jip* 老柏軒集 in *Han-guk munjip chonggan*, Supplementary Volume, 145:607b.

48. The recent use of the explanatory method *hoengseol/suseol* (橫說/竪說) on the part of Yi Seung-hwan followed the framework of *hoenggan/sugan*. Yi Seung-hwan, *Hoengseol-gwa Suseol* (Hoengseol and Suseol) (Seoul: Humanist, 2012).

49. The terms "the difference in sameness (同中有異)" and "the sameness in difference (異中有同)" derive from Toegye's work. Regarding the four beginnings and the seven feelings, he said that although both of these perspectives are possible, he adopted the perspective of "the difference in sameness." Yi Hwang. "Toegye dap Gobong sadan chiljeong bun igi byeon" 退溪答高峯四端七情分理氣辯 (Toegye's Response to Gobong on the Schematization of the Four and the Seven as *Li* and *Gi*), in *Gobong jeonjip*, the right side of page 5.

Chapter 7

The Politics of the Royal Court

Upon the death of King Myeongjong (明宗, reign: 1545–1567), Toegye was appointed by the Royal Court to write his biography. In the following year (1568), he was called to the Royal Court by King Seonjo (宣祖, reign: 1567–1608). With great expectations for the new king's reign, he participated in *gyeong-yeon* (經筵, a lecture for the king) many times and presented his letter of counsel "Mujin yukjo so (戊辰六條疏, Memorandum on Six Points in 1568)" to the king. However, he ultimately returned to his hometown after compiling *Seonghak sipdo* (聖學十圖, *Ten Diagrams of Sage Learning*) for King Seonjo, which he produced in order to help his young monarch to become a sage king.

Two years later in 1570, at the news of Toegye's death, Yulgok mourned deeply, and later in 1581 requested the enshrinement of Toegye's tablet in the National Shrine of Confucius. Although Yulgok greatly admired Toegye even after his death, he continued to establish his own philosophical position, which differed from Toegye's. Two years after the death of Toegye (1572), Yulgok even criticized him in the course of a debate with Ugye on the theory of the four beginnings and the seven feelings. Three years later (1575), Yulgok published a new textbook on sage learning titled *Seonghak jibyo* (聖學輯要, *The Essentials of Sage Learning*) for King Seonjo, which offered a different perspective than Toegye's *Ten Diagrams on Sage Learning*.

Yulgok raised a clear objection about the structure and some of the contents of *Ten Diagrams on Sage Learning* when it was published by Toegye.[1] After the latter's death, he seemed to have decided to write a new textbook on Confucianism that was comparable to or capable of replacing Toegye's. However, when he finally completed *The Essentials of Sage Learning* and presented it to King Seonjo, he discovered that the king was very attached to Toegye's *Ten Diagrams on Sage Learning*. When presenting his text to King

Seonjo, Toegye had asked him to make copies of it in the form of a booklet and a folding screen and to always keep them nearby. As a result, while the followers of Yulgok made persistent efforts to encourage the adoption by the Royal Court of *The Essentials of Sage Learning* as a course of *gyeong-yeon*, or lectures, it took a century to achieve their goal.[2]

Based on their philosophical learning, accumulated through the study of Confucian classics and engagement in scholarly debates, Toegye and Yulgok wrote *Ten Diagrams on Sage Learning* and *The Essentials of Sage Learning*, respectively, in order to propose to the king the optimal way to learn and practice the philosophy of Confucianism. Both were textbooks for sage learning, which were presented to King Seonjo, but their readership was not limited to the king. Considering the fact that the ultimate goal of studying Confucianism or Neo-Confucianism was to become a sage, these books were also compiled for the edification of all interested scholars. Toegye and Yulgok believed that the ultimate goal of studying these texts was for the reader to learn how to practice what he has learned in real life and to guide ordinary people in that direction. The scholarly explorations of Toegye and Yulgok were supplemented by their practical, political positions and actions. Therefore the intense dispute over the theories of *li-gi* and of the heart-mind and nature between the two may seem meaningless unless it is understood and evaluated in light of their opinions and stances on real-world politics.

In fact, their political philosophy, which focused on the ideal of cultivating "a sage on the inside and a virtuous king on the outside" is in evidence throughout their letters, their memorials and petitions to the king, and in their poetry and other writings. Among these texts, *Ten Diagrams on Sage Learning* and *The Essentials of Sage Learning* are the writings that are most representative of their systematic philosophical positions on politics. However, considering that these books were basically "textbooks" for sage learning, with all the abstraction that such texts entail, it is also necessary to pay attention to their petitions to the king written as policy or political proposals that were set forth in light of the specific state of affairs of the period in which they were written. Among these petitions, those with the most systematic content and the clearest positions were "Memorandum on Six Points in 1568," which was presented to the king by Toegye in his later years, and "Dongho mundap (東湖問答, Questions and Answers at the Eastern Lake)" (1569) and "Maneon bongsa (萬言封事, Memorial in Ten Thousand Words)" (1574), presented by Yulgok to King Seonjo. In this chapter, these three texts will first be compared in order to examine their stances on important issues, and then *Ten Diagrams on Sage Learning* and *The Essentials of Sage Learning* will be reviewed with a view to understanding the ideal political philosophy and society that the two scholars espoused.[3]

THE KING AND HIS RETAINERS

The role of the king was very important in Joseon, which was an absolute monarchy. However, the role of his retainers was also a significant factor in the king's exercise of power and in his governance of the country. In particular, in Joseon, a country in which the official intelligentsia had played a crucial role since its foundation, including through several political upheavals, the king's retainers both assisted him in governing and kept his power in check. The roles of the king and his retainers and their relationship were very important issues because they determined one's political position in Joseon. The strands of thought of Toegye and Yulgok were clearly different in this regard, and this led to a separation in Joseon intellectual political life between the Toegye School and the Yulgok School, or between *namin* (南人, the Southerners) and *seo-in* (西人, the Westerners).

The two scholars' memorials and petitions to the king clearly display the difference in their opinions in this issue. While Toegye's "Memorandum on Six Points in 1568" focuses on the status and role of the king, Yulgok's "Questions and Answers at the Eastern Lake" and "Memorial in Ten Thousand Words" emphasize the relationship between the king and his retainers. This contrast was caused not only by their differing perceptions of the state of affairs in the country and by their philosophical viewpoints but also by their respective personal circumstances.

"Memorandum on Six Points in 1568"[4] is a petition presented by Toegye, at the time a renowned sixty-eight-year-old scholar, to King Seonjo, a newly crowned seventeen-year-old monarch. At the repeated request of King Seongjo, Toegye entered the Royal Court at the end of July 1568 and, in early August, presented this petition to the king while giving lectures and offering counsel at *gyeong-yeon*. He continued to attend *gyeong-yeon* for the king, staying in Hanyang for a period, but finally decided to return to his hometown. In December, prior to his departure from the Royal Court, Toegye completed *Ten Diagrams on Sage Learning*, intended for presentation to the king. In early March in the following year (1569), he was finally able to return to his hometown with the permission of the king. He had stayed by King Seonjo's side for approximately seven months, and "Memorandum on Six Points in 1568," written during this period, displays the thinking of a scholar who had great expectations for his young king and concerns over the royal family and the Royal Court. It consists of the following six core counsels:

First, recognize the significance of the royal lineage and do your utmost to practice filial piety and to display benevolence.

Second, prevent slander and maintain a friendly relationship between the two palaces.

Third, establish a firm foundation for politics by immersion in sage learning.

Fourth, rectify the attitudes of your people by illuminating the path toward the Way.

Fifth, trust and communicate with your retainers to govern the country.

Sixth, be sincere in your efforts at self-cultivation and self-examination in order to respect the love of Heaven.

The first counsel stresses that the royal lineage is more important than blood kinship, in this way emphasizing that securing the legitimacy of the kingship is the most urgent matter for King Seonjo to attend to, as it is basic to good governance.

The second counsel is in regard to the relationship between King Seonjo and Queen Insun (仁順王后), the wife of King Myeongjong, who resided in a separate palace. It stipulates that King Seonjo should not let others come between Queen Insun and him.

The third counsel points out that study and self-cultivation based on Confucianism are the basis of politics. It emphasizes that heightened philosophical awareness and the resulting moral personal practices are also necessary to conducting effective politics, just as two wheels are essential to a wagon.

The fourth stricture counsels that the king should serve as a model of the adherence to Confucian values. It holds that he should emulate previous kings, positively influence the minds of his people, and edify them in order to govern the country.

The fifth counsel emphasizes the roles of the king and his vassals. It indicates that a country is like a human body in which the king plays the role of the head, *daeshin / da-chen* (大臣, ministers) play the role of the stomach and the chest, and *daegan / tai-jian* (臺諫, advisors and inspectors) play the role of the eyes and ears. The king should make good use of them in order to govern the country.

The sixth counsel points out that the king's position is bestowed by Heaven and that Heaven promulgates natural disasters to warn the king of imminent hardship, out of its affection for him. Therefore the king should govern the country based on his thorough understanding of the way of Heaven.

The third through the sixth counsels are similar to the general contents of other memorials or petitions to the king, including Yulgok's. However, the first and second counsels should be examined closely because Toegye put special emphasis on them through their placement in his text. These counsels reflected Toegye's awareness of the state of affairs of the time and were influenced by his philosophical perspective on politics.

The placement of the counsel "Recognize the significance of the royal lineage and do your utmost to practice filial piety and to display benevolence" at the start of the petition was related to the fact that King Seonjo, whose father, Deokheunggun, was a son of King Jungjong (the eleventh king of Joseon) and his concubine, was crowned as the fourteenth king of Joseon in succession to King Myeongjong (the thirteenth king). The fact that a child of a concubine's son, King Seonjo, succeeded his half-uncle King Myeongjong meant that it was eminently possible that a cloud could be cast over his legitimacy. In particular, because it was still early in his reign, Toegye advised King Seonjo to authoritatively prevent such a controversy by setting a good example by displaying benevolence and demonstrating filial piety toward the royal lineage. Toegye claimed, "Nothing is more important than the royal lineage linked to the king's position (君位一統),"[5] stressing that once the king acceded to the throne, he should accord primacy to this lineage and never be influenced by personal affection for his biological parents.

The second counsel, "Prevent slander and maintain a friendly relationship between the two palaces," shows Toegye's awareness of urgent contemporary issues. This stricture is related to the fact that Yoon Wonhyeong, a brother of Queen Munjeong who covertly acted as regent during King Myeongjong's reign, mismanaged his responsibilities and acted independently in his handling of the affairs of state. As he had directly experienced such mismanagement by maternal relatives of the king, Toegye pointed out that a relationship of trust between King Seonjo and Queen Insun, who was acting as regent, should be established in order to prevent the possible recurrence of such a situation.

At the root of these two counsels was Toegye's philosophical position that all political activities derive from the king's authority. According to him, in the political system of the monarchy of the time, the royal lineage linked to the king is the most important facet, and based on its legitimacy, the king should govern the country as the head of the royal family and the Royal Court, in doing so guiding the work of competent ministers, advisors, inspectors, and administrators. This position led to Toegye's emphasis on the self-cultivation of the king, and this admonition took a more intensive form in the priority placed on the reverent "study of the mind" of the king in *Ten Diagrams on Sage Learning* published several months later. Later, in the *yesong / li-song* (禮訟, disputes on the observance of propriety) (1659, 1674), "the Southerners (南人)" stressed the distinctiveness of royal succession, and in the eighteenth century, *geun-gi namin* (近畿南人, the Southerners residing in the areas adjacent to Gyeong-gi province) supported political reform centered on an evolution into a king-centered system, in this way adhering to Toegye's position.

This stance cannot be considered separately from the personal situation of Toegye, who had entered his later years. He was sixty-eight years old, which was a very advanced age at that time, and in fact he would pass away only two years later. Instead of engaging in an attempt to realize his own political ideal in the contemporary Royal Court, in all likelihood he hoped that his young monarch would mature into a sage king. However, Yulgok, a promising young scholar in his thirties with only four or five years of experience as a public official, was in a different situation. He attempted to open a new era along with the *sarim* (士林, a collective name for virtuous scholars called *seonbi*) by offering philosophical guidance to King Seonjo. However, in Yulgok's view, the king was reluctant to accept the opinions of his retainers and to put the implications of their counsel into practice, even while he pretended to seek a wide spectrum of advice. Throughout his two relevant texts on this subject, Yulgok consistently stressed the relationship between the king and his retainers, especially the importance of the latter and the attitude of the king toward them.

Written after Toegye completed "Memorandum on Six Points in 1568," Yulgok's "Questions and Answers at the Eastern Lake" also reflects the situation in the early years of King Seonjo's reign. At that time, Yulgok had an opportunity to take up *saga dokseo* (賜暇讀書), a kind of sabbatical leave for the purpose of research offered to civil officials. After approximately a month of the *saga dokseo* period, he presented "Questions and Answers at the Eastern Lake" to King Seonjo. Yulgok, an enthusiastic thirty-four-year-old intellectual in public service, wrote this text for his young king who had recently ascended to the throne, and this text was significantly different from that of Toegye, an elderly scholar, in terms of its perspectives and positions. "Questions and Answers at the Eastern Lake"[6] is composed of the following chapters:

Chapter 1 The Role of the King
Chapter 2 The Role of Retainers
Chapter 3 The Difficulties in Achieving Agreement between the King and His Retainers
Chapter 4 The Absence of the Learning of the Way (道學) in Joseon
Chapter 5 The Inability to Restore the Old Way in the Joseon Royal Court
Chapter 6 Discussion of the Current State of Affairs
Chapter 7 Practical Endeavor with Sincerity as the Key to Self-Cultivation
Chapter 8 Discrimination against Villainous Retainers as the Key to the Selection of Talented Officials
Chapter 9 Discussion of the Optimal Method of Ensuring the People's Welfare
Chapter 10 Discussion of the Optimal Mode of Education
Chapter 11 The Rectification of Names (正名) as the Basis of Governance

Throughout the first three chapters, Yulgok stressed that even a great king is not capable of governing the country effectively without outstanding retainers. Yulgok defined the formation of "a good relationship" between the king and his retainers as the process of "establishing mutual trust based on the righteous way and on basic principles."[7] In other words, it means cooperation between the king and his retainers based on Confucian values and philosophical positions. The role of retainers is emphasized throughout the text except in chapters 9 and 10, which discuss specific measures required to deal with given states of affairs. The last chapter, "The Rectification of Names as the Basis of Governance," also makes the case for a clear reevaluation of Yoon Wonhyeong's monopoly of power and a recognition of his misdeeds that occurred during King Myeongjong's reign, and their resultant victims. Therefore Yulgok closed his text by stressing that the just evaluation of retainers is the basis of good governance.

Although it is a little different in structure, "Memorial in Ten Thousand Words" also consists of two themes: the relationship between the king and his retainers and the necessity of measures to deal with the contemporary state of affairs. In Yulgok's view, the essence of governance was the king's trust in his retainers, his resultant acceptance of their opinions, and his capacity to deal with specific urgent issues based on them. Written five years after "Questions and Answers at the Eastern Lake," this text shows Yulgok's more thoroughgoing disappointment with and concern over King Seonjo's rule and the political situation of the time. He believed that the main contemporary problems were the king's distrust in his retainers and the irresponsibility of the latter. The structure of "Memorial in Ten Thousand Words"[8] is as follows:

1. Introduction: It is important to know when to act (知時) and to endeavor to engage in practical matters (務實) in the political sphere.
2-1. Adaptation to Circumstances (時宜): The king should enact new laws and reform existing laws according to the demands of the times in order to improve the lot of his people.
2-2. Practical Achievement (實功): The king should speak and act in good faith in the course of his work and not utter empty words.
3-1. Self-Cultivation (修己): The king should display his will, strive to attain sage learning, be on good terms with wise scholars, and never be unduly influenced by personal relationships.
3-2. Ensuring the People's Welfare (安民): The king should seek the loyalty of his retainers, reform the harsh tax system, pursue thrift and frugality, and modify military policy in order to bolster national defense.
4. Conclusion: When accepting a wise proposal from his retainers, the king should task competent officials to work on its implementation with utmost sincerity and trust and to firmly advance it.

The admonition concerning "knowing when to act" and the qualification "according to the demands of the times" in the introduction and chapter 2-1 respectively imply the necessity of reform according to changing circumstances, and the notions of "practical matter" and "practical achievement" in the introduction and chapter 2-2 entail that governance should be helpful in practical terms. The contents of these chapters reveal the difficulty that Yulgok experienced in the Royal Court. He wrote that, despite the need for reform designed to meet the changing demands of the times, the retainers as well as the king opposed this reform. He also said that the core component of ideal governance is to be helpful to the people but that he could not observe such governance in the contemporary world.

The detailed suggested methods of arriving at practical solutions in chapter 2-2 are mostly concerned with the relationship between the king and his retainers, and their respective roles. In this chapter, Yugok maintains that there was no trust between the king and his retainers and that the latter were not willing to assume responsibility for their actions. Thus, the king did not implement the suggestions of his retainers and even refused to appoint virtuous people as high-ranking officials. Contrary to Yulgok's previous theoretical claims about the relationship between the king and his retainers in "Questions and Answers at the Eastern Lake," this chapter clearly expresses his disappointment with King Seonjo. Chapters 3-1 and 3-2, which suggest measures to deal with such issues, also argue that the king should keep well-meaning scholars by his side, be open to the counsel of his retainers, and seek their loyalty in order to achieve an ideal mode of governance.

Of course, Yulgok also pointed out that in order to appoint people of good faith, to avoid bestowing responsibility on calculating or cunning people, and to realize governance based not on selfish interests but on benevolence and righteousness, the king should study sage learning and be engaged in self-cultivation. However, Yulgok's text also emphasized that the king should assign tasks to his retainers based on his trust in them, and the retainers should in turn proffer their opinions in good faith and perform their tasks based on their trust in the king. While Toegye consistently laid stress on the importance of the legitimacy of the king and on monarch-centered governance based on said legitimacy, Yulgok focused on the need for cooperative governance involving the king and his retainers. Furthermore, in *The Essentials of Sage Learning*, Yulgok asserted that the Confucian ideals of retainers were more important than the royal succession of the king. This position led to the stance adopted by *seo-in* (the Westerners) in the *yesong* dispute in the seventeenth century, which did not admit the distinctiveness of the proprieties observed by the royal family because it considered the king to be a scholar like others, and to the political position of *seo-in*, the official intelligentsia who checked the king's power and assumed leadership roles in politics through the formation of powerful families during the eighteenth and nineteenth centuries.

THE UNIFIED MIND OF THE KING

Toegye met King Seonjo in person, participated in lectures for the king (*gyeong-yeon*) nine times, and even presented a petition titled "Memorandum on Six Points in 1568" to him, but the new young king seems to have fallen somewhat short of his expectations.[9] As an old man, Toegye probably had to consider the fact that there was not enough time left for him to directly participate in practical politics. Thus, before returning to his hometown, he compiled *Ten Diagrams on Sage Learning* and dedicated it to King Seonjo, hoping that the young monarch would become a true sage king in the fullness of time.

Ten Diagrams on Sage Learning is a booklet that explains the core of sage learning through ten diagrams and descriptions. Sage learning was "the course of study required to become a sage," but for King Seonjo it had the additional dimension of providing guidance on becoming a sage king. However, *Ten Diagrams on Sage Learning* did not include any content directly related to politics. The book contains ten chapters regarding the duty of human beings and the study and self-cultivation methods required to fulfill this duty, based on the principles behind the creation of the universe and the structure of the human mind. As Toegye explained, the structure of this book, which begins with the origin and creation of the universe, adhered to that of *Jin-si lu* (近思錄, *Reflections on Things at Hand*, c. 1175) compiled by Zhu Xi and Lü Zuqian (呂祖謙, 1137–1181).[10] However, while the latter part of *Jin-si lu* is mostly about the essence and methods of politics, *Ten Diagrams on Sage Learning* ends with an apolitical theory of self-cultivation.

Each of the ten chapters of *Ten Diagrams on Sage Learning* contains a diagram and the related and salient writings of the sages and a brief supplementary explanation by Toegye. Except for these explanations, the book is simply a collation of the writings and diagrams of the ancient sages. Therefore it is more important to focus on the entire structure of this book rather than on each chapter in order to better understand Toegye's intent.

Toegye divided the ten chapters into two parts. Chapters 1 through 5 in the first part collectively argue that "the root of sage learning is the Way of Heaven (天道), but its achievements should illuminate humanity and seek to encourage virtuous deeds,"[11] and chapters 6 through 10 in the second part maintain that "the basis of sage learning is the heart-mind and nature (心性), but its core imperative is the call to study assiduously every day and to cultivate a spirit of reverent mindfulness and awe (敬畏)."[12] Toegye thought that the core of the theory of sage learning should include the concepts of the Way of Heaven and of the heart-mind and nature. Thus, he wrote about them in chapters 1 and 2, and 6 and 7, respectively, and described the methods by which individuals could assimilate these concepts in chapters 3 to 5 and 8 to

10. The entire process of study, self-cultivation, and practice, whose goals are "to illuminate humanity and seek to encourage virtuous deeds" and "to study assiduously every day and to cultivate a spirit of reverent mindfulness and awe," is based on the Way of Heaven and on the heart-mind and nature, the root of which fields of learning should be assimilated through such every-day commitment. It is possible that Toegye felt that "the governance of a sage king," which was not even mentioned in this book, could probably be achieved naturally as a result of such study and self-cultivation.[13]

In order to examine Toegye's thought concerning the Way of Heaven and the heart-mind and nature in *Ten Diagrams on Sage Learning* in detail,

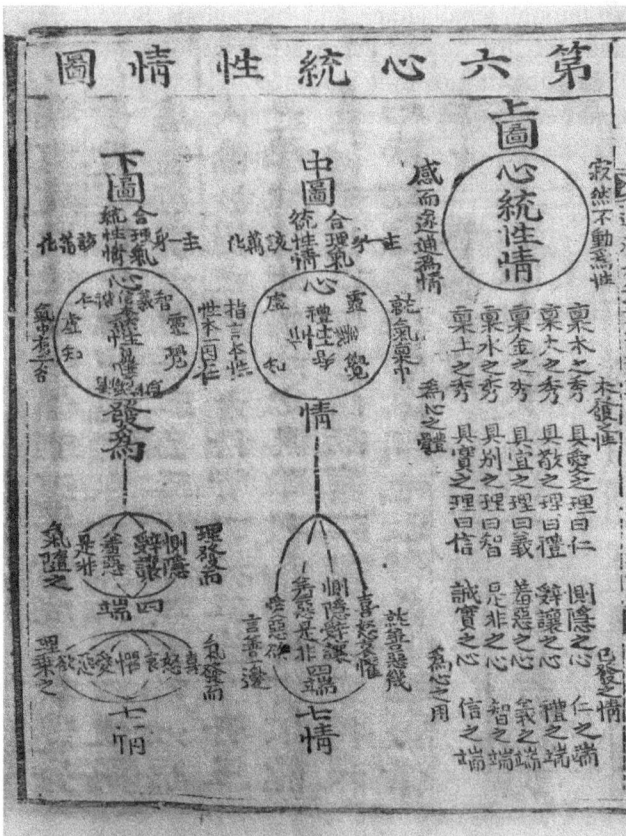

Image 7.1 "The Diagram of the Saying, 'The Heart-Mind Combines and Governs Nature and the Feelings.'" *Source* "Simtongseongjeong do 心統性情圖" (Vol.7, p. 22) in *Toegye seonsaeng munjip* 退溪先生文集. Author: Yi Hwang 李滉. Publisher: Dosan seowon 陶山書院, Korea Date of publication: 1697. Used here with permission from Korea University Library.

"The Diagram of the Saying, 'The Heart-Mind Combines and Governs Nature and the Feelings' (心統性情圖)," which was supplemented explicitly by Toegye, and the section on the theory of self-cultivation, which emphasized the importance of a reverential attitude toward the Mandate of Heaven (天命) and toward *Sangje* (上帝, the Lord on High), should be examined closely. "The Diagram of the Saying, 'The Heart-Mind Combines and Governs Nature and the Feelings" is composed of three illustrations: the top illustration (上圖) by Cheng Fu-xin (程復心), a scholar in the Yuan Dynasty, and two illustrations by Toegye, the middle illustration (中圖) and the bottom illustration (下圖).

Cheng Fu-xin's illustration summarizes the basic relationship between the heart-mind, human nature, and feelings from the perspective of Neo-Confucianism, but Toegye seems to have thought that it was not adequate. He supplemented it with his two illustrations, one of which displays the ideal state in which the heart-mind combines and governs human nature and feelings (心統性情), the other of which expresses his theory of the four beginnings and the seven feelings, which proposed that moral feelings should be distinguished based on the standards of good and evil. These supplementary illustrations were placed in the middle and bottom positions, respectively. The middle illustration presents the structure of the heart-mind, human nature, and feelings in an ideal state in which the moral feelings that stem from the original nature of the heart-mind are manifested. The bottom illustration displays feelings, which originated from human nature possessed of two opposite attributes, the original/innate pure nature and physical nature. These opposed forms of nature are wedded to the two separate categories of the four beginnings, which are pure and good moral feelings, and the seven feelings, which are moral feelings that are prone to becoming evil.

Considering the fact that the purpose of *Ten Diagrams on Sage Learning* was to help the king, who was born an ordinary man, to develop into a sage king through study and self-cultivation, the key message of Toegye seems to be contained in the bottom illustration. The essence of his theory of the four beginnings and the seven feelings was to distinguish moral feelings based on the standards of good and evil and to make it clear which direction people should take. He explained, "The heart-mind contains both *li* and *gi* and controls human nature and feelings. The manifestation of human nature in feelings is a microcosmic omen in the heart-mind and the core of all changes, through which good and evil are distinguished."[14] In this way, he emphasized the importance of maintaining an attitude of reverent mindfulness (敬) and of being engaged in intense study in order to develop one's original nature, even before the manifestation of the original moral nature in the form of feelings.[15]

Although Toegye consistently stressed "reverent mindfulness" as a basic concept necessary for the furtherance of study and self-cultivation, it is still noteworthy that he closed his *Ten Diagrams on Sage Learning* with an emphasis on reverence for and awe before the Lord on High (上帝) and the Way (道).[16] He regarded *li* (理), the Way (道), and the Supreme Polarity (太極) as the various aspects of the Mandate of Heaven (天命) and proposed that the Lord on High and the Way were also different names for *li*. As a universal principle or norm that slowly or incrementally emanates from the origin of existence, filling the entire universe and nature, in Neo-Confucianism *li* is conceived of as an entity that has been assimilated into the original moral nature (性卽理). Toegye believed that sage learning can be fully practiced by maintaining reverence for and awe before the Lord on High, the source of *li*, as an external entity.

Gyeong (敬, reverent mindfulness) is a core concept of Toegye's form of learning and cultivation. Although *gyeong* in Neo-Confucianism is variously interpreted as enjoining us "to focus the mind and not to let it wander (主一無適)," "to maintain an orderly and focused body and mind (整齊嚴肅)," and "to always maintain a clear-minded and alert state (常醒醒)," it originally meant a reverential attitude toward God. Therefore *gyeong* can be understood as denoting a sole focus on God, carried out with reverence and solemnity. In this respect, it a priori connotes awe (畏). As long as one focuses on God with a reverential attitude, it is immaterial whether the subject of one's awe is understood as a universal norm, such as *li* or the Way, or as the personified reigning presence of Heaven, that is, the Lord on High.

The Lord on High (上帝) and Heaven (天) as concepts denoting a God imbued with personality, which frequently appeared in the literature of pre-Qin Confucianism, were replaced by abstract concepts such as *li*, the Supreme Polarity, or the Way in Neo-Confucianism. Toegye was a scholar who strongly emphasized the role of *li*. However, even during his era, *Sangje*, as a concept denoting a God imbued with personality, was still current, and Toegye supported two positions simultaneously by reinterpreting the role of *li* and also stressing reverence for *Sangje*. This stance was open to criticism because it contradicted the tenets of Toegye's philosophy, but he seems to have thought that the coexistence of internal self-cultivation achieved through *li* and an external relationship with *Sangje* would be effective in the realization of an ideal form of morality.[17]

Unlike Yulgok, who focused on the process of purifying matter or temperament (*gi*) that interfered with the realization of *li* in one's study and self-cultivation, Toegye focused solely on *li* itself, which is equal to the original nature (性), the Way (道), the Mandate of Heaven (天命), and the Lord on High (上帝). According to Toegye, focusing on *li* with a reverential attitude, from the starting point at which the heart-mind is not yet revealed or manifested until the state in which the heart-mind is revealed, is the most effective way to realize one's original moral nature and to fully act in accordance with universal norms. He believed that study and self-cultivation carried out in this way was the most certain method of becoming a sage and therefore that governance by a sage would be achieved as a result of such study and self-cultivation.

This demonstrates why, when Toegye wrote *Ten Diagrams on Sage Learning*, he focused on the studies and self-cultivation of the king, who was the central figure in the political administration of Joseon. He presented *Ten Diagrams on Sage Learning* to the king in tandem with the following letter of dedication:

> Everything is determined by the mind of the king, which is but one mind that must carry the weight of many responsibilities. There, numerous desires war for priority and evil threatens to spread. A single act of negligence, neglect, or self-indulgence would lead to torrential or sea-borne flooding and to mountains collapsing. Who would be able to stop it?[18]

For Toegye, the core figure in the governance of a country is the king who is at the center of the political system, and it is crucial that the king's mind embraces *li*. The success of a system of governance depends on the cultivation and capacity for introspection of the king's mind. Through *Ten Diagrams on Sage Learning*, Toegye proposed his political view that in order to achieve the most ideal life of a sage and to display the quality of the governance of a sage king, the king should focus on preserving *li* (human nature/the Way/ the Mandate of Heaven/the Lord on High), which is a universal principle of nature and society as well as a moral norm, by maintaining a consistent reverential attitude, and thereby propagate it naturally across the world, instead of paying attention to transient or superficial circumstances or events that may become evil.

THE ROYAL SUCCESSION BASED ON CONSANGUINITY AND THE LINEAGE OF THE CONFUCIAN SAGES

Compared to Toegye's *Ten Diagrams on Sage Learning*, Yulgok's *The Essentials of Sage Learning* contains relatively concrete methods for engaging in public and private activities ranging from self-cultivation to politics. This book focuses not on exploring the fundamental principles of politics but on the process of putting these principles into practice, in that it employs *susin / xi-shen* (修身, self-cultivation), *jega / qi-jia* (齊家, establishing harmony in the family), *chiguk / zhi-gua* (治國, governing a country), and *pyeongcheonha / ping-tian-xia* (平天下, bringing peace to the world) from among the eight concepts in *The Great Learning* as basic elements of its structure. However, Yulgok thought that, although *The Great Learning* contained methods aimed at enabling initiates to learn the core tenets of the voluminous "Four Books and Six Classics (四書六經)," it was too simplistic. He initially highly evaluated *Da Xue yan-yi* (大學衍義, *The Extended Meaning of The Great Learning*) by Zhen De-xiu (眞德秀) as a supplementary text to *The Great Learning*, but later criticized it, saying that, "As it consists of too many volumes and unfocused sentences, it is akin to a volume of history that describes the course of events, rather than a substantial, systematic text."[19] With hopes of publishing a new sage learning textbook as systematic as *The Great Learning*, which would contain more considered explanations than those contained in *The Extended Meaning of The Great Learning*, Yulgok compiled *The Essentials of Sage Learning*.

Unlike Toegye's *Ten Diagrams on Sage Learning*, which was compiled with a focus on self-cultivation and the study of the mind, *The Essentials of Sage Learning* was produced as a textbook on sage learning that focused on *jega*, *chiguk*, and *pyeongcheonha / ping tian-xia*. This intention is also evident in the structure of the book. Its chapters are organized in the sequence of "practicing self-cultivation (*sugi / xiu-ji* 修己)," "maintaining discipline in the family (*jeongga / zheng-jia* 正家)," "becoming engaged in politics (*wijeong / wei-zheng* 爲政)," and "supporting the lineage of the sages and worthies (*seonghyeon dotong / sheng-xian dao-tong* 聖賢道統)." The last chapter was included in order to emphasize that the governance of a sage should be based on a course of study that leads from Fu Xi (伏羲) to Confucius to Zhu Xi.

However, based on the length and depth of the discussion on "practicing self-cultivation," it seems clear that Yulgok also put special emphasis on this issue. This was probably because there was no difference between Toegye and Yulgok in terms of their belief that the concepts of *chiguk* and *pyeongcheonha* stem from the moral studies and the efforts at self-cultivation of a ruler, which are then disseminated among families, villages, and countries and eventually across the world. Although it did not display as many dimensions as Toegye's *Ten Diagrams on Sage Learning*, almost half of *The Essentials of Sage Learning* consists of the chapter on "practicing self-cultivation," which is composed of three sub-sections. However, unlike Toegye, who focused on the complete preservation and realization of *li* (human nature/the Way/the Mandate of Heaven/the Lord on High), Yulgok placed special stress on changes in individuals' physical matter or material disposition (氣質) in his chapter on "practicing self-cultivation."

He emphasized that shaped matter or temperament can be transformed through study and argued that the primary goal of studying is precisely this. He put emphasis on forms of study that accomplish this by describing cases in which violent people who read Confucius's *The Analects* became calm and in which those who studied diligently, refusing to succumb to their desires, became sturdy and handsome.[20] He also claimed that a scholar whose material disposition or physical matter was unchanged after study was proceeding in his studies incorrectly.[21]

However, it is significant that Yulgok proposed *ipji / li-zhi* (立志, establishing one's goal) as his first counsel, prior to the need to amend one's material disposition (矯氣質), in the chapter dealing with "practicing self-cultivation." According to Yulgok, the starting point of study is the establishment of a goal. That is, any individual (not solely the king) should firstly delineate a clear objective when beginning his studies. He also suggested *ipji* (establishing a goal) as the first step in a course of study in *The Secret to Dispelling Ignorance* (擊蒙要訣, 1577), a study guidebook for beginning scholars written two years after the completion of *The Essentials of Sage Learning*.

According to Yulgok, the *ji / zhi* (志, a goal) of *ipji* entails that the tenor of one's "intention (意)" is fixed. That is, if some feelings arise from one's original nature, the functions of one's intention, which are the processes of calculating, comparing, examining, and considering (計較商量), begin to take effect and to determine the direction of one's mind. This result is called *ji* (志). Of course, it only takes a short period of time to form moral feelings and judgments, and thus, it is very difficult to establish a set hierarchy among feelings (情), intentions (意), and goals (志). However, Yulgok argued that they could be assigned the order of feelings, intentions, and goals for the sake of convenience.[22] Through the role of these feelings, intentions, and goals, changes in material disposition occur, which are the key to the form of sage learning that focuses on *susin*, *jega*, *chiguk*, and *pyeongcheonha* and to the type of governance instituted by a sage. In other words, one's intention and goal eventually purify one's material disposition in order to achieve the fulfillment of the essence of *li*. The studies and governance of the king put this theory into practice in the personal dimension of study and self-cultivation and in the dimension of politics, respectively. In addition, in either the personal or political dimension, establishing the ultimate goal of becoming a sage and of realizing the ideal of a sage constitutes *ipji*.

Toegye thought that the focus of sage learning is on the realization of the unified mind (一心) of the king and on the study of the original nature inside his mind (性卽理). He believed that the ideal politics is to spread morality in the world, a morality that arises from the original nature of the king's mind, which has been cultivated. However, Yulgok regarded the king as the embodiment of *li* and the officials surrounding him as a spectrum of political disposition or a range of physical matter. He argued that the key to effective politics is to realize the ideal of the king as a purely good and perfect center

(= *li*, 理) by having exceptional people surround him as embodiments of the range of physical matter or the spectrum of material disposition of the king.

> In my humble opinion, the most important goal of the king's studies is to trans-
> form the physical matter or material disposition of the king and the most urgent
> task of the king's governance is to appoint faithful and wise officials through
> the recommendations of others. In terms of changing physical matter or material
> disposition, the king should be as careful as if he were administering medicine
> to cure a disease, and in terms of appointing faithful and wise people on the
> strength of recommendations, there should be no bias toward those from the
> upper or the lower classes.[23]

Yulgok said that the essence of the king's learning is to change his material disposition and that the first priority of the king's governance is to appoint faithful and wise people to positions of responsibility. The king's learning that is geared toward changing his own material disposition is composed of his studies and self-cultivation, while his governance, which relies on his appointment of well-meaning officials, transforms the retainers or the range of physical matter that surrounds him, or in other words, the "*li* of the nation." Just as study and self-cultivation are important to the king on a personal level, the creation of an environment in which ideal morality can be realized is important on the political. This was the image of the ideal cooperative governance of the king and his retainers that Yulgok devised in the form of the theory of *li-gi*.

Another aspect of Yulgok's text to be noted here is the lineage of the sages who adhere to Confucian ideals (聖賢道統) listed at the end of *The Essentials of Sage Learning*. This was added by Yulgok himself, and it was therefore unconnected to the system of *The Great Learning*, which Yulgok regarded as a standard text. What was emphasized in this lineage is not "the royal succession according to consanguinity (王統)" but the succession of Confucian ideals (道統) that leads from Fu Xi (伏羲) to Zhou Gong (周公) to Confucius to Mencius and finally to Zhu Xi. Yulgok did not deny the importance of the unified mind of the king.[24] However, he pointed out that, after the kinship-based succession of the royal line had been determined, the Confucian ideals were never transmitted without the assistance of sages and worthies.[25] The logical outcome is that, after the method of succession of the royal line changed from a reliance on abdication (禪讓) to kinship-based succession (世襲), not only the role of the king but also that of the officials around him became important.[26] In addition, by maintaining the legacy of the Confucian ideals that had been advanced through history, the officials were enabled to both help the king and to check his power. Yulgok went further than simply appealing to the king to trust his retainers and proposing a form of cooperative governance between the king and the retainers in "Questions and Answers at the Eastern Lake" and "Memorial in Ten Thousand Words." In *The Essentials of Sage Learning* he unfolded his principle that the maintenance of Confucian ideals on the part of retainers is a more legitimate basis than the royal succession of the king for ruling the country.

From Yulgok's viewpoint, the objective of transforming material disposition or physical matter was a key to profound study and effective politics, and the role of retainers in adhering to Confucian ideals was more important than the king's royal lineage. In order to achieve sage governance, not only should the kingship be based on Neo-Confucianism, which had inherited the accumulated tradition of the Confucian sages, but retainers who inherited the same tradition should also be *in situ*. Of course, almost all of the respected intellectuals who studied Neo-Confucianism, including Zhu Xi and Toegye, attempted to check the real-world power of the king based on their academic and philosophical reputations and the influence they had won on that basis. In particular, Toegye attempted to keep the central power in check by establishing *seowon / shu-yuan* (書院, Confucian academies) as spaces for truth seeking and public discussion based on truth and the accumulated tradition of the Confucian sages, and this emphasis on balancing the power of the king continued throughout the whole of the Joseon era.[27] However, Toegye conceded in *Ten Diagrams on Sage Learning* that his recommended method of realizing a secure and stable form of learning in order to constitute a check on power merely plays an auxiliary role in the governance of the king, which is primarily based on the centrality of the monarch's unified mind.

Yulgok inherited these ideas and methods from Toegye but placed more emphasis on the role of the sages and wise men around the king in assisting and checking his power based on the accumulated tradition of the Confucian sages. On this basis, he argued that the power and authority of the king is realized and checked by the retainers or range of physical matter that surround him. Of course, given that the king plays a crucial role in gathering these respected people around him, the king's will based on the legitimacy of the royal succession, and the devotion of his vassals based on the accumulated tradition of the Confucian sages together comprise the quality of governance of a sage king.

NOTES

1. Yi I, "Sang Toegye seonsaeng munmok" 上退溪先生問目 (Inquiries Presented to Master Toegye), in *Yulgok jeonseo*, 44:182a–184b.

2. *The Essentials of Sage Learning* was finally adopted as a formal *gyeong-yeon* textbook at the end of the seventeenth century. Refer to Ji Du-hwan, "Joseon hugi

gyeong-yeon gwamok-ui byeoncheon" (Changes in the Courses of Gyeong-yeon in Late Joseon), *Han-gukhak nonchong* 18 (1995).

3. Discussions on the political philosophies of Toegye and Yulgok are developed from my article: Kim Hyoungchan, "The Theory and Practice of Sage Politics: The Political Philosophies and Neo-Confucian Bases of Yi Hwang and Yi I," *Acta Koreana* 17, no. 1 (2014).

4. Yi Hwang, "Mujin yukjo so," in *Toegye jip*, 29:183d–195b.

5. Ibid., 029:184a.

6. Yi I, "Dongho mundap," in *Yulgok jeonseo*, 44:316a–331d.

7. Ibid., 44:319b.

8. Yi I, "Maneon bongsa," in *Yulgok jeonseo*, 44:097b–111c.

9. Yi Hwang, "Jin Seonghak sipdo cha" 進聖學十圖箚 (Dedication Letter for *Ten Diagrams on Sage Learning*), in *Toegye jip*, 29:197d–200a.

10. Yi Hwang, "*Seonghak sipdo*: Je-1-Taeguek do" 聖學十圖: 第一太極圖 (*Ten Diagrams on Sage Learning*: Chapter 1: The Diagram of the Supreme Polarity), in *Toegye jip*, 29:201c.

11. Yi Hwang, "*Seonghak sipdo*: Je-5-Baengnokdonggyu do" 聖學十圖: 第五白鹿洞規圖 (*Ten Diagrams on Sage Learning*: Chapter 5: The Diagram of the Rules of the White Deer Hollow Academy), in *Toegye jip*, 29:206c.

12. Yi Hwang, "*Seonghak sipdo*: Je-10-Sukeung yamae jam do" 聖學十圖: 第十夙興夜寐箴圖 (*Ten Diagrams on Sage Learning*: Chapter 10: The Diagram of the Admonition on Rising Early and Retiring Late), in *Toegye jip*, 29:213a–b.

13. This description of the structure of *Ten Diagrams on Sage Learning* is a partial summary of my article, "Seonghak sipdo haeje" (A Bibliographical Introduction to *Ten Diagrams on Sage Learning*), in *Yeokjuwa haeseol Seonghak* (*Ten Diagrams on Sage Learning*: Translation Notes and Interpretations), ed. Han-guk sasang yeon-guso at Korea University (Seoul: Yemun seowon, 2009).

14. Yi Hwang, "*Seonghak sipdo*: Je-6-Simtongseongjeong do" 聖學十圖: 第六心統性情圖 (*Ten Diagrams on Sage Learning*: Chapter 6: The Diagram of the Saying "The Heart-Mind Combines and Governs the Nature and the Feelings"), in *Toegye jip*, 29:207d.

15. Ibid., 29:207d–208a.

16. Yi Hwang, "*Seonghak sipdo*: Je-9-Gyeongjae jam do" 聖學十圖: 第九敬齋箴圖 (*Ten Diagrams on Sage Learning*: Chapter 9: The Diagram of the Admonition for Mindfulness Studio), in *Toegye jip*, 29:211a–213b.

17. For the details on combining the study of *li* and the reverence for *Sangje*, refer to Kim Hyoungchan, "Joseon yuhak-ui i gaenyeome natanan jonggyojeok seonggyeok yeon-gu: Toegye-ui ibal-eseo Dasan-ui sangje-kkaji" (A Study of the Religious Character of the Concept of *Li* in Korean Confucianism: From Toegye's Concept of the Issuance of *Li* to Dasan's *Sangje*), *Cheorak yeon-gu* 39 (2010).

18. Yi Hwang, "Dedication Letter for *Ten Diagrams on Sage Learning*," in *Toegye jip*, 29:198a.

19. Yi I, "Seonghak jibyo-seo" 聖學輯要–序 (Preface to *The Essentials of Sage Learning*), in *Yulgok jeonseo*, 44:422d.

20. For the details of the method of changing material disposition or physical matter and its effect, refer to Kim Hyoungchan, "Gijil byeonhwa, yokmang-ui jeonghwareul wihan seongnihakjeok giheok" (Changing Material Disposition : Neo-Confucian Strategizing for the Purification of Desire), *Cheorak yeon-gu* 38 (2009): 203.

21. Yi I, *The Essentials of Sage Learning*, in *Yulgok jeonseo*, 44:471a.

22. Ibid., 44:458b–d.

23. Yi I, "Dedication Letter for *The Essentials of Sage Learning*," in *Yulgok jeonseo*, 44:420d.

24. Yi I, *The Essentials of Sage Learning*, in *Yulgok jeonseo*, 45:61a.

25. Ibid., 45:80c.

26. Since the ancient China era, the efforts to make up for the weak points in a monarchical system based on royal bloodline through recruiting competent scholar-officials had been frequently made. Song Jaeyoon examines the power relationship between emperors and premiers based on the Southern Song scholars' interpretations of *Zhou li* (The Rites of Zhou). Song Jaeyoon, "Hwangjewa Jaesang: Namsongdae (1127–1279) gwollyeok bullip iron" (Emperors and Premiers: Souther Song (1127–1279) Theories on Separation of Powers), *Toegye hakbo* (The Journal of Toegye Studies) 140, (Seoul: Toegyehak yeon-guwon, 2016).

27. For Toegye's thought and achievements regarding *seowon* (Confucian academies), refer to Kim Hyoungchan, "Toegye-ui seowongwan-e daehan cheorakjeok haemyeong" (A Philosophical Elucidation of Toegye's View of the Confucian Academies), *Toegye hakbo* 136 (2014).

Chapter 8

Conclusion

The Mind of the King and the Retainers' Adherence to Confucian Ideals

Toegye and Yulgok were intellectual descendants of those who envisioned, created, and administered a Joseon polity that was based on the philosophy of Neo-Confucianism. They were scholars who were weaned on Neo-Confucianism from their childhoods and who regarded themselves as the primary guiding force of the country. They were initiated into and stewarded academic discussions about broad-ranging topics spanning metaphysics, including the theories of *li-gi* and of the heart-mind and nature, and practical and political philosophy, in the process touching on issues such as the theory of self-cultivation. They were also poets who wrote and recited prodigiously, as well as public officials and public figures who directly participated in real-world politics.

The two have been evaluated as being in a contrasting or conflictual relationship both academically and politically, but in fact their common features far outweigh their differences. Toegye and Yulgok had common Confucian values, a Neo-Confucian worldview and academic basis for their thought, and a common political philosophy. However, in terms of their theories of *li*, *gi*, and the heart-mind and nature, it is clear that Yulgok was critical of Toegye's thinking. In a factional political system, this academic critique was later interpreted as stemming from an antipathetic stance, and this evaluation of the conflictual relationship between these two scholars has figured far too prominently in academic and other commentary. Of course, it cannot be denied that this conflictual or tense relationship exerted significant influence on scholarship and politics for a long time in Joseon. However, when considering the commonalities between Toegye and Yulgok, the reason for this relationship and its advantages and disadvantages can be identified.

This book has traced the process by which Toegye and Yulgok made different academic and political choices, regardless of the common traits in their thinking. The letters exchanged and dialogues conducted between the two have been productive materials through which to examine this process. As Yulgok established his own distinctive theory and, free from the shadow cast by Toegye, began to participate in the political sphere, their intellectual differences began to reveal themselves in their political viewpoints. The differences in the philosophical and political positions of the two were formed throughout the period of their long-term interaction and can be found in the dialogues between them, the debate regarding the four beginnings and the seven feelings, and the academic opinions they offered in their political writings.

When reading a text, Toegye focused on understanding the intention of the writer in the fullest context possible, while Yulgok analytically and logically examined the content of a text and advanced sharp criticisms. While Toegye employed a method that was focused on examining differences within a given context and giving clear explanations to enable easy understanding, Yulgok preferred a method that was focused on causally explaining nature, society, and human beings within the framework of a consistent system. Toegye tried to reveal the truth that lay beyond the language used by examining matters that were difficult to explain in ordinary language, whereas Yulgok wanted to clarify both metaphysical and physical issues or questions surrounding nature and the human being by organizing them into a single system. Unlike Toegye, who attempted to understand why his opponent made an argument and sought to advise or persuade him of an alternative view, Yulgok clearly organized his opinions as if he was writing a textbook in order to make an argument. It seems that their personalities and proclivities differed at a profound level in that Toegye thought that it was implausible that ordinary people like himself could reach the level of a sage, while Yulgok believed that he himself could attain the status of a sage with sufficient effort.

However, they shared common values and academic groundings, derived from Confucianism and Neo-Confucianism, and influenced each other through dialogue and discussion over a long period of time. It is undeniable, though, that Toegye influenced Yulgok more than vice versa, based on his seniority, academic experience, and intellectual maturity. When they met for the first time in 1558, it was ten years since Toegye had retired from his position as magistrate of Pung-gi, and he was concentrating on his studies in his hometown. It was the period when his fully mature academic achievements began to manifest themselves. As for Yulgok, at this time he was eagerly studying Confucian classics and preparing for a state-run examination, and thus there were many queries he was eager to put to Toegye and many things he felt he could learn from him. In fact, the dialogues conducted through letters between them later contributed to Yulgok making meaningful progress in his philosophy. In their correspondence, Yulgok queried Toegye's positions on the following issues: self-cultivation based on the philosophy of the human mind (人心) and the moral mind (道心), which should be exercised when the mind is stimulated rather than when it is calm; the need to distinguish human perception that can recognize the truth and animal perception that can only recognize physical objects; and the schematization of the intentional levels of self-cultivation and the consideration of their roles. Based on these discussions, Yulgok was able to progress in his own scholarship and in his political positions, and as a result he eventually decided to take a separate path from Toegye's.

In the process of discussing the four beginnings and the seven feelings, Toegye tried to clarify the origin of the moral feelings, judgment, and behavior. Of course, Zhu Xi had already argued that the root of moral feelings is the original or innate human nature that is consistent with the order of nature (性卽理) and had explained the relationship between the original nature and feelings in the proposition, "The original nature is manifested in feelings (性發爲情)." However, in Toegye's view, this was not an adequate explanation of the impetus behind the moral tendency to produce moral feelings, judgment, and behavior. From the perspective of the theory of *li-gi*, he focused on the idea that the aspect or dimension of things with actual functioning is *gi*, while the cause of its functioning is *li*, and he argued that "*li* issues (理發)" and "*li* arrives of its own accord (理自到)" in order to explain the metaphysical dynamic of *li*. This stance was controversial, as Toegye employed vocabulary that had been established in order to describe the functions of objects in the phenomenal world as predicates of the abstract concept of *li*. He did this in order to provide a vivid explanation of the role of *li*, which enables the actual functioning of *gi*. It seems clear that Toegye was attempting to explain the purely good moral tendency of the original human nature in a way that was consistent with *li* as a universal principle and the voluntary metaphysical impulses that fulfill such a moral tendency. He argued that in the process of the revelation of moral feelings, judgment, and behavior, the function of *li* is not a physical one, as is the case with *gi*, but can instead be seen as "a metaphysical moral impulse" that enables the physical functioning of *gi*. Toegye was concerned about the possible misconception of *li* as a "dead thing" when its function is overlooked and when it is regarded as playing the role of *gi*. He believed that a morally good life should allow the metaphysical impulse of this original nature (性卽理) to well up naturally, without being suppressed or distorted by the external environment.

From the perspective of Toegye, personal self-cultivation should focus on fostering the potential of the original nature in the form of pure *li* before the manifestation of the mind. If this theory were applied to the field of politics, study and self-cultivation would begin to focus on the cultivation of the king's mind, which is the starting point of all acts of governance. The importance of the mind of the king, of education and training carried out in order to cultivate the mind, and of a variety of strategies and obstacles designed to prevent the mind of the king from succumbing to various temptations, all of which were consistently emphasized by Toegye, emerged from this philosophical and political perspective.

Yulgok displayed as much confidence as Toegye in the purely good completeness or perfection of the original human nature that was consistent with the *li* of nature. However, he believed that human beings cannot autonomously increase, decrease, or modify the *li* of nature and of the original human nature because these concepts are derived from the arena of metaphysics. Therefore he strove for a method of adjusting *li* through the strength and conviction of one's will, which is exercised subsequent to the moment when the *li* of nature and of the original human nature are manifested in phenomena. Due to this perspective, in the debate over the four beginnings and seven feelings with Ugye, Yulgok focused on divining the optimal method of guiding feelings into the right or moral direction after they have been revealed, rather than on the relationship between the original human nature and feelings. As a result, his thinking began to revolve around how to enhance the relationship between the human mind and the moral mind, that is, how to consistently sustain the mind revealed as the moral mind and how to transmute the mind revealed as the human mind into the moral mind. In addition, because any arbitrary adjustment of the purely good and complete *li*, which is a universal principle of nature, is impossible, Yulgok began to focus on the role of study and self-cultivation in revealing the purely good and complete characteristics of *li*, through which activities he hoped to transform the *gi* surrounding *li* and to make it clear and pure through the action of the human will.

For Yulgok, study and self-cultivation on a personal level meant the complete revelation of *li* or of the original nature, which has been distorted by one's *gi*. This could be achieved by purifying one's *gi* through the exercise of one's will, which would enable one's mind to function in a more moral way. In the political domain, he thought that the ideal method of governing was to enable the king to perform his tasks through the employment of respected and able retainers. In this light, Yulgok saw the relationship between the king and his retainers as identical to that between *li* and *gi*. He entered the Royal Court when virtuous scholars called *sarim* (士林) were returning to the fold. He stressed the role of retainers in the governance of the country, working in partnership with the king. Furthermore, he attempted to realize a morally ideal polity by assigning primacy to the philosophical and ideological legitimacy of the intelligentsia in public office who had inherited the accumulated tradition of the Confucian sages over the royal succession of the king based on consanguinity.

In a monarchical country, the king and public officials are in the seat of governance. In order to achieve a form of governance based on "the Way of the king (王道)," benevolent governance (仁政), and virtuous governance (德治), which are the components of ideal governance in Confucianism, the king should always seek to square his personal desire or gain with the common interests of the people through continuous study and self-cultivation. Without constant self-cultivation, it is impossible for the king, who wields ultimate power and is often enticed toward taking the wrong path, to avoid temptations and to maintain the capacity to make the right judgments. Toegye seems to have believed that this regimen on the part of the king requires not only the capacity for reasonable and rational judgment but also voluntary moral emotion that comes from deep within the individual. Toegye suggested a way to realize a moral life and a just state, which he was confident was achievable through the potential for good of human moral instincts and through the role of the king. He explained that the king's moral emotions, judgments, and behavior stem from a metaphysical moral impulse consistent with the principle of nature.

However, the king's role is not the sole consideration in achieving a just society because his retainers are entrusted with a degree of power in order to play a part in establishing and executing policies on behalf of the king, and in this way they have a decisive influence on the lives of the people. This power may far surpass the personal abilities of these public officials, but they wield it in order to contribute to the common good through its use. Public officials are also exposed to many temptations to use their power for personal gain. In order to overcome such inducements and to ensure they use their power for the public good, the practice of self-cultivation is necessary for them as much as for the king. King Seonjo did not display an active commitment to the practice of effective politics, contrary to Yulgok's expectation. Yulgok had hoped the king would wisely govern the nation based on the opinions of his retainers. He seems to have thought that more power should be granted to selected and recommended members of the intelligentsia. Thus, he wrote and presented to King Seonjo a sage learning textbook, which claims that the accumulated tradition of the Neo-Confucian sages is more legitimate than the royal succession of the king based on the royal bloodline.

As discussed earlier, the king and his retainers govern a country in a monarchical system. The king decides the direction his governance of the country should take, selects retainers, and adopts the policies suggested by them. The retainers institute and execute policies while respectfully taking into account the king's will. Although the final decisions on the direction of governance and on policies to be adopted are taken by the king, whether he or his retainers play the more decisive role in this process may vary depending on the political situation. The power of the king and his retainers should be at the service of furthering national prosperity and security, but it is always possible that they may misuse or abuse their power for personal gain, and in fact there are many temptations to do so. Various political or institutional mechanisms are created in order to prevent this outcome, but in reality it is impossible to control all the political variables. In fact, laws and institutions are merely minimal controlling mechanisms designed to prevent extreme political situations from arising. Ultimately, the best safeguard is the cultivation, evaluation, and selection for senior positions of people with sufficient ability and self-control to handle significant power, and Neo-Confucianism is a discipline that aims to produce such virtuous people by cultivating the capacity for self-cultivation from childhood. The reason why Toegye and Yulgok were immersed in the discussion of *li*, *gi*, and the heart-mind and nature was because in order to foster, select, evaluate, and monitor those who might rise to senior public positions, forms of education and training that enhance their understanding, adjustment, and control of human impulses were necessary. Such forms of education, training, and monitoring were necessary for the king, as well as for his retainers. Toegye and Yulgok chose to emphasize the role of the king or that of retainers depending on the prevailing political situation and their own personal circumstances, and such a political system based on mutual checks between the king and his retainers began to predominate in Joseon.

Shortly after the death of Toegye and Yulgok, the Japanese invasion of Korea in 1592 occurred, an event that demonstrated that the two scholars had not been able to create as ideal and strong a country as they had hoped to. However, Joseon was able to survive for approximately another three hundred years, in that time enduring numerous national and international crises, and the academic and political framework established by Toegye and Yulgok played a significant role in this political longevity.

Glossary

M-R System

Bak Se-dang [Pak Se-dang] 朴世堂
bonyeon jiseong [bonyŏn chisŏng] / ben-ran-zhi-xing 本然之性
bungdang jeongchi [pungdang chŏngch'i] / peng-dang zheng-zhi 朋黨政治
Bu-wang zhang 補亡章
Byeoljip [Pyŏljip] 別集

chaengmun [ch'aengmun] / ce-wen 策文
Cheng Fu-xin(Lin-yin) 程復心(林隱)
Cheng Min-zheng 程敏政
Cheng Ming-dao 程明道
Cheondo chaek [Ch'ŏndo ch'aek] 天道策
Cheong-hyang so [Ch'ŏng-hyang so] 請享疏
Cheonin simseong habilji do [Ch'ŏnin simsŏng habilchi do] 天人心性合一之圖
Cheonmyeong do [Ch'ŏnmyŏng do] 天命圖
Cheonmyeong dohae [Ch'ŏnmyŏng dohae] 天命圖解
Cheonmyeong doseol [Ch'ŏnmyŏng dosŏl] 天命圖說
Cheonmyeong doseol huseo [Ch'ŏnmyŏng dosŏl husŏ] 天命圖說後敍
Cheonmyeong gudo [Ch'ŏnmyŏng gudo] 天命舊圖
Cheonmyeong sindo [Ch'ŏnmyŏng sindo] 天命新圖
che yong [ch'e yong] / ti yong 體用
chiguk [ch'iguk] / zhi-gua 治國
chiji [ch'iji] / zhi-zhi 致知
chiljeong [ch'ilchŏng] / qi-zheng 七政
chiljeong [ch'ilchŏng] / qi-qing 七情
chong [ch'ong] 總

daegan [taegan] / tai-jian 臺諫

daeseol [taesŏl] 對說
daeshin [taesin] / da-chen 大臣
Da Xue huo-wen 大學或問
Da Xue yan-yi 大學衍義
Da Xue zhang-ju 大學章句
dohak [dohak] / dao-xue 道學
Dongho mundap [Tongho mundap] 東湖問答
Du-le-yuan-ji 獨樂園記
Du Zhong Yong fa 讀中庸法

Eulsa sahwa [Ŭlsa sahwa] 乙巳士禍
eum yang [ŭm yang] / yin yang 陰陽

Fu Xi 伏羲

Gapja sahwa [Kapcha sahwa] 甲子士禍
geogyeong [kŏgyŏng] / ju-jing 居敬
geun-gi namin [kŭn-gi namin] 近畿南人
Gi Dae-seung(Gobong) [Ki Tae-sŭng(Kobong)] 奇大升(高峯)
Gi Jeong-jin(Nosa) [Ki Chŏng-jin(Nosa)] 奇正鎭(蘆沙)
gijil [kijil] / qi-zhi 氣質
gijil jiseong [kijil chisŏng] / qi-zhi-zhi-xing 氣質之性
Gimyo sahwa [Kimyo sahwa] 己卯士禍
gisim suryeom buryong ilmul [kisim suryŏm buryong ilmul]
    / qi-xin shou-lian bu-rong yi-wu 其心收斂, 不容一物
Gobong jeonjip [Kobong jŏnjip] 高峯全集
Gobong jip [Kobong jip] 高峯集
gudo jangwon gong [kudo jangwŏn gong] 九度壯元公
Gwon Geun(Yangchon) [Kwŏn Kŭn(Yangch'on)] 權近(陽村)
gyeong [kyŏng] / jing 敬
gyeonghak [kyŏnghak] / jing-xue 敬學
Gyeongmong yogyeol [Kyŏngmong yogyŏl] 擊蒙要訣
gyeongmul [kyŏngmul] / ge-wu 格物
gyeongmul gungni [kyŏngmul gungni] / ge-wu qiong-li 格物窮理
gyeong-oe [kyŏng-oe] / jing-wei 敬畏
gyeongsin [kyŏngsin] / jing-shen 敬身
gyeong-yeon [kyŏng-yŏn] / jing-yan 經筵

Hanseong [Hansŏng] 漢城
Han Won-jin(Namdang) [Han Wŏn-jin(Namdang)] 韓元震(南塘)
Heo Yeop(Chodang) [Hŏ Yŏp(Ch'odang)] 許曄(草堂)
hobal [hobal] / hu-fa 互發
hoenggan [hoenggan] 橫看

Hu Bing-wen(Yun-feng) 胡炳文(雲嶧)

hwaryeon gwantong [hwaryŏn gwant'ong] / huo-ran-guan-tong 豁然貫通

Hwaseokjeong [Hwasŏkchŏng] 花石亭

inseol [insŏl] 因說

ipji [ipchi] / li-zhi 立志

Jaseongnok [Chasŏngnok] 自省錄

jega [chega] / qi-jia 齊家

jeon [chŏn] 專

Jeong Jae-gyu(Nobaekheon) [Chŏng Chae-gyu(Nobaekhŏn)] 鄭載圭(老柏軒)

jeongje eomsuk [chŏngje ŏmsuk] / zheng-qi yan-su 整齊嚴肅

Jeong Ji-un(Chuman) [Chŏng Chi-un(Ch'uman)] 鄭之雲(秋巒)

Jeongmi sahwa [Chŏngmi sahwa] 丁未士禍

jeongsim [chjŏngsim] / zheng-xin 正心

Jeong Yak-yong(Dasan) [Chŏng Yak-yong(Tasan)] 丁若鏞(茶山)

Jeonseumnok nonbyeon [Chŏnsŭmnok' nonbyŏn] 傳習錄論辯

jijiji [chijiji] / zhi-zhi-zhi 知之至

Jinsa [Chinsa] 進士

Jin-si lu 近思錄

Jinul [Chinul] 知訥

Jo Gwang-jo(Jeongam) [Cho Kwang-jo(Chŏngam)] 趙光祖(靜菴)

Jo Mok(Wolcheon) [Cho Mok(Wŏlch'ŏn)] 趙穆(月川)

Joseon [Chosŏn] 朝鮮

Juja eollon dong-i go [Chuja ŏllon dong-i go] 朱子言論同異考

Juja seo jeoryo [Chuja sŏ chŏryo] 朱子書節要

Kim Chwi-ryeo [Kim Ch'wi-ryŏ] 金就礪

Kim Goeng-pil [Kim Koeng-p'il], 金宏弼,

Kim In-hu(Haseo) [Kim In-hu(Hasŏ)] 金麟厚(河西)

Kim Jeong-guk(Sajae) [Kim Chŏng-guk(Sajae)] 金正國(思齋)

Kim Jong-jik [Kim Chong-jik] 金宗直

Kim Seong-il [Kim Sŏng-il] 金誠一

li [li] /li 理

libal [libal] / li-fa 理發

ligi [ligi] / li-qi 理氣

lihak [lihak] / li-xue 理學

liilbunsu [liilbunsu] / li-yi-fen-shu 理一分殊

lijado [lijado] / li-zi-dao 理自到

Li Ji 禮記

Li Tong(Yan-ping) 李侗(延平)

litong-giguk [lit'ong-giguk] 理通氣局

Li yun 禮運
Luo Qin-shun(Zheng-an) 羅欽順(整庵)
Lu Xiangshan 陸象山
Lü Ziyue 呂子約
Lü Zuqian 呂祖謙

Maneon bongsa [Manŏn bongsa] 萬言封事
mibal [mibal] / wei-fa 未發
mubudo [mubudo] / wu-bu-dao 無不到
Mujin yukjo so [Mujin yukcho so] 戊辰六條疏
mulgyeok [mulgyŏk] / wu-ge 物格
munmok [munmok] / wen-mu 問目
Muo sahwa [Muo sahwa] 戊午史禍
musil yeokhaeng [musil yŏkhaeng] / wu-shi-li-xing 務實力行
Myeongjong [Myŏngjong] 明宗

Naejip [Naejip] 內集
naeseong oewang [naesŏng oewang] / nei-sheng-wai-wang 內聖外王
namin [namin] 南人
No Su-sin(Sojae) [No Su-sin(Sojae)] 盧守慎(蘇齋)

Oejip [Oejip] 外集
ogi [ogi] / wu-qi 五器
orye [orye]/ wu-li 五禮
osang [osang] / wu-chang 五常

pyeongcheonha [p'yŏngch'ŏnha] / ping-tian-xia 平天下

sadan [sadan] / si-duan 四端
sadeok [sadŏk] / si-de 四德
saga dokseo [saga doksŏ] 賜暇讀書
samjae [samjae] / san-cai 三才
Sangje [Sangje] / Shang-di 上帝
sangseongseong beop [sangsŏngsŏng bŏp] / chang-xing-xing-fa 常惺惺法
sarim [sarim] 士林
seo-in [sŏ-in] 西人
Seong-gyun-gwan [Sŏng-gyun-gwan] 成均館
Seonghak jibyo [Sŏnghak chibyo] 聖學輯要
Seonghak sipdo [Sŏnghak sipto] 聖學十圖
Seong Hon(Ugye) [Sŏng Hon(Ugye)] 成渾(牛溪)
seonghyeon dotong [sŏnghyŏn dot'ong] / sheng-xian dao-tong 聖賢道統
Seongnihak [Sŏngnihak] / Xing-li-xue 性理學

Seongsan [Sŏngsan] 星山
seong-ui [sŏng-ŭi] / cheng-yi 誠意
Seonjo [Sŏnjo] 宣祖
seowon [sŏwŏn] / shu-yuan 書院
seul [sŭl] / se 瑟
Shi Jing 詩經
Shin Hu-dam(Habin) [Sin Hu-dam(Habin)] 愼後聃(河濱)
Shu Jing 書經
Shun 舜
Silhak [Sirak] 實學
Si-ma Wen-gong 司馬溫公
Simgyeong huron [Simgyŏng huron] 心經後論
simhak [simhak] / xin-xue 心學
sindok [sindok] / xin-du 愼獨
Sin Saimdang [Sin Saimdang] 申師任堂
Si-shu 四書
Si-shu da-quan 四書大全
Si-shu zhang-tu 四書章圖
sodang-yeon [sodang-yŏn] / suo-dang-ran 所當然
Sokjip [Sokchip] 續集
Songgye won myeong ihak tongnok [Songgye wŏn myŏng ihak t'ongnok]
    宋季元明理學通錄
soyiyeon [soyiyŏn] / suo-yi-ran 所以然
sugan [sugan] 豎看
susin [susin] / xi-shen 修身
Swae-eon [Swae-ŏn] 瑣言

Toegye jip [T'oegye jip] 退溪集
Tong-shu 通書

ui [ŭi] / yi 意
uiri [ŭiri] / yi-li 義理

Wang Yangming 王陽明
wijeong [wijŏng] / wei-zheng 爲政
wonhyeongyijeong [wŏnhyŏngyijŏng] / yuan-heng-li-zhen 元亨利貞
Wonhyo [Wŏnhyo] 元曉

Xing-li da-quan 性理大全
Xing li shi yi 性理拾遺
Xin Jing 心經
Xin Jing fu-zhu 心經附註

Xun Zi 顏子

Yan Yuan 顏淵
Yan Zi 顏子
Ye-an [Ye-an] 禮安
yeokhaeng [yŏkhaeng] / li-xing 力行
Yeonbo [Yŏnbo] 年譜
yesong [yesong] / li-song 禮訟
yibal [yibal] / yi-fa 已發
Yi Byeong-hyu(Jeongsan) [Yi Pyŏng-hyu(Chŏngsan)] 李秉休(貞山)
Yi-chuan(Cheng Yi) 伊川(程頤)
Yi Eon-jeok [Yi Ŏn-jŏk] 李彥迪
Yi Hae(Ongye) [Yi Hae(Ongye)] 李瀣(溫溪)
Yi Hang-no(Hwaseo) [Yi Hang-no(Hwasŏ)] 李恒老(華西)
Yi Hwang(Toegye) [Yi Hwang(T'oegye)] 李滉(退溪)
Yi I(Yulgok) [Yi I(Yulgok)] 李珥(栗谷)
Yi Ik(Seongho) [Yi Ik(Sŏngho)] 李瀷(星湖)
Yi Jin-sang(Hanju) [Yi Chin-sang(Hanju)] 李震相(寒洲)
yinsim dosim [yinsim tosim] / ren-xin dao-xin 人心道心
yinuiyejisin [yinŭiyejisin] / ren-yi-li-zhi-xin 仁義禮智信
Yi Sang-jeong(Daesan) [Yi Sang-jŏng(Taesan)] 李象靖(大山)
Yi Sik(Taekdang) [Yi Sik(T'aektang)] 李植(澤堂)
Yu 禹
Yulgok jeonseo [Yulgok chŏnsŏ] 栗谷全書

Zeng Shen 曾參
Zeng Zi 曾子
Zhang Zai 張載
Zhang Zai Ji 張載集
Zhao Shun-sun(Ge-an) 趙順孫(格菴)
Zhen Chun(Bei-xi) 陳淳(北溪)
Zhen De-xiu 眞德秀
Zhong Yong 中庸
Zhong Yong zhang-ju 中庸章句
Zhong Yong zhang-ju xu 中庸章句序
Zhou Dun-yi(Lian-gu) 周敦頤(濂溪)
Zhou Gong 周公
Zhu Xi 朱熹
Zhu Zi chuan-shu 朱子全書
Zhu Zi yu-lei 朱子語類
Zi-si 子思
Zi-zhi tong-jian 資治通鑑

Selected Bibliography

I. ORIGINAL TEXTS

Da Xue 大學 (*The Great Learning*)
Li Ji 禮記 (*The Book of Rites*)
Lun Yu 論語 (*The Analects*)
Meng Zi 孟子 (*Mencius*)
Shi Ji 史記 (*The Records of the Grand Historian*)
Shu Jing 書經 (*The Book of Documents*)
Zhong Yong 中庸 (*The Doctrine of the Mean*)

Gi, Dae-seung 奇大升. *Gobong jeonjip* 高峯全集 (The Complete Works of Gobong). Seoul: Daedong munhwa yeon-guwon at Sungkyunkwan University, 1979.
———. *Gobong jip* 高峯集 (The Collected Works of Gobong). Seoul: Minjok munhwa chujinhoe, 1988.
Hu, Guang 胡廣 et al., ed. *Si-shu da-quan* 四書大全 I, II. Jinju, Gyeongnam: Suri, 2012.
———, ed. *Xing-li da-quan* 性理大全. Seoul: Bogyeong munhwasa, 1994.
Jeong, Jae-gyu 鄭載圭. *Nobaekheon jip* 老柏軒集 (The Collected Works of Nobaekheon). Seoul: Han-guk gojeon beonyeogwon, 2012.
Jeong, Yak-yong 丁若鏞. *Jeongbon Yeoyudang jeonseo* 定本 與猶堂全書 (The Standard Edition of the Complete Works of Yeoyudang). Seoul: Dasan haksul munhwa jaedan, 2012.
———. *Yeoyudang jeonseo* 與猶堂全書 (The Complete Works of Yeoyudang). Seoul: Minjok munhwa chujinhoe, 2002.
Seong, Hon 成渾. *Ugye jip* 牛溪集 (The Collected Works of Ugye). Seoul: Minjok munhwa chujinhoe, 1988.
Wu, Chucai 吳楚材, and Diaohou Wu 吳調候, ed. *Gu-wen Guan-zhi* 古文觀止. Taipei: Da Zhong-guo tu-shu gong-si, 1958.

Yi, Eonjeok 李彦迪. *Hoejae jip* 晦齋集 (The Collected Works of Hoejae). Seoul: Minjok munhwa chujinhoe, 1988.

Yi, Hwang 李滉. *Toegye jip* 退溪集 (The Collected Works of Toegye). Seoul: Minjok munhwa chujinhoe, 1988.

Yi, I 李珥. *Yulgok jeonseo* 栗谷全書 (The Complete Works of Yulgok). Seoul: Minjok munhwa chujinhoe, 1988.

Zhang, Zai 張載. *Zhang Zai Ji* 張載集 (The Collected Works of Zhang Zai). Beijing: Zhong-hua shu-ju, 1978.

———. *Zhang Zi quan-shu* 張子全書 (The Complete Works of Master Zhang). Taipei: Taiwan Zhong-hua shu-ju, 1996.

Zhen, De-xiu, and Min-zheng Cheng 眞德秀·程敏政. *Xin Jing fu-zhu* 心經附註 (Supplementary Annotations to the Classic of the Heart-Mind). Daejeon, Chungnam: Hangmin munhwasa, 2005.

Zhu, Xi 朱熹. *Si-shu zhang-ju ji-zhu* 四書章句集注 (Collected Commentaries on the Four Books in Chapters and Verses). Beijing: Zhong-hua shu-ju, 1983.

———. *Zhu Zi quan-shu* 朱子全書 (The Complete Works of Master Zhu). Shanghai: Shanghai gu-ji chu-ban-she, 2002.

II. ORIGINAL TEXTS (TRANSLATION EDITIONS)

Han, Won-jin 韓元震. *Juja eollon dong-i go* 朱子言論同異考 (*Discrepancies in Speeches and Writings of Master Zhu*). Translated and annotated by Sin-hwan Gwak. Seoul: Somyeong Publishing Company, 2002.

Han-guk jeongsin munhwa yeon-guwon jaryo josasil 한국정신문화연구원 자료조사실(The Complete Works of Yulgok in Korean). Edited by *Gugyeok Yulgok jeonseo* 국역 율곡전서. Seongnam, Gyeong-gi: Han-guk jeongsin munhwa yeon-guwon, 1996.

Han-guk sasang yeon-guso at Korea University 고려대 한국사상연구소 (*Ten Diagrams on Sage Learning*: Translation Notes and Interpretations). Edited by *Yeokjuwa haeseol Seonghak sipdo* 역주와 해설 성학십도. Seoul: Yemun seowon, 2009.

Jeong, Seok-tae 정석태. *Toegye seonsaeng yeonpyo irwol jorok* 退溪先生年表日月條錄 (*The Chronology of Toegye's Daily Records*). Seoul: Toegyehak yeon-guwon, 2006.

Jeong, Sun-mok 정순목, trans. and ed. "Toegye seonsaeng eonhaengnok" 退溪先生言行錄 (Memoirs of Master Toegye's Words and Deeds), *Toegyehak Yeon-gu nonchong* 退溪學 硏究論叢 (Collected Studies on Toegye's Learning) 10. Daegu, Gyeongbuk: Toegye yeon-guso at Kyungpook National University, 1997.

Kalton, Michael C. *The Four-Seven Debate*. Albany: State University of New York Press, 1994.

———. *To Become a Sage*. New York: Columbia University Press, 1988.

Toegyehak chongseo pyeon-gan wiwonoe 퇴계학 총서 편간 위원회. Edited by *Gugyeok Toegye jeonseo* 국역 퇴계전서 (The Complete Works of Toegye in Korean). Seoul: Toegyehak yeon-guwon, 2003.

Yi, Gwang-ho 이광호, trans. and ed. *Toegye-wa Yulgok, saeng-gageul datuda* 퇴계와 율곡, 생각을 다투다 (The Exchange of Opinions between Toegye and Yulgok). Seoul: Hong-ik Publishing Company, 2013.

Yi, Hwang 李滉. *Toegye si puri* 퇴계시 풀이 (The Interpretations of Toegye's Poetry). Translated by Jang-wu Yi and Se-hu Jang. Gyeongsan, Gyeongbuk: Yeungnam University Press, 2007–2011.

Yi, I 李珥. *Seonghak jibyo* 聖學輯要 (The Essentials of Sage Learning). Translated by Tae-wan Kim. Seoul: Cheong-aram Media, 2007.

III. BOOKS

Bae, Jong-ho 배종호. *Han-guk yuhaksa* 한국유학사 (A History of Korean Confucianism). Seoul: Yonsei University Press, 1974.

Chan, Wing-tsit 陳榮捷. *A Source Book of Chinese Philosophy*. Princeton, NJ: Princeton University Press, 1963.

Chen, Lai 陳來. *Zhu Zi zhe-xue yan-jiu* 朱子哲學研究 (A Study of Master Zhu's Thought). Shanghai: Huadong shifan Universitu Press, 2000.

Choe, Seok-gi 최석기 et al., ed. Juja 朱子 (*Zhu Zi*). Jinju, Gyeongnam: Suri, 2005.

Chung, Edward Y. J. *The Korean Neo-Confucianism of Yi T'oegye and Yi Yulgok*. Albany: State University of New York Press, 1995.

Flanagan, Owen. *Moral Sprouts and Natural Teleologies*. Milwaukee: Marquette University Press, 2014.

Geum, Jang-tae 금장태. *Yulgok pyeongjeon* 율곡평전 (The Critical Biography of Yulgok). Seoul: Jisik-gwa gyoyang, 2011.

Han, Yeong-wu 한영우. *Yulgok Yi I pyeongjeon* 율곡 이이 평전 (A Critical Biography of Yulgok Yi I). Seoul: Minumsa, 2013.

Han-guk cheorak sasang yeon-guhoe 한국철학사상연구회, ed. *Nonjaeng-euro boneun han-guk cheorak* 논쟁으로 보는 한국철학 (Korean Strands of Philosophy in View of the Salient Debates). Seoul: Yemun seowon, 1995.

Han-guk cheorak sasang yeon-guhoe 한국철학사상연구회, ed. Gangjwa han-guk cheorak 강좌 한국철학 (Lectures on Korean Philosophy). Seoul: Yemun seowon, 1995.

Hyeon, Sang-yun 현상윤. *Joseon yuhaksa* 조선유학사 (A History of Joseon Confucianism). Seoul: Shimsan, 2010 (1949).

Jang, Ji-yeon 장지연. *Joseon yugyo yeonwon* 조선유교연원 (The Origin of Confucianism in the Joseon Dynasty). Seoul: Myeongmundang, 2009 (1922).

Johnson, Mark. *Moral Imagination: Implication of Cognitive Science*. Chicago: University of Chicago Press, 1993.

Kim, Gyeong-ho 김경호. *In-gyeok seongsuk-ui saeroun jipyeong: Yulgok-ui ingannon* 인격 성숙의 새로운 지평: 율곡의 인간론 (A New Horizons for the Maturation of Personality: Yulgok's Theory of the Human Being). Goyang, Gyeong-gi: Jeongbo-wa saram, 2008.

Lewis, Mark Edward. *Writing and Authority in Early China*. Albany: State University of New York Press, 1999.

Qian, Mu 錢穆. *Zhu Zi xue ti-gang* 朱子學提綱 (The Outline of Master Zhu's Learning). Translated by Wan-jae Yi and Do-geun Baek. Daegu, Gyeongbuk: Yimun Publishing Company, 1990.

Ro, Young-chan. *The Korean Neo-Confucianism of Yi Yulgok*. Albany: State University of New York Press, 1989.

Takahashi Susumu 高橋進. *Toegye gyeong cheorak* 퇴계 敬철학 (Toegye's Philosophy of *Gyeong*). Translated by Choe Bak-gwang. Seoul: Dongseo munhwasa, 1993.

Song, Jaeyoon 송재윤. *Traces of Grand Peace: Classics and State Activism in Imperial China*. Cambridge, MA: Harvard University Asia Center, 2015.

Yi, Sang-eun 이상은. *Toegye-ui saeng-aewa hangmun* 퇴계의 생애와 학문 (Toegye's Life and Learning). Seoul: Yemun seowon, 1999.

Yi, Seung-hwan 이승환. *Hoengseol-gwa Suseol* 횡설과 수설 (Horizontal Explanation and Vertical Explanation). Seoul: Humanist, 2012.

Youn, Sasoon 윤사순. *Critical Issues in Neo-Confucian Thought: The Philosophy of Yi T'oegye*. Translated by Michael C. Kalton. Seoul: Korea University Press, 1992.

———. *Han-guk yuhak sasangnon* 한국유학사상론 (A Study on Korean Confucian Thought). Seoul: Yemun seowon, 1997.

———. *Han-guk yuhaksa* 한국유학사 (A History of Korean Confucianism) I, II. Seoul: Jisik saneop sa, 2012.

———. *Toegye cheorak-ui yeon-gu* 퇴계철학의 연구 (A Study of Toegye's Philosophy). Seoul: Korea University Press, 1980.

Yu, Jeong-dong 유정동. *Yugyo-ui geunbon jeongsin-gwa han-guk yuhak* 유교의 근본정신과 한국유학 (The Basic Confucian Spirit and Korean Confucianism). Seoul: Yugyo munhwa yeon-guso at Sungkyunkwan University, 2014.

Yu, Myeong-jong 유명종. *Han-guk yuhak yeon-gu* 한국유학연구 (A Study of Korean Confucianism). Daegu, Gyeongbuk: Yimun Publishing Company, 1988.

———. *Seongnihak-gwa Yangmyeonghak* 성리학과 양명학 (Philosophies of Zhu Zi and Yangming). Seoul: Yonsei University Press, 1994.

IV. CRITICAL ARTICLES IN KOREAN

An, Byeong-ju 안병주. "Toegye-ui hangmun-gwan: 'Simgyeong huron'-eul jungsimeuro" (퇴계의 학문관: "心經後論"을 중심으로, Toegye's View of Learning: Focusing on "Postscripts to the Classic of the Heart-Mind"). *Toegyehak yeon-gu* (Toegye Studies Journal) 1. Seoul: Toegyehak yeon-guso of Dankook University, 1987.

Han, Jae-hoon 한재훈. "Toegye yehak sasang yeon-gu" (퇴계 禮學思想 연구, A Study on Toegye's Ritual Thought). PhD diss., Korea University, Seoul, 2012.

Hong, Won-sik 홍원식. "Toegyehak, geu jonjae-reul mutda" (퇴계학, 그 존재를 묻다, What Are Toegye Studies?). *Oneurui dong-yang sasang* (Today's Eastern Thought) 4. Seoul: Yemun dong-yang sasnag yeon-guso, 2001.

Jeong, Won-jae 정원재. "Jisikseol-e ipgakhan Yi I cheorak-ui haeseok" (知覺說에 입각한 이이 철학의 해석, An Interpretation of Yi I's Philosophy on the Basis of the Theory of Perception). PhD diss., Seoul National University, Seoul, 2000.

Ji, Du-hwan 지두환. "Joseon hugi gyeong-yeon gwamok-ui byeoncheon" (조선후기 경연과목의 변천, Changes in the Courses of Gyeong-yeon in Late Joseon). *Han-gukhak nonchong* (Theses of Korean Studies) 18. Seoul: Han-gukhak yeon-guso of Kookmin University, 1995.

Kim, Gi-hyeon 김기현. "Toegye-ui 'li' cheorag-e naejaedoen segyegwanjeok hamui" (퇴계의 "理"철학에 내재된 세계관적 함의, The Worldview Implied in Toegye's Philosophy of *Li*). *Toegye hakbo* (The Journal of Toegye Studies) 116, Seoul: Toegyehak yeon-guwon, 2001.

Kim, Hyoungchan 김형찬. "Andong Kimmunui jisik nonjaenggwa jisik gwolly-eogui hyeongseong: Nong-am Kim Chang-hyeop-ui hangmunjeok ipjang-eul jungsimeuro" (安東 金門의 지식논쟁과 지식권력의 형성: 농암 김창협의 학문적 입장을 중심으로, Knowledge Debates of the Kims of Andong and the Formation of Knowledge Power: The Academic Position of Nong-am Kim Chang-hyeop). *Minjok munhwa yeon-gu* (Korean Cultural Studies) 56. Seoul: Minjok munhwa yeon-guwon at Korea University, 2012.

———. "Dodeok gamjeonggwa dodeok bonseong-ui gwan-gye: Toegye-ui munje uisige daehan geomto" (도덕감정과 도덕본성의 관계: 퇴계의 문제의식에 대한 검토, The Relationship between Moral Emotions and Moral Nature: A Review of Toegye's Philosophical Quest for Moral Spontaneity). *Minjok munhwa yeon-gu* (Korean Cultural Studies) 74. Seoul: Minjok munhwa yeon-guwon at Korea University, 2017.

———. "Han-guk cheorak-eseo-ui segyehwa galdeung" (한국철학에서의 세계화 갈등, The Conflicts within Korean Philosophy Ensuing from Globalization). In *Cha-i-wa galdeung-e daehan cheorakjeok seongchal* (차이와 갈등에 대한 철학적 성찰, A Philosophical Reflection on Differences and Conflicts), edited by Han-guk cheorakhoe (The Society of Korean Philosophy). Seoul: Cheorakgwa hyeonsil sa, 2007.

———. "Gijil byeonhwa, yokmang-ui jeonghwa-reul wihan seongnihakjeok gihoek" (氣質變化, 욕망의 정화를 위한 성리학적 기획, Transforming Material Disposition: Neo-Confucian Strategizing for the Purification of Desire). *Cheorak yeon-gu* (The Journal of Philosophical Studies) 38. Seoul: Cheorak yeon-guso at Korea University, 2009.

———. "Igironui irwonnonhwa yeon-gu" (理氣論의 一元論化 연구, A Study on the Monistic Tendency of the Theory of *Li-Gi*). PhD diss., Korea University, Seoul, 1996.

———. "Joseon yuhak-ui i gaenyeom-e natanan jonggyojeok seonggyeok yeon-gu: Toegye-ui ibal-eseo Dasan-ui sangje-kkaji" (조선유학의 理 개념에 나타난 종교적 성격 연구: 퇴계의 理發에서 다산의 上帝까지, A Study on the Religious Character of the Concept of *Li* in Korean Confucianism: From Toegye's Concept of the Issuance of *Li* to Dasan's *Sangje*). *Choerak yeon-gu* (The Journal of Philosophical Studies) 39. Seoul: Cheorak yeon-guso at Korea University, 2010.

———. "Ma-eum-ui ligiwa jayeon-ui ligi" (마음의 理氣와 자연의 理氣, The *Li-Gi* of the Mind and the *Li-Gi* of Nature). *Han-gukhak nonjip* (Korean studies Journal) 40. Daegu, Gyeongbuk: Han-gukhak yeon-guwon at Keimyung University, 2010.

———. "Naeseong oewang-eul hyang-han du gaji gil: Toegye cheorak-eseo-ui liwa sangjereul jungsimeuro" (내성외왕을 향한 두 가지 길: 퇴계철학에서의 리와 상제를 중심으로, The Two Paths toward Becoming a Sage on the Inside and a Virtuous King on the Outside: Focused on the Concepts of *Li* and *Sangje* in Toegye's Philosophy). *Cheorak yeon-gu* (The Journal of Philosophical Studies) 34. Seoul: Cheorak yeon-guso of Korea University, 2007.

———. "Samunnanjeok nollan-gwa saseo-ui jaehaeseok" (斯文亂賊 논란과 四書의 재해석, On the Issue of Enemies of Confucianism and the Reinterpretation of the Four Books). *Han-guk sasang-gwa munhwa* (Korean Thought and Culture) 63. Seoul: Han-guk sasang munhwa hakhoe, 2012.

———. "Toegye-ui seowongwan-e daehan cheorakjeok haemyeong" (퇴계의 서원관에 대한 철학적 해명, A Philosophical Elucidation on Toegye's View of the Confucian Academies). *Toegye hakbo* (The Journal of Toegye Studies) 136. Seoul: Toegyehak yeon-guwon, 2014.

Kim, Jong-seok 김종석. "Ma-eum-ui cheorak: Toegye simhak-ui gujobunseok" (마음의 철학—퇴계심학의 구조분석, The Philosophy of the Heart-Mind: A Structural Analysis of Toegye's Study of the Heart-Mind). *Minjok munhwa nonchong* (Korean Cultural Studies) 15. Gyeongsan, Gyeongbuk: Minjok munhwa yeon-guso at Yeungnam University, 1994.

Kim, Tae-nyeon 김태년. "Namdang Han Won-jin-ui jeonghak hyeongseong-e daehan yeon-gu" (남당 한원진의 正學 형성에 대한 연구, A Study of Han Won-jin's Construction of Orthodoxy and Herasy). PhD diss., Korea University, Seoul, 2006.

Kim, Yong-heon 김용헌. "Gobong Gi Dae-seung-ui sachil nonbyeon-gwa Cheonmyeong do" (고봉 기대승의 사칠논변과 천명도, Gobong Gi Dae-seung's Involvement in the Controversy on the Four-Seven and the Diagram of the Mandate of Heaven). *Jeontong-gwa hyeonsil* (Tradition and Reality) 8. Gwangju, Jeonnam: Gobong haksulwon, 1996.

Lee, Gi-yong 리기용. "Yulgok Yi I-ui Insim dosim non yeon-gu" (율곡 이이의 인심도심론 연구, A Study on the Human Mind and the Moral in the Philosophy of Yulgok Yi I). PhD diss., Yonsei University, Seoul, 1995.

Mun, Seok-yun 문석윤. "Toegye-eseo ibalgwa idong, ido-ui uimi-e daehayeo" (퇴계에서 理發과 理動, 理到의 의미에 대하여, On the Meaning of Toegye's Expressions, "The Issuance of *Li*," "The Mobility of *Li*," and "The Arrival of *Li*"). *Toegye hakbo* (The Journal of Toegye Studies) 110. Seoul: Toegyehak yeon-guwon, 2001.

———. "Toegye-ui *Seonghak sipdo* sujeong-e gwanhan yeon-gu (퇴계의 "성학십도" 수정에 관한 연구, A Study on Toegye's Revision of *Ten Diagrams on Sage Learning*). *Toehye hakbo* (The Journal of Toegye Studies) 130. Seoul: Toegyehak yeon-guwon, 2011.

Nam, Ji-man 남지만. "Gobong Gi Dae-seung-ui seongniseol yeon-gu" (고봉 기대승의 성리설 연구, A Study of Gobong Gi Dae-seung's Theory of Nature and Principle). PhD diss., Korea University, Seoul, 2009.

Sin, Gwi-hyeon 신귀현. "Toegye Yi Hwang-ui 'Simgyeong buju' yeon-guwa geu-ui simhak-ui teukjing" (퇴계 이황의 "심경부주" 연구와 그의 心學의 특징, Toegye's Study on *Supplementary Annotations to the Classic of the Heart-Mind* and the Characteristics of His Study of the Mind). *Minjok munhwa nonchong*

(Korean Cultural Studies) 8. Gyeongsan, Gyeongbuk: Minjok munhwa yeon-guso of Yeungnam University, 1987.

Song, Jaeyoon 송재윤. "Hwangjewa Jaesang: Namsongdae (1127~1279) gwollyeok bullip iron" (황제와 재상: 남송대 [1127~1279] 권력분립이론, Emperors and Premiers: Southern Song [1127~1279] Theories on Separation of Powers). *Toegye hakbo* (The Journal of Toegye Studies) 140. Seoul: Toegyehak yeon-guwon, 2016.

Takahashi Susumu 高橋進. "Dong-asia-e isseo-seo 'gyeong' cheorak-ui seongnip-gwa jeon-gae" (동아시아에 있어서 "敬"철학의 성립과 전개, The Formation and Development of the Philosophy of *Gyeong* [敬] in East Asia). *Toegye hakbo* (The Journal of Toegye Studies) 44. Seoul: Toegyehak yeon-guwon, 1984.

Yi, Jang-wu, and Se-hu Jang 이장우 · 장세후, trans. and ed. "Toegye si yeokhae (74)" (퇴계시 역해 [74], An Interpretation of Toegye's Poetry [74]). *Toegye hakbo* (The Journal of Toegye Studies) 130. Seoul: Toegyehak yeon-guwon, 2011.

Yu, Sae-rom 유새롬. "17-segi seo-in-ui haktong uisikgwa Yulgok yeonbo-ui pyeon-chan" (17세기 서인의 학통의식과 율곡연보의 편찬, The Seo-in Members' Consciousness of Their Scholastic Mantle and the Publication of the Chronology of Yulgok). *Han-guksaron* (The Journal of Korean History) 52. Seoul: Department of Korean History at Seoul National University, 2006.

V. CRITICAL ARTICLES IN ENGLISH

Clark, Andy. "Connectionism, Moral Cognition, and Collaborative Problem Solving." In *Mind and Morals*, edited by Larry May, Marilyn Friedman, and Andy Clark. Cambridge, MA: MIT Press, 1998.

Dreyfus, Hubert I., and Stuart E. Dreyfus. "What Is Morality? A Phenomenological Account of the Development of Ethical Expertise." In *Universalism vs. Communitarianism*, edited by David Rasmussen. Cambridge, MA: MIT Press, 1990.

Kim, Hyoungchan. "Internalizing Morals and the Active Intervention of a Moral System: Zhu Xi and Yi Hwang's Theories of kyŏngmul 格物 and mulgyŏk 物格." *Journal of Korean Religions* 6, no. 2. Seoul: Institute for the Study of Religion at Sogang University, 2015.

———. "The *Li-Ki* Structure of the Four Beginnings and the Seven Emotions and the Intent of the Four-Seven Debate." *Acta Koreana* 18, no. 2. Daegu, Gyeongbuk: The Academia Koreana at Keimyung University, 2015.

———. "The Theory and Practice of Sage Politics: The Political Philosophies and Neo-Confucian Bases of Yi Hwang and Yi I." *Acta Koreana* 17, no. 1. Daegu, Gyeongbuk: The Academia Koreana at Keimyung University, 2014.

———. "Toegye's Philosophy as Practical Ethics: A System of Learning, Cultivation, and Practice of Being Human." *Korea Journal* 47, no. 3. Seoul: Korea National Commission for UNESCO, 2007.

Tu, Wei-ming. "Yi T'oegye's Perception of Human Nature: A Preliminary Inquiry into the Four-Seven Debate in Korea Neo-Confucianism." In *The Rise of Neo-Confucianism in Korea*, edited by William Theodore de Bery and JaHyun Kim Haboush. New York: Columbia University Press, 1985.

Index

About the Author

Hyoungchan Kim is a professor of Korean philosophy at Korea University, South Korea. He specializes in Korean philosophy and Confucianism and its potential for contemporary ethics and social philosophy. He has also edited *East Meets West* and written several books, including *Natural Philosophy of Korean Confucianism* (coauthor) and *Old Dreams*.

About the Translators

Shon Yoo-taek is a former professor of English (currently lecturer in English) at Suwon University, South Korea.

Yoon Heeki is a research professor at the Institute of Foreign Language Studies, Korea University, South Korea.

Dara Seamus Fox is an assistant professor at the Institute of Foreign Language Studies, Korea University, South Korea.

www.ingramcontent.com/pod-product-compliance
Lightning Source LLC
Chambersburg PA
CBHW021815270326
41932CB00007B/189